D1711691

Disability Income Insurance
The Unique Risk

Disability Income Insurance
The Unique Risk

Second Edition

Charles E. Soule
Executive Vice President
The Paul Revere Life Insurance Company

Dow Jones-Irwin
Homewood, Illinois   60430

Dow Jones-Irwin is a trademark of Dow Jones-Irwin & Company, Inc.

Project editor: Jane Lightell
Production manager: Ann Cassady
Compositor: Arcata Graphics/Kingsport
Typeface: 10/12 Sabon
Printer: R. R. Donnelley & Sons

Library of Congress Cataloging-in-Publication Data

Soule, Charles E.
    Disability income insurance.

    Includes index.

    1. Insurance, Disability—United States. I. Title.
HD7105.25.U6S68   1989   368.3′86′00973   88–25747
ISBN 1-55623-182-2

Printed in the United States of America
1 2 3 4 5 6 7 8 9 0 DO 5 4 3 2 1 0 9 8

To Albert F. Soule, Sr.
a man of integrity, energy, and industry

Preface

The purpose of this book is to explain to insurance professionals the important concepts, risks, and patterns of disability income insurance.

A significant part of the disability income industry's difficulties, concerns, and misunderstandings stems from inadequate recognition of its unique characteristics and risks. This book is an attempt to identify these qualities and to bring together under one cover what I consider the most significant considerations today for the home office manager and professional in the disability income business. In addressing this objective, I will frequently compare the disability income industry with the life insurance business. The great majority of disability income insurance is sold and administered by companies, home office personnel, and salespeople who are primarily life insurance oriented; their emphasis and experience with disability income is secondary. To compare the differences between life and disability income insurance, therefore, may be particularly helpful to those people whose background is primarily life insurance, but who find they have some responsibilities for the disability income product line.

My career experience has been with The Paul Revere Companies, a firm that markets a full line of individual and group products but whose major line throughout its 85-year history has been individual disability income. Because of the depth of its experience and the size of its policyholder file, Paul Revere has the advantage of a broad and reliable data base on which to make management decisions. My first

10 years in the business were spent as a disability income underwriter, and I consider this discipline to represent my basic professional training. This book will discuss contracts, premiums, claims, and sales concerns. I ask the reader to remember that these subjects are observed through the eye of an underwriter, with whatever advantages or limitations that may be associated with that angle of observation.

Some people in the industry will disagree with some of my observations and conclusions. That is because the disability income business is still in its developmental stages. It can be molded and directed in a way that few major lines of insurance still can be. That is what makes it so exciting and competitive. The unknowns are still enormous; the flexibility of contract language is in a way unbounded; the premium differentials from company to company are substantial and in some instances dangerous. The underwriting rules and requirements differ more substantially than in life insurance; claim practices are continually being modified to respond to consumer attitude changes; and complicating the whole sphere of operations is the fact that claimants can significantly affect claim situations.

There are two important characteristics of individual buyers of disability income that are particularly important and are distinctive from the characteristics considered in underwriting a life insurance applicant. The first is stability. The stability of the risk in his or her home, occupation, and community is a much more important element to both claim and persistency results in disability insurance than in life insurance.

The second element is the motivation of the individual. It is important to remember that, contrary to normal patterns in life insurance, in disability insurance the policyholder may deliberately and consciously make the decision to present a claim. This is not an infrequent occurrence. The motivation of the policyholder under such circumstances, as well as the motivation to return to work once disabled, is a key element that affects the development and patterns in the disability income business.

Stability and motivation factors affect product language, rate development, underwriting considerations, and, of course, claim management. The reader should keep in mind the impacts that stability and motivation have had and will continue to have on the disability income industry.

Charles E. Soule

Acknowledgments

My sincere thanks to the following individuals who provided advice and suggestions for this text:

Donald E. Boggs
John H. Budd
Eleanor L. Clifford
Russell P. Deal
Joseph R. Gagliano
Kenneth B. Hedenburg
W. Duane Kidwell
Charles T. Lanigan
Lorna E. Long
Gordon L. Newell
Arthur F. Newman
Ronald S. St. Jean
Arthur J. Taylor

C. E. S.

Contents

Insurance. Extended Elimination Period. Excess Risk. Quota Share. Recapture. Experience Refunds. Reinsurance Services: *Market Analysis. Product Development. Pricing. Underwriting Support. Claims Support. Evaluation.* Future Trends and Support.

Historical Highlights
and
Developments

1

Throughout the following pages of this book, the disability income industry will be referred to as "disability income" or "disability." Individuals who have been associated with our business for any length of time know well that we have had a fundamental problem in agreeing upon an appropriate and accurate term to describe our business. As a result the disability industry has also regularly been referred to as "health insurance," "loss of time," "accident and health," "accident and sickness," "income replacement," "loss of income," "A & S," "A & H," "accident insurance," "long-term disability," "LTD," and even facetiously sometimes as "sick and hurt." Some of these terms are misleading in that they might be construed and interpreted to mean hospital or medical care coverage. Therefore, this book will arbitrarily use the terms *disability income* and *disability* throughout the text, since they are the most descriptive.

EARLY HISTORY—1890–1929

The industry, as we know it today, had its real beginnings in the latter part of the 19th century. Early forms of disability income coverage had appeared prior to that time; however, they traditionally provided only accident protection or were limited benefits attached to ordinary life insurance contracts. Gradually, several companies, many

1

of the fraternal type, experimented with the sale of separate disability income contracts.

Regardless of the form of disability coverage during these early years, contracts were very limited in both the amount of benefits payable and the length of time the benefits were paid. In addition, the contracts during this early period were of the cancellable type, where the company retained the right to either terminate the policy or increase the premium on relatively short notice.

In the early 20th century, what we now refer to as guaranteed-renewable contracts began to appear in a very restricted form. These contracts could not be terminated during the term of the policy, regardless of claim experience. However, the premium could be increased on groups of lives and on notice from the insurer.

The Armstrong investigation, which had a tremendous impact on regulating life insurance practices, also had a significant effect upon the fledgling disability income industry. Anyone who has taken a basic insurance course is well aware of the significance of the Armstrong investigations and the subsequent dominance by the state of New York in regulating and directing the insurance industry. This in-depth investigation of life insurance industry practices in the state of New York came about because of serious abuses within the industry. This investigation was authorized by the New York legislature in 1905 and addressed abuses in sales, investments, and management practices. The recommendations were enacted by the New York legislature and established high standards for the industry, correcting many abuses that had developed during the late 19th century. It does not seem possible that any future commission or committee at a state level could have the nationwide impact on an industry that these investigations in the early 20th century had on the insurance business.

One important outcome of the Armstrong investigation and subsequent legislation was in the area of policy language and provisions. Subsequently, the first health insurance policy provision regulations came into being in 1912. These were called the Uniform Standard Provisions Law and also applied to disability income.

In the late teens (1916), the first non-cancellable and guaranteed-renewable disability income contracts appeared; and the predecessor of the Paul Revere Life Insurance Company introduced its first contract in 1918 (see Figure 1–1). The principle of "non-can" disability income coverage was a most revolutionary one at that time. The company not only guaranteed to continue the contract for the specified life of the policy (generally to age 55 or 60), but also guaranteed a stated level premium throughout that period of time. It abdicated its right to change the premium or cancel the contract, which had been characteristic of all disability contracts up to that time. The innovators in the industry during those years displayed not only courage but a great deal of foresight and knowledge, since their basic contract language continues today.

FIGURE 1-1

CHARTERED IN MASSACHUSETTS

THIS POLICY IS NON-CANCELLABLE AND PROVIDES INDEMNITY FOR LOSS OF LIFE, LIMB, SIGHT AND TIME BY ACCIDENTAL MEANS, OR OF TIME BY DISEASE, AS HEREIN LIMITED.

The Masonic Protective Association

of Worcester, Massachusetts

DOES HEREBY INSURE

subject to the provisions and limitations contained herein

whose occupation is

against loss resulting from (1) bodily injuries effected directly and independently of all other causes by accidental means (excluding self-destruction, or any attempt thereat, while sane or insane) and due solely to external, violent and involuntary causes; and (2) disability from disease.

ACCIDENT INDEMNITIES

A. **TOTAL DISABILITY.** If such injuries result in continuous total disability from the date of the accident requiring the regular and personal attendance of a licensed physician and lasting for at least five days, the Association will pay an indemnity at the rate of _____ Dollars per week for the period of such disability, as hereinafter limited.

B. **PARTIAL DISABILITY.** If such injuries continuously from the date of the accident result in partial disability lasting for at least five days which prevents the insured from performing a majority of the duties of his occupation and which necessitates the regular and personal attendance of a licensed physician, or if such partial disability follows a period of total disability as above, the Association will pay for the period of such disability, not exceeding twenty-six weeks, one-half the weekly indemnity provided in Clause A, as hereinafter limited.

C. **SPECIFIC LOSSES.** If such injuries result in continuous total disability from the date of the accident and within ninety days of the accident in the loss of both hands or both feet at or above the wrists or ankles, or similarly of one hand and one foot, or of the entire and irrecoverable loss of the sight of both eyes, the Association will pay for one and only one of such losses, in lieu of any other indemnity, the sum of _____ Dollars per week for a period of eighty weeks; or similarly for the loss of one hand or foot as above, it will pay a like sum for a period of forty weeks, or twenty weeks for loss of sight of one eye as above, as hereinafter limited, or, if the insured has not requested payment in the form of an Income Bond, the commuted value of such weekly payments accruing for any such loss as provided in paragraph E below. Loss in any such case shall terminate this policy and all liability under it, except for the payment of the indemnity provided for such loss.

D. **ACCIDENTAL DEATH.** Or, if such injuries result in continuous total disability from the date of the accident and within ninety days of the accident in the death of the insured (death from accidental drowning included) the Association will, in lieu of any other indemnity, pay to the beneficiary hereunder the sum of _____ Dollars per week for a period of eighty weeks, as hereinafter limited, or, if the insured has not requested payment in the form of an Income Bond, the commuted value of such weekly payments accruing for such loss as provided in paragraph E below.

SPECIAL INDEMNITY (50% INCREASE)

E. If any loss described in Clauses C or D results from injuries sustained during any period for which a premium has been paid on this policy annually in advance, the Association will pay the indemnity therein mentioned for an additional number of weeks equal to one-half the number already therein provided for such loss. Upon written request of the insured, the Association, within thirty days after receipt of proof of loss under this or either of the two preceding clauses, will pay the same by delivery of an Income Bond, in the form attached hereto, providing for the payment of the indemnity promised for such loss, the first payment amounting to four weeks' indemnity, to be made upon delivery of said Bond, and subsequent payments of a like amount every four weeks thereafter. If such request be not made by the insured, any indemnity payable under this or either of the two preceding clauses shall amount to the commuted value at 5% of the weekly indemnities provided for such loss, and the same shall be paid in cash within thirty days after receipt of proof of loss, such commuted value in the event of loss from death being _____ Dollars if premiums have been paid quarterly, or _____ Dollars if they have been paid annually as above described.

SICKNESS INDEMNITIES

F. **CONFINING SICKNESS INDEMNITY.** If any disease results in continuous total disability lasting at least five days confining the insured within house or hospital and requiring the regular and personal attendance of a licensed physician, the Association will pay at the rate of _____ Dollars for the first week, and at the rate of _____ Dollars per week for the remainder, of the period of such disability, as hereinafter limited.

G. **NON-CONFINING SICKNESS INDEMNITY.** If any disease results in continuous total disability lasting at least five days requiring said medical attendance but not necessitating confinement to the house or hospital, or in such non-confining total disability following a period of confinement as above, the Association will pay for the period of such disability, one-half the indemnity provided in Clause F, as hereinafter limited.

CONTINUATION OF INSURANCE

H. The Association agrees that during the term of this policy the sole condition for its continuance shall be the timely payment by the insured of the premiums hereon.

Form 62 A Protective Income

Between 1918 and 1929, following the end of World War I, the disability income industry grew significantly, and many companies entered the business. One development that was later to cause serious financial losses for many companies was the emergence of liberal definitions of disability, particularly on disability income riders attached to life insurance contracts. The amount of indemnity was normally a percent of the face amount of life insurance. However, unfortunately, the contract language and underwriting did not distinguish carefully between the disability risk and the life insurance risk. Since this type of disability benefit on a life insurance policy was written primarily by companies with life insurance rather than disability income skills, important protection elements were missing. Several of these types of contracts contained disability income provisions that increased the amount of disability benefits substantially as an individual remained disabled longer. Consequently, the motivation and incentive for recovery were substantially diminished. Here was perhaps the first clear evidence in the disability business of the subjective nature of determining disability, and of course, it was quite a bit different from the normally objective determination of death for life insurance payments. The will to work, enhanced or retarded by the economic climate, is the most significant single factor differentiating disability income from life insurance. Although the economic climate is the key variable that affects the "will to work" quality, the social environment and attitude of the public as they differ from one segment of society to another and as they change through time have a direct impact upon disability experience. Later on in this book, this important subject will be discussed in more depth.

DEPRESSION YEARS—1929–1940

From 1929 to 1940, as with many other American businesses, the disability income industry experienced its most critical period. In the early 1930s, with the deepening Depression and with large numbers of workers unemployed, disability writers suffered both increases in the number of claims and increases in the average length of claims. Losses for the industry as a whole were substantial, and those companies that had written contracts with overly liberal definitions and had written indemnities without regard to the earned income of the insured suffered the greatest losses. As a result, several companies withdrew from the disability marketplace; some companies failed financially; and all companies took steps through underwriting and rating approaches to readjust their positions in the marketplace. The disability rider on life insurance contracts essentially disappeared from the marketplace, and several well-established mutual life insurance companies withdrew entirely from the disability income business, not to return until the mid 50s and 60s. Many of the largest insurers of disability income during this most critical period in its history were forced to withdraw from the business, and the scars and memories remained vivid through the 1950s.

Those insurers of disability income who had looked to it as a principal source of growth and profits—and there were only a handful of them—survived the Depression in much better financial condition than those who had considered disability income to be a secondary product line. In addition to discovering the "will to work" and motivation factors mentioned previously, a second lesson for the youthful industry became apparent during this period: The volatile nature of disability insurance requires that the insurer devote significant and substantial resources to managing this product line. If an insurer develops a disability income product solely as an accommodation to other individual products, the company will eventually suffer serious financial consequences. Proper management requires frequent evaluation, fine tuning, and changes in direction because of the direct relationship between disability claims experience and changes in the socioeconomic condition and climate in which we live. Life insurance claim results are clearly not as sensitive to these factors; however, through the 1920s and into the early 1930s, those life insurers writing disability income failed to make this important distinction.

WAR YEARS—1940–1950

During the war years from 1940 through 1950, sales began to grow again in disability income. However, there was very little enthusiasm or incentive for companies to experiment with significant changes or liberalizations in product language or underwriting rules. The typical disability income contract called for up to $200 per month of disability benefits, had a definition of disability that was strictly determined by the applicant's ability to work in "any occupation," and had a maximum period for which benefits were to be paid that was rarely more than two or three years. In addition, contracts typically carried an "aggregate" clause, which accumulated the total number of days of disability paid for all claims under the contract. The contract terminated when the total number of days of disability accumulated equaled the benefit period, even though several separate disabilities may have been involved. It is clear that the experience of the industry during the Depression had the effect of deterring innovative product and contract approaches and had resulted in a holding pattern in the industry.

INFLUENCE OF HOSPITAL/MEDICAL CARE

In the latter 1940s, but more significantly in the early 1950s, the development of another health insurance product began to affect the growth and sales in the individual disability income line. Individual hospital contracts appeared, and then later on in the mid 50s, major medical contracts began to appear in large volume and were offered to the public. Because much of this business was sold by individual life and disability income salespeople, I believe that its emergence during this period tended to slow down the growth of disability income sales. This book is not intended to discuss the hospital/medical care product line or its contractual approaches. However, the significant growth of the hospital product line of insurance through the 50s and well into the 60s affected both the level of sales and the further development and experimentation with new approaches in the disability income product line.

Aside from the fact that the purposes of hospital/medical care coverage were different from those of disability income, there was another factor surrounding hospital/medical care that concerned managers in the disability business. Disability income insurance, similar to life insurance, requires the salesperson to have well-developed sales skills and in-depth product knowledge. Neither life nor disability income is "bought"; it must be "sold." However, hospitalization coverage grew in acceptance in the public's mind—as far as its necessity was concerned—until virtually every American believed that a hospital/medical care program was as important as automobile and homeowner's insurance. Therefore, hospitalization is in fact "bought" by the consumer to a much greater extent than is either life or disability income. Home office managers consequently developed concern that to the extent that individual hospitalization sales increased, the professional quality and technical development of their sales force was somewhat impaired.

Finally, but by no means least, the reimbursement nature of the hospitalization contract tended to develop a core of claimants who were less satisfied with the performance of their policy at claim time than were disability income claimants. Because the disability income contract typically pays a flat indemnity per month, the claimant had little argument with the level of benefits. With a hospital contract, in which the claimant was typically left with some charges to pay out of pocket (for either basic daily room charge, hospital services, or surgical benefits), the claimant was frequently less than satisfied with the performance of the contract.

Inevitably, because of the rapid growth of individual hospitalization premiums (in some companies reaching one third to one half of total individual health insurance sales), many insurers developed concerns through the mid and late 60s over the possibility of a national health insurance program. If such a program came to pass, they concluded, large blocks of in-force premiums would lapse, which would cause substantial upheaval in both home office and field force operations. Furthermore, large writers of individual hospitalization believed that even though a national health insurance program might well provide room for the private sector, this protection would primarily benefit the group hospitalization writers, where the volume of premium was significantly greater than on the individual side.

CHANGES IN CONTRACT LANGUAGE— 1950–1960

In the early 1950s contractual language changes began to emerge in the disability income product line. The most significant of these was the elimination of the aggregate type of benefit period and the emergence of a benefit period approach that could be recycled. As mentioned previously the aggregate type of contract accumulated the days of disability during the entire life of the contract. Although benefits for any one period of disability were limited to typically a two- or three-year benefit period, when the total days of disability for all claims combined exceeded this two- or three-year period, benefits ceased under an aggregate clause. It was not infrequent for an individual under such a contract to receive claim payments for several claims over a 20-year period; but between ages 50 and 65, when the longer disabilities occurred, the policyholder found the contract had "run out." To correct this weakness, companies eliminated the aggregate provision and issued contracts with a recycled benefit period—a new benefit period for each disability. Although the period of time benefits might be paid for any one disability were restricted to 2, 3, 5, and sometimes 10 years, the benefit period was recycled for each new period of disability.

A second development during the early 1950s was the experimenting with longer accident benefit periods within the disability income contract. The longer benefit period appeared initially on accident-only contracts and was typically a lifetime benefit. That is, if an individual was totally disabled from performing any occupation for which he or she was reasonably fitted by education, training, and experience, then the indemnity amount would be payable for the person's life. Throughout the 50s significant amounts of accident-only coverage continued to be sold, even though contracts with both accident and sickness coverage were gaining more popularity with both the consumer and the insurer. Accident-only contracts, however, were available at significantly lower premiums, and the risk of accidental disability to the consumer was clearly more tangible than sickness, particularly at the younger ages. Throughout the development of the disability income business, the accident-only contract was frequently used for experimenting with new contractual and extra-benefit approaches. Lifetime accident, short elimination periods, and medical reimbursement benefits are examples of approaches first developed for the accident-only contract and subsequently for accident and sickness contracts.

Another contractual development that occurred during this period had to do with the maximum life of the contract. Until the early 1950s most disability contracts terminated at age 60. In some instances benefits were payable beyond age 60 if the disability occurred before that age, and in some other contracts the level of benefits was actually cut in half at age 55 or 60. This approach changed in the 1950s, and most disability contracts extended the maximum contract age to 65 to coordinate with the typical retirement age at that time. In addition, the reduction to half benefits for older ages began to disappear, so that contracts written in the mid 1950s and since that time honor claims up to age 65 without a restriction as to the amount of indemnity and then continue payments for the length of the benefit period.

Gradually, another refinement in the maximum-age question began to appear. Recognizing that many individuals (particularly the self-employed) continue to work after age 65, some companies developed language that would allow the contract to continue after age 65 as long as the insured remained actively at work. This period was initially extended to age 70, but many contracts today extend this to age 72.

During the 1950s and into the early 1960s, individual disability income sales continued to grow, and non-cancellable contracts began to appear from more and more companies. The contractual changes discussed in this chapter affected both non-cancellable and guaranteed-renewable contracts. With the growth of both non-cancellable and guaranteed-renewable contracts, the volume of cancellable or optionally renewable contracts began to diminish. It should be mentioned at this point that the non-cancellable contract during this period and continuing to today carries a guaranteed-renewable provision after age 65. In other words, although the level of premium is guaranteed through age 65, at that point companies have the option of increasing the premium for individuals who continue their contracts beyond that point. Until recent years few non-cancellable companies took advantage of this option, but with the claims experience problems of the mid 1970s, some companies did begin to increase their premiums on this block of policyholders.

The Uniform Standard Provisions Law was gradually replaced in the 1950s by the Uniform Individual Accident and Sickness Policy Provision Law. This new law was less rigid than its predecessor and allowed more flexiblity in designing contracts.

GROWTH AND COMPETITION—1960–1968

In the early 1960s a further contractual change involved an optional Uniform Provision clause called the Relation to Earnings Provision. This language had been available to companies to include at their option in the contract and provided for coordination of the amount of claim payments under a contract with other individual contracts, a language approach intended to limit overinsurance problems. The use of this language was particularly popular with insurers in those contracts that provided long periods of benefits. From its inception and clearly following the severe losses of the 1930s Depression, the industry recognized a relationship between the level of benefits and the amount of income. Disability income is different from life insurance because the value of a life cannot be objectively determined. Disability income is more closely related to casualty insurance, where the amount of indemnity to be insured can be more directly tied to the potential loss. In disability insurance, therefore, similar to casualty coverage, the closer the level of insurance approaches the actual loss, the greater the tendency for claim. The Relation to Earnings language was intended to mitigate overinsurance situations. Unfortunately, the language allowed under the Uniform Provisions was complicated and very difficult to administer and explain. Consequently, in the late 1950s and early 1960s, even though the risk of overinsurance was a concern, competitive pressures caused companies to remove the Relation to Earnings clause from their contracts, particularly in the professional and business markets.

By the mid 1960s the industry had progressed and prospered for more than 25 years, and the need and demand for disability income coverage was greater from the consumer and from the salesperson. Many predominantly life insurance companies who had dropped their disability income products and riders during the Depression of the 1930s began to reexamine their decision, and one of the primary motivations in this reexamination was the fact that their sales forces were demanding the product. Several well-established and high-quality life insurance writers, particularly mutual companies, found their agents brokering disability business through four or five specialty disability income companies. They were naturally concerned that these relationships with other companies might ultimately lead to the brokering of life insurance business by their agents and loss of control of their captive sales force.

During the early 1960s and building rapidly through the later 1960s and early 1970s, the Paul Revere Life Insurance Company, the Provident Life and Accident Insurance Company, the Monarch Life Insurance Company, the Union Mutual Life Insurance Company, and the Guardian Life Insurance Company began to capture substantial blocks of premium income through their brokerage disability operations. The majority of this brokerage business came from well-established agents of large and well-known life insurance companies who either did not offer disability income products for sale or who offered such products but did not support them with adequate training and marketing programs. These disability income specialists initially showed reluctance to expand substantially their brokerage marketing, since they feared it would exhibit the same type of characteristics that had traditionally been a part of life insurance brokered business. Industry experience had clearly shown in the past that brokered life business tended to be "shopped business"—with a greater degree of antiselection and with poorer persistency. Interestingly, the experience of disability income brokerage business did not, and to this day does not, carry these same characteristics. Companies writing disability income brokerage have found it to be of high quality and unusually persistent. The explanation for the different experience between brokerage life and disability income clearly results from the fact that the source of disability income brokerage business was primarily the high-quality, well-established, and professional life insurance salesperson who was looking for a "quality" outlet for disability income needs to service clients. These salespeople were not "shopping" business to get the most attractive rate or commission, but rather were motivated to locate a quality disability income contract to serve their clients.

During the 1960s, "programming" of disability benefits began to appear. The purpose of programming was to provide insurance coverage that recognized an individual's salary continuation and group insurance through a variety of elimination periods and benefit periods that worked around these other coverages.

INCREASED LIMITS AND INCREASED LIABILITIES—1968–1974

Another important development occurred in the mid and late 1960s that opened up the disability income marketplace to substantial growth in premium and sales. Until this time few companies offered monthly indemnities exceeding $1,000 per month, even though a need could be identified for professionals and businesspeople who earned incomes at levels large enough to justify $2,000 to $3,000 per month of indemnity. One of the reasons for these low issue limits was that reinsurance facilities for these larger indemnities were lacking. Also the conservative approach to limits was again a holdover from the serious financial losses suffered in the 1930s. In the mid 1960s reinsurance facilities began to open up. At the same time direct writers, following several years of profitable experience, began to relax their issue-limit maximums. By the end of the 1960s, issue limits of $2,500 per month were common, and this trend continued through the early 1970s to the point where issue limits of $3,000 and $3,500 were more and more frequently seen. Coupled with this increase in issue limits was the fact that the professional and self-employed business market was identified as a source of large-premium, persistent, and quality business. The substantial growth in premium of the disability industry in the 1970s can be directly attributed to significant penetration of the professional and white-collar market. It was here that the brokerage disability income companies primarily concentrated their efforts and experienced very substantial success.

Coupled with the penetration of the professional marketplace, the growth of brokerage business, and the increase in issue limits was the significant extension of the maximum benefit period for which indemnities were payable under disability income contracts. As mentioned previously, through the mid 1950s benefit periods longer than three years were unusual, and benefit periods beyond five years were seen in only a very few instances. In addition, because of insurers' concerns that significant amounts of indemnity paid for longer periods of time would tend to extend the normal length of a disability, it was common practice for a company to offer lower levels of indemnity for 5-year coverage and 10-year coverage than for 2- and 3-year benefit periods. Similar to the situation in the indemnity area, the encouragement of significant profits on disability income business over the previous 20 years caused companies to begin to extend the maximum benefit period beyond a 10-year period to age 65 for sickness coverage. Although lifetime accident benefits were common in the early 1950s, because of the more subjective risk of sickness claims, it was not until the mid and late 1960s that many companies began to offer long-term sickness benefit periods. The high-quality aspects of the professional and white-collar markets made it natural for insurers to offer the large-indemnity/long-benefit period contract exclusively in this occupation grouping, and this generally continues through today.

The emergence of the larger indemnity and longer benefit period contracts was significant. Up through the early 1960s the maximum liability for an insurer for one claim was rarely more than $500 a month for 10 years, or $60,000. By 1970, the potential liability for one disability on a $2,000-per-month contract with a benefit period to age 65 represented a total liability of $720,000 at age 35 and, of course, even greater amounts at the younger ages. In a 10-year span, liability had increased more than 12-fold! The mandatory claim reserves required for open claims, particularly those open longer than 60 days, grew in proportion to the increase in liability. Claim reserves on a single claimant could frequently exceed $100,000 and occasionally were as high as a quarter of a million dollars.

It is proper to point out that with this rapid change in the characteristics of the disability business, neither underwriting rules or approaches nor claim approaches kept full pace with the rapid increase in potential liability. Companies continued to underwrite without adequate recognition of the change in either the amount of indemnity or the length of the benefit period.

GOVERNMENT ENCROACHMENT

Another event that began to affect the business in the mid and late 1960s was the encroachment of both the federal and state governments into the disability income business. In 1958, Congress enacted legislation that provided disability benefits under the Social Security program for individuals disabled after age 60. In 1965, this was extended to essentially all participants in the Social Security program, although an elimination period of one year was necessary. Also during the 60s several states considered developing their own cash sickness or disability programs to cover disabilities that were not covered under the Workers' Compensation program. These governmental disability programs are discussed in more detail in Chapter 20.

By the late 1960s the level of both federal and state disability payments had reached the point at which insurers recognized that they could no longer ignore these benefits in considering applicants for private individual disability income coverage. It is an accepted fact that the greater the amount of disability benefits available to an insured, the greater the possibility of claim, and the greater the possibility of a claim being extended. Insurers, therefore, commenced to reduce the normal amount of disability benefits they would write, dependent upon the level of governmental coverage. Since the amount of disability insurance covered by insurers is directly related to the earned income of the applicant, and since both federal and state programs offered a greater proportion of income protection to the lower-income individual, this lower-income marketplace began to disappear.

In 1972, Congress enacted more changes in the Social Security disability program, including a built-in inflation factor that increased the total amount of benefits even further and encroached more into those markets that had historically been the domain of the private insurers. This 1972 federal legislation was to cause substantial problems for the disability income trust fund under Social Security in later years (see Table 1–1). In fact, because of the way in which the disability income formula operated, the actual yearly inflation increase in Social Security benefits tended to run much higher than the rate of inflation (see Figure 1–2). Many individual disability income insurers had built their reputations and blocks of business in the middle-income and blue-collar markets, and both Social Security and state cash sickness programs eliminated many of these markets by the mid 1970s. To write three-year benefit period disability income contracts on individuals with incomes of less than $12,000 after 1974 meant that an insurer was consciously providing

TABLE 1–1
Social Security Income versus Benefit Payment Growth ($ millions)

Year	Disability trust fund income	Disability benefit payments
1970	$ 4,800	$ 3,300
1975	8,000	8,800
1980	13,900	15,900
1981	17,100	17,700
1982	22,000	17,400
1983	18,000	17,500
1984	15,900	17,900
1985	17,200	18,800
1986	18,400	19,900

1982 *World Almanac;* 1988 *World Almanac.*

FIGURE 1-2
Comparison of Social Security OASDI Benefit Increases to Consumer Price Index, Using 1970 as Base Year

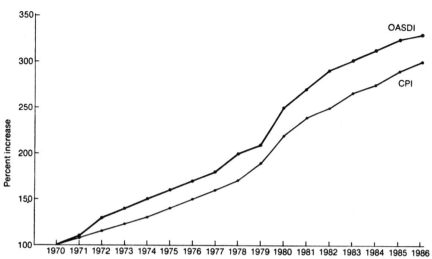

to a policyholder coverage that exceeded prudent levels of replacement income.

By 1977 the disability income trust fund under Social Security was so rapidly being depleted that Congress was faced with taking immediate corrective action. Consequently, legislation was passed in 1978 that began to correct some of the serious overinsurance problems that existed within the Social Security system—the most important of which was removing and correcting that part of the law that provided for benefits increasing at almost twice the rate of inflation. In 1980 additional legislation was passed that tightened up still further on the disability income part of the Social Security system. Specifically, this 1980 law introduced a formula that related the maximum benefits payable to the claimant's predisability earnings, set up tighter administrative guidelines, and generally attempted to remove the more serious abuses. Although the 1983 Social Security legislation did not significantly affect the disability income program, it represented clear evidence that Congress was reluctant to further expand Social Security benefits. There was simply no public support for increased taxes to support increased benefits, and no available trust fund surpluses.

RECESSION—1974–1976

The mid-1970s recession, the deepest since the Great Depression of the 30s, caused serious and broad losses throughout the disability industry. Liberalizations in contract language, underwriting, and claim

practices, along with overinsurance caused by government encroachment, combined to cause significant losses in the disability business.
The industry had failed to remember the cyclical nature of the disability
income product and that it must resist over-liberalizing rates, language,
and underwriting procedures during good economic times, since the
inevitable recession will come. The magnitude of the mid-70s recession
was accentuated by the magnitude of the socioeconomic changes in the
previous several years. Since disability income experience is so directly
affected by the stability and motivation of the policyholder, as the public's
attitude and expectations of the government providing various types
of benefits became more prevalent, this same expectation extended to
disability contracts. During the recession, and particularly because of
its severity, the change in social attitude became evident in claims experience.

Losses in the disability business from 1974 through the end of
the decade continued at levels greater than at any time during the postwar
period (see Figure 1–3). Some companies began to change their contracts
and underwriting rules to recognize the socioeconomic differences. Premium rates increased at the lower occupation classes; shorter elimination
periods began to disappear; and by the end of the 1970s, only a small
portion of individual disability income premium was being derived from
applicants with incomes less than $20,000 per year. Governmental en-
croachment was indeed a major factor in aggravating these claims losses
during the recessionary period.

FIGURE 1–3
Non-Can Disability Profits/Percent of Premium, Using 1972 as Base Year

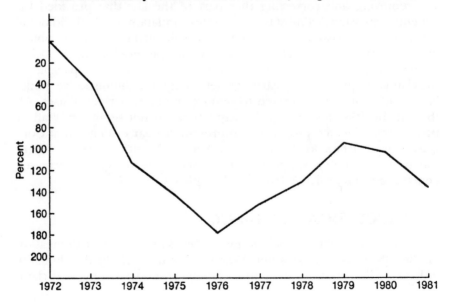

1980s

By the early 1980s, the industry had begun to reestablish its confidence in underwriting, product language, and rate structure. However, very substantial changes in markets and products had resulted. New premium volume was even more concentrated in the professional, white-collar markets, and the lower-income, blue-collar markets had been essentially abandoned to the federal government out of necessity. The more moderate recession of 1981–1983 did not cause the types of problems that the industry had experienced in the mid 70s. Although group writers did experience some claims losses in their disability income product line during this early 1980s recession, total individual disability experience showed that the steps that had been taken in the previous few years had corrected most of their problems.

With the favorable economic environment through 1986, the disability industry experienced substantial growth. This period was characterized by further liberalizations in contract language, increased issue limits, more relaxed underwriting, and increased competition as companies expanded their portfolios and their emphasis on disability income. Many life insurance companies committed more resources towards their disability income product line, a partial reaction to the readjustment of their portfolios as a result of the problems of universal life products. Sales and profits in life insurance had become more difficult, and consequently disability income became more attractive.

These product liberalizations began to appear as claim problems by 1986. Companies, therefore, began to adjust their premium rates, underwriting, contract language, and marketing techniques to restore the necessary margin to the product line. This cycle of sales expansion and product liberalization, followed by product restriction and sales contraction, continues to be a characteristic of the disability business. The 1980s cycle was simply one more evidence of this phenomenon.

Life versus
Disability Income

2

At the outset of this book it was stated that the text would make comparisons between life and disability income in several instances. The majority of disability coverage is written by companies who are primarily life insurers and whose disability income personnel often have dual responsibilities between life and disability insurance. Before going further in this book and particularly before getting into the specific disciplines of the disability business, it will be helpful to discuss further the areas of similarity and difference between life and disability.

First and foremost, of course, and overriding all other discussions of this subject is the level of maturity of the two insurance lines. Life insurance has been sold in large volume for a much longer period of time than has disability income, and therefore, the statistical base on which to make sound underwriting and actuarial judgments is much more reliable. Second, because disability income insurance is sensitive to the economy, it is much more volatile than life insurance and consequently carries more risk with it. The combination of a lack of credible statistical information and a volatile product cause me to believe that the stability and reliability of actuarial data will never reach the level of industry acceptance we find in life insurance. Let's look briefly at some of the important areas in which life/disability income differences exist. These areas are contract language, rates, selection and underwriting, claims handling, administration, sales, and governmental influence.

CONTRACT LANGUAGE

One of the most obvious areas of difference is contractual language. Although there are many language similarities, substantial differences are caused by the nature of the products being defined. Both types of contracts have insuring clauses, language relating to payment of premiums, notice of claims, incontestable period description, preexisting conditions, and other standard clauses. Beyond this, however, the disability income contract is somewhat more complicated because of its more numerous and technical definitions.

The word *disability* itself must be defined from several angles to differentiate accident from sickness disabilities, total from partial disabilities, and even permanent from temporary disabilities. When comparing this need with the need to define death in a life insurance contract, the difference in complexity is readily understood. In addition, disability contracts require other definitions: when indemnity payments commence, the elimination period, how long indemnity payments are payable, the benefit period, how recurrent disabilities are handled, the requirement of physician's care, frequency of claim payments, and so on.

In addition, disability contracts tend to offer a wide variety of optional benefits, which require further definition. Life insurance contracts normally offer some additional benefits—such as waiver of premium, accidental death, and guaranteed insurability coverage. Optional disability benefits are more numerous and would include lifetime accident coverage, hospital confinement benefits, medical reimbursement benefits, guaranteed insurability, cost of living, accidental death and dismemberment, waiver of premium, partial benefits, overhead expense, loss of use provisions, and some other benefits that are less common.

RATES

Because of the larger number of variable factors affecting disability claims, such as the economy and the motivation of the claimant, the actuary's job is also made more difficult. The reliability of morbidity data, both because of the lack of great volume and its volatile nature, tend to make one conclude that disability income rate-making is frequently more of an art than a science. During the past 20 years, more reliable statistical information has been developed on both the frequency of claim and the rate of recovery, and with each passing actuarial study, the "art" does become more of a "science." In the early 1980s the Society of Actuaries researched and developed new disability tables on which to base disability income reserves which will replace the 1964 Commissioner's Disability Table. These new tables were adopted by the National Association of Insurance Commissioners and are being implemented in the various states. Some of the elements that contribute to the complexity and volatility of disability income rate-making, in contrast to life insurance, are the greater number of variables affecting rates. Life insurance rates vary primarily by age, sex, and type of policy form. Disability insurance rates vary not only by policy form, age, and sex, but also by occupation class, elimination period, benefit period, and by the large variety of extra benefits.

In addition, there are different types of disability products—optionally renewable, guaranteed renewable, and non-cancellable—each of which requires different actuarial assumptions because of the difference in the rate-guarantee provision.

SELECTION AND UNDERWRITING

The disability income underwriting process, particularly that for non-cancellable, follows closely the process for life insurance. A fairly extensive application must be completed by the applicant and the agent. Attending physicians' statements are ordered frequently; inspection reports are regularly required for the larger indemnity amounts; and medical examinations are also required for the larger indemnities and longer benefit periods where more is at risk. Supplementary information is often requested—such as detailed income questionnaires, blood pressure questionnaires, and diabetes questionnaires.

Income and occupation are of much more significance in disability income underwriting than in life insurance underwriting. The indemnity approved by the underwriter must bear a direct relationship to the applicant's earned income, and every applicant must be classified into one of four or five occupational class groupings, which determine the level of premium rate.

Perhaps one of the best measures of the difference between life and disability is a comparison of the frequency of rejected and substandard cases in life and disability insurance. Typically, 1 to 3 percent of all life insurance applicants are found to be uninsurable; however, rejection rates in disability income are normally found to be in the 6 to 10 percent range. In life insurance 3 to 5 percent of all applicants are found to be impaired and require an extra premium at time of issue; however, in disability income between 15 and 20 percent of all applicants are found to be impaired enough to require either an extra premium charge, an exclusion endorsement, or a combination of both.

In addition, some 15 percent of all remaining disability applications are changed and modified in some other way, such as reducing the indemnity because of insufficient income or overinsurance or changing the occupation class because of information developed during underwriting. When the total impact of these changes is measured, we find that in life insurance some 8 percent of applications are changed from the way they were submitted to the underwriter; however, in disability income close to 40 percent of all applications are changed or modified in some way.

CLAIMS HANDLING

The most important point to remember in distinguishing life from disability claims handling is a most simple and fundamental one. There's only one death claim in life insurance; there can be many disabilities in disability income! The second point to remember (and perhaps more important to the claims examiner) is that the claimant for disability income is a participant in the claim process and indeed has some control over the extent of the claim itself. The claimant's stability, motivation, and employment circumstance all are as important in determining the length of a claim as is the nature of the disability itself. In life insurance the determination of the claim is quite definite indeed; but in disability insurance both the determination of disability itself and then its continuation are frequently quite subjective and vulnerable to abuse through malingering.

One interesting development in the current field of disability claim handling is in the area of rehabilitation—another area that does not exist in life insurance. Historically, disability income companies have not had active or successful programs encouraging rehabilitation; however, in recent years more attempts have been made in this area.

ADMINISTRATION

The administration of in-force policies also involves many similarities between life and disability insurance—for example, their common functions and department names, such as billing and collections, policyholder service, rewrites, policy changes. The administrative difference between the two product lines tends to be more a matter of degree than of actual function. It is more frequent in disability insurance for an individual to replace an old policy when increasing coverage than is the case in life insurance. Since the disability income contract does not have a cash value, there is less incentive to continue the old contract. Because of the high percentage of applications that are either rated, modified, or changed in some other way, the percentage of reconsiderations of the original underwriting decision is at a higher level in disability than in life insurance. This reconsideration activity is not confined simply to the first few months after issue but may continue for several years.

SALES

In the sales process the maturity of the disability business in contrast to life insurance becomes quite apparent. Most insurance salespeople are trained first in life insurance and consider this their primary product line. If they sell disability income at all, it is clearly as a secondary product. Company promotional material, sales aids, and various levels of product support are highly developed in life and disability insurance. Proposals for business markets, estate needs, and various types of advanced life sales needs are available to the salesperson. However, although sales support for disability income products has increased markedly over its position several years ago, the level of such support is still very limited. Those few companies that write large volumes of disability income tend to be ones with more highly developed sales support material in the areas of basic disability product knowledge, business disability income, buy and sell, overhead expense, key person, and so on.

Many of the large disability income writers firmly believe that the disability income sale is the most fundamental and basic personal insurance sale that should be made to the consumer. The argument is that the odds of suffering a long-term or permanent disability before an individual retires are much greater than the odds of dying before retirement, and in such a circumstance the economic drain on the family is much more severe. With the proper protection for disability income, the insured not only can provide income for the family but can also pay for his or her life insurance premium. Therefore, there may be a difference in philosophy between the primary disability salesperson and the primary life insurance salesperson; that is, which product should be sold first.

There is one other important point to consider regarding sales when comparing the two product lines. Although in both products the role of the salesperson as a field underwriter in the selection process is an important one, in disability insurance, field selection is especially critical to the success of the product line. For all of the reasons mentioned above, the agent is in the best position to measure the stability, motivation, and general character of the applicant in the disability income process, and this evaluation has a much more direct bearing on the claims experience than would be true in life insurance.

GOVERNMENTAL INFLUENCE

Although the governmental influence factor is not of the same type as those factors mentioned previously in contrasting life and disability insurance, it is important and deserves special attention. First, let us consider similarities in government influence on life and disability insurance.

- Both product lines are regulated at a state level and are regulated to approximately the same degree.
- Both are subject to the requirements of the Uniform Provisions Law.
- Both are subject to New York State extraterritorial jurisdiction.
- Both must file policy forms in states before they can be sold.
- Both are subject to a variety of other sales and promotional regulations.

One of the differences is that many states require filing and approval of disability income premium rates before contracts can be sold, whereas the same type of procedure does not exist in life insurance.

Government encroachment into the insurance business through Social Security at the federal level affects both life and disability markets. Its effect is more immediate and significant, however, on disability income insurance, since the relationship of indemnity and income has such a direct bearing on frequency and length of claim. It was mentioned in the previous chapter that when Social Security disability benefits expanded rapidly during the early 1970s, claims experience also escalated because of overinsurance problems. State cash sickness benefits and Workers' Compensation benefits (not to mention no-fault automobile insurance) provide governmental benefits that place them in competition with the private sector. During the past 10 years insurers have attempted to develop disability income products that program and coordinate around governmental coverages to the extent allowed by law.

Disability income and life insurance do represent similar products from contractual, actuarial, underwriting, claims, and administration viewpoints—more similar than other products that exist in the insurance industry. Yet there are still many differences. Disability income is an infant when compared with the sophistication and the reliability of data available in life insurance. On the other hand, this lack of maturity represents tremendous opportunity for experimentation and innovation in a product line that is not yet fully developed and mature. It presents an opportunity for creativity, along with the excitement and challenge of the risk associated with a volatile product.

Stability
and
Motivation

3

To the person whose entire experience has been in the life insurance arena, the prominence given to stability and motivation in this book may be difficult to understand. However, it is here that the greatest difference between disability and life insurance exists, and it is here that the success or failure of the disability income product is determined. Some disabilities can be objectively determined; however, others are much more subjective. Some individuals will continue to work with a given physical impairment; others will become disabled. Some people are affected by psychosomatic disabilities when economic pressures become severe; others are not. Some individuals will use disability to finance early retirement; others with the same physical impairment will work well beyond retirement age. Some claimants are anxious to become involved in rehabilitation programs; others with even less serious impairments are not.

The listing of different circumstances in which people are differently motivated can go on endlessly, but the importance of the will to work is basic to disability income insurance. Furthermore, as the work ethic of the society in which we live changes, our products are directly affected and must be adjusted. Disability income claim experience is very dynamic, reflecting to a considerable extent the changes in the society in which we live. It is only natural that the product that insures the economic stability of an individual and his or her family would be affected by the changes in attitude, motivation, stability, and mores of that family unit.

CHANGES IN THE WORK ETHIC

Since the end of World War II, the United States and indeed the entire Western world has seen a substantial change in traditional work-ethic patterns. This degree of change accelerated in the late 1960s and early 1970s, and the will-to-work level was significantly depressed at the time the economy entered into the deep recession of the mid 1970s. This circumstance and internal problems within the disability income industry itself were the major reasons for the substantial claim losses during this period. It may be considered somewhat reactionary to discuss seriously the subject of work ethic at a time when accepted personal attitudes toward one's employment are undergoing such marked changes. Nevertheless, it is important for the student of disability income to understand that there has been movement away from traditional work-ethic patterns and that this movement has required a reevaluation and modification of some of the basic assumptions of disability insurance.

AGE OF ENTITLEMENT

The so-called "age of entitlement," during which a greater percentage of the population looks increasingly toward government to provide a variety of social programs, tends to make the individual not only more dependent upon the government, but also more dependent upon such private institutions as insurance companies. The traditional attitude of the public in regard to insurance was that it was protection they paid for and hoped never to have to use. To some extent that attitude has been replaced in a significant part of the population with a new attitude that says in effect, "If I've paid for it, I should expect at least to get my money back." To the extent that this type of a change has taken place, the assumptions and premiums supporting disability contracts must also be changed. The life insurance contract is not affected as directly by such changes in the work ethic. Hospital and medical care contracts are affected to some degree; however, the scarcity of hospital beds tends to place controls on excessive overutilization. The primary control that exists in disability insurance is the self-motivation of the claimant, along with the controls the insurer places on abuses in the claims process.

GOVERNMENTAL COVERAGE

Although the change in traditional work-ethic patterns began to emerge noticeably after World War II, the degree of change accelerated markedly in the late 1960s and early 1970s. During this period disability benefits under such governmental programs as Social Security, state cash sickness, and Workers' Compensation all expanded to meet the public's growing demand and expectation for a wider range of governmental benefits. Not only did significant overlaps between governmental and private coverages cause overinsurance, but some governmental programs overlapped other government programs. Also during this period Social Security disability benefits in particular grew at a pace that far exceeded the rate of inflation. Later on in this book governmental programs, and particularly Social Security, will be discussed in more depth.

MID–1970s RECESSION

For the disability insurer, the problems of changes in the work ethic, the age of entitlement, excessive governmental coverages, and some unsound industry practices came to a head in the recession of the mid 1970s, the deepest recession in four decades. From 1974 through 1977, disability insurers suffered the greatest losses they had suffered since the Depression of the 1930s. Several companies pulled out of problem markets; some companies pulled out of the disability business altogether; and some companies suffered such losses that they went into receivership (see Figure 3–1). If industry managers had forgotten the lesson of the 1930s—that disability income insurance is a very cyclical business—then the mid 1970s was all too real a reminder. It is impossible to quantify which excess had the greatest impact upon disability insurance claims during this period. Was it the work ethic, or excessive governmental benefits, or excessive industry practices? Overshadowing each element, however, was the basic change in the attitude of the public and its stability and motivation. Actuarial assumptions that the disability industry had worked with for many decades had to be adjusted.

CHANGES IN THE DISABILITY BUSINESS

As a result of this period, fairly recent in history, the characteristics of the disability business changed considerably. By 1980 private insurers were writing considerably less disability insurance at the low- and middle-income ranges on which governmental programs had encroached severely. Policies with first-day accident coverage had basically disappeared from the marketplace because of adverse experience. Indeed, the minimum elimination period for sickness gradually increased from 7 days to 15 days, and many companies began to offer only 30-day elimination periods. Premium rates increased, particularly at the lower occupation classes, where the most serious claims problems had been experienced during the mid 1970s recession. And finally, disability underwriters began to take more and more notice of stability characteristics of the applicant.

As already mentioned, claim loss problems again began to surface in the 1986 period. Although it is not possible at this writing to be precisely certain of the factors causing this latest deterioration in claims,

FIGURE 3–1

Statutory Profits (Non-Can Disability)—Argus Charts of Health Insurance, 1967–1979

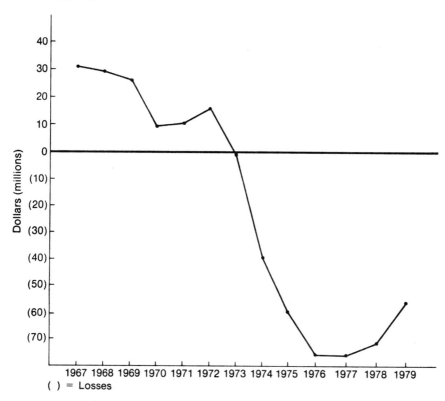

( ) = Losses

Source: The National Underwriter Company.

stability and motivation are clearly some of the causes. Professional risks, especially dentists and physicians, are causing higher claim costs than assumed in the rates. As individual risks they have lost some of the unique motivational characteristics of the past; that is, independent workers, self-employed, with very high incomes, stature, and scarcity. An oversupply of these professionals, earning less income, employed by group practices, under more government regulation, and subject to increasing costs and threats of litigation, cause changes in the behavior at time of claim.

RELATIONSHIP OF STABILITY TO CLAIMS EXPERIENCE

The stability of the applicant in family, community, and employment situations began to receive more attention. However, even with this attention, the ability of underwriters to draw reliable conclusions based upon subjective information was at best limited. It is somewhat of a fundamental of disability insurance, however, that there is a direct correlation between claim experience and stability. In life insurance the goals of the company and the insured are usually the same; both wish the insured a long and healthy life. In disability insurance, however, the goals of the company and the insured may well be in conflict. The company would always prefer that the insured remain healthy and certainly not submit more than his or her "share of claims"; however, there are circumstances in which it is to the insured's advantage to become disabled or to remain disabled. The stability of one's job, how well one is motivated, personal family problems, whether one is single or married, whether or not one has a family to support, and whether or not one is interested in early retirement—all these factors mesh together to create circumstances in which a disability policyholder may elect to become totally disabled, either temporarily or permanently.

A basic problem for the disability income underwriter is how to determine and identify that applicant who represents a high risk for future claims because of certain financial or stability characteristics, entirely separate from what the applicant's medical or physical condition may be.

The key is motivation! We all know individuals who because of their personal drive or motivation will return to work sooner than other people. The disability underwriter knows that the employer will generally return to work sooner than the employee, the professional person sooner than the laborer, the married individual sooner than the single risk, and the high-income earner sooner than the low-income earner. Stability patterns in the applicant's history are, therefore, of significant importance to the disability underwriter. Statistics show clearly that the single, 22-year-old unskilled worker will not only lapse more quickly, but will generate poorer claims experience than will the married, 35-year-old in a skilled occupation.

During the past decade a few companies have begun to experiment with a persistency rater (perhaps more accurately called a stability rater) to attempt to measure the expected persistency of a particular applicant. Since industry statistics do clearly indicate that there is a direct relationship between persistency and claims experience, a reliable method of screening out risks with potential unfavorable persistency can have an important and favorable impact upon claims experience.

FACTORS THAT INFLUENCE STABILITY RATING

A large number of factors may affect the stability rating, and following are some of the more significant ones:

1. *Age*—Industry studies indicate that risks under age 30, and particularly under 25, are not only poor persistency risks, but also experi-

ence higher claims rates, particularly for accidents. The claim rate then begins to come down in the late 20s and follows a more natural curve that increases with age. Since there is also a relationship between unemployment and frequency of disability, and since younger workers are more subject to unemployment in poor economic times, the younger age risk is also a greater disability risk from this angle.

2. *Marital Status*— As a group single risks do not represent the same stability pattern for disability insurance as do married policyholders. The same factors that contribute to this group of risks having poorer persistency can also be translated to a somewhat higher risk for disability.

3. *Occupation* —Generally speaking, the more skilled the occupation, the greater the stability; but perhaps more important than the physical characteristics of the job is whether or not the insured is the employer or employee. The employers—including managers, supervisors, and lead workers—are simply more stable disability income risks. They are less apt to stay home from work with a minimal impairment and are likely to return to work sooner than would the employee. The motivation gap between these two groups tended to widen as the entitlement ethic more and more replaced the traditional work ethic. The distinction between the groups has various shadings. For example, the employee who is a skilled worker tends to be more stable than the less-skilled employee.

4. *Income* —Closely associated with the pattern of persistency based upon occupation is the impact of income. Generally, the higher the income, the better the persistency, and the better the claims experience. The key question is, "Is it the income, the occupation, or the employer/employee status that causes the change in stability?" The chances are it's some combination of all of these items.

5. *Sex* —Industry studies indicate that in the past male risks have exhibited better persistency and lower morbidity than have female risks. Consequently, premium rates for women have been higher than for men—not only because of the expectation of higher morbidity, but also because of expected poorer persistency. The reason behind the study results is less clear. Natural physiological differences may cause increased morbidity in females but obviously should have no effect on persistency. More important, as we measure female risks within the same occupation and income groupings, we find persistency to be very close to that of male risks. The fact that women in the past tended to move in and out of the labor force was a major element in adverse persistency. As women more and more assume equal status and stability in the work force and in their earned income, I believe the current persistency differences by sex will disappear.

6. *Mode* —Similar to life insurance studies, the mode of premium payment has a direct effect upon the expected persistency of the policyholder and consequently is a measure of the stability of the risk. Quarterly business is clearly the poorest payment mode; annual is by far the best;

and semiannual and preauthorized monthly checks fall somewhere between. Claims experience predictably follows a similar pattern to the
persistency pattern by mode. Here again though, we must ask whether
the prime problem is the mode itself or whether poorer stability risks
associated with age, occupation, and income happen to be purchasing
one mode more frequently than another. The lower-income risk tends
not to buy the annual mode. The answer, I believe, is a little bit of
both factors, since even the most affluent professional occupational
groupings seem to show better persistency and more favorable morbidity
for the annual mode than do the same professional groupings buying
the quarterly mode. To say it another way, two individuals with identical
stability characteristics, except for the mode of payment, will still show
a different pattern for both persistency and morbidity.

7. *Job Stability* —The number of years an individual has remained
in his or her present occupation is naturally a measure of stability; and
the greater the number of years, the more favorable the stability. Perhaps
the employee who has worked for the same employer for an extended
period of time is more likely to feel a greater obligation to return to
work more quickly following a disability.

8. *Early Retirement* —After listing all of the variable elements
above, it should be pointed out that circumstances change throughout
one's lifetime that affect the level of motivation and consequently affect
morbidity. Perhaps one of the most obvious factors is the desire for
early retirement as the individual approaches age 65. The impact of
this factor is accentuated by the fact that a large percentage of insured
risks as they approach age 65 are suffering from physical impairments
that under the proper circumstances could be considered totally disabling.
A change in any one of the other stability factors as an individual approaches age 65 may be enough to trigger early retirement. An important
factor in such a decision is the amount of disability income the insured
may expect to receive as a percentage of income. Consequently, the
ratio of indemnity to income takes on greater importance as retirement
approaches—the greater the ratio, the poorer the motivation for the
insured to continue working.

9. *Overinsurance* —The ratio of income to indemnity is actually
important at all ages and is a critical element in the stability and motivation
of the risk. If the insured can expect to receive an amount when disabled
that is close to the amount received when working, the incentive to
remain working or return to work is diminished.

10. *Net Worth and Unearned Income* —Separate from an individual's
earned income and the factors surrounding one's employment situation
is the level of unearned income and net worth available when the insured
is disabled. Simply stated, if an individual is not solely dependent upon
earned income for living expenses, then morbidity may increase. Naturally, the degree of net worth and unearned income is important, as
well as the source of it, and this will be discussed in a later chapter.

FIGURE 3–2
Attained Age—Lapse Ratio (first year)

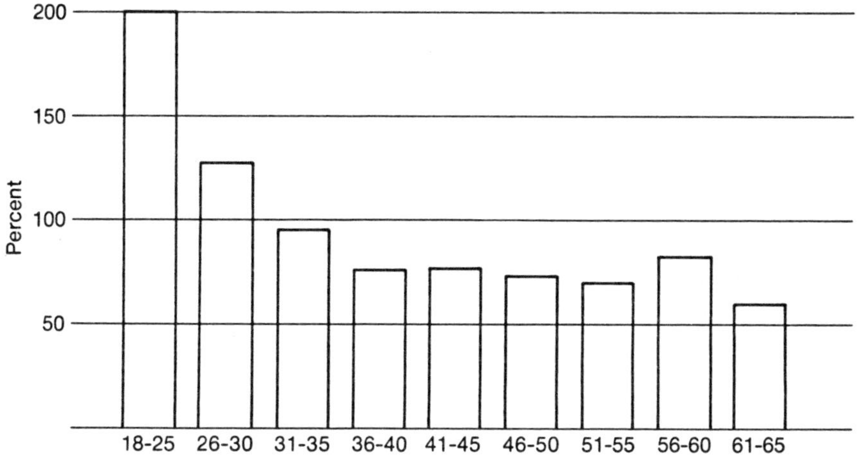

Note: Ratios are based upon comparing lapse rates with the total lapse rate for all ages.

11. *Combination of Factors* —Finally, these factors when combined will either greatly enhance or further limit the level of stability and motivation. The 22-year-old, single, unskilled, low-income applicant purchasing disability income on a quarterly mode represents a first-year lapse rate in excess of 50 percent and in addition is a high claims risk (see Figure 3–2). Similarly, the 35-year-old, married, professional risk with a high income is a better risk for the quarterly mode than is the previous individual but not as good a risk as the same person purchasing on an annual basis.

The significance of stability and motivation, therefore, weave through disability income experience, claim considerations, underwriting concerns, and actuarial assumptions in a continuous pattern. Since the characteristics themselves tend to be subjective, they cannot be quantified with precise accuracy. The impact is that stability and motivation create an important backdrop for very basic industry decisions and must be understood by the student of the business. In this area of stability and motivation, the disability income professional faces the greatest challenges and greatest dangers. Indeed, we have only begun to scratch the surface in understanding stability and motivation.

Other Disability Coverages

4

In addition to individual disability, the prime subject of this book, there are several other forms of disability income protection. All of them were developed during the 20th century, but most of their growth has occurred since the end of World War II. Included in this chapter are various forms of group disability coverage, franchise coverage, limited special-risks contracts, and a variety of governmental coverages, both state and federal.

A subcommittee of the Disability Insurance Committee of the Health Insurance Association of America completed a study in the late 1970s listing the variety of disability income programs available to the public and identified some 42 such programs (see Figure 4–1). Many were governmental, many were private, and most of them to one extent or another overlapped other forms of coverage, thereby causing overinsurance. The importance then of these "other coverages" is the potential for overinsurance that may result and indeed has resulted.

GROUP AND FRANCHISE

The earliest form of "group insurance" was the employer's personal decision to continue an employee's salary for some period of time in the event of disability. This was done without insurance and continues today. Typical employer salary continuation programs are tied to the employee's length of service and may continue benefits for a few weeks

FIGURE 4–1
Listing of Compensation Systems

Federal Disability Compensation Systems
- Primary Social Security Disability Benefits
- Dependents' Social Security Disability Benefits
- Armed Services Disability Benefits
- Veterans Administration Disability Benefits
- Veterans Administration Pension Disability Benefits
- Civil Service Disability Benefits
- Federal Employees Compensation Act
- Black Lung Benefits Act of 1972
- Longshoremen's and Harbor Workers' Compensation Act
- Railroad Retirement Act

Employer-, Union-, and Association-Sponsored Compensation Systems
- Employer/Union or Association Group Life Waiver of Premium
- Employer/Union or Association Hospital Indemnity
- Employer/Union or Association Accidental Death & Dismemberment
- Employer/Union or Association Travel Accident
- Employer/Union Group Long-Term Disability
- Employer/Union Group Short-Term Disability
- Employer/Union Group Life Total and Permanent Disability (TPD) Benefit
- Employer/Union Retirement Disability
- Employer Deferred Compensation Plans
- Employer Profit Sharing and Savings Plans
- Association Disability Income

State and Local Government Compensation Systems
- Workers' Compensation
- State Cash Sickness
- State Vocational Rehabilitation
- Supplemental Security Income
- Aid to Families with Dependent Children
- Food Stamps

Individually Purchased Insurance Industry Compensation Systems
- Disability Income
- Automobile No-Fault Disability
- Automobile (other than No-Fault) Disability
- Hospital Indemnity
- Disability Buy/Sell
- Travel Accident
- Accidental Death & Dismemberment
- General & Individual Liability
- Business Overhead Expense
- Mortgage Disability Income
- Creditor Disability Income
- Individual Insurance Waiver of Premium

Miscellaneous Sources of Income
- Underground Employment
- Recoveries through Litigation
- Unearned Income

Source: *Compensation Systems Available to Disabled Persons in the United States,* Health Insurance Association of America, 1979.

or even up to a year, the length of time usually depending upon the employer's financial resources.

Since the end of World War II, group weekly income (usually of short duration—13 weeks, 26 weeks, or 52 weeks) began to grow in popularity. One important stimulus for its growth was union bargaining. It was natural for employees to bargain for longer group disability benefits, commonly referred to as LTD, for long-term disability. Today, LTD benefits typically extend to age 65. They were originally marketed in the higher-income occupations, and employees of lower income were restricted to shorter-term weekly income. By the end of the 1970s, however, long-term disability benefits became more popular in all group plans of significant size and for all classes. A later chapter deals with group disability in more detail.

A parallel development occurred during the same period since World War II and is widely referred to as franchise disability income. Group insurance requires an employer-employee relationship; and the marketing, product design, rating, administration, and underwriting all assume this relationship. Franchise coverage is designed for non-employer–employee groups in which there is some other type of occupational relationship, normally a profession or trade. Associations of professional people are the most common holders of franchise coverage, and various types of insurance, including disability, are marketed to members of the association. Franchise disability income, particularly in the medical and legal professions, has expanded widely since the early 1960s.

The advantage of group and franchise coverages over individual disability income is twofold. First, significant administrative savings in both the selection and billing processes lower the unit cost to the insured. Second, the process of group underwriting tends to control antiselection, particularly in large groups, because of the law of averages.

There are some problems and disadvantages with group and franchise coverages; the most common problem is that the contract itself is not as liberal as the individual contract. Group coverage is not portable in that it cannot be carried from one employer to another, and at this time conversion benefits under group weekly income and LTD are uncommon. The premium under the contract is not guaranteed, and indeed the contract itself can be cancelled by either party with relatively short notice.

Group and franchise contracts are normally coordinated with both state and federal disability benefits, so that there is not a duplication of benefit payments. The primary advantage, then, of group and franchise is the relatively low cost in comparison with individual coverage, and the primary disadvantage is the lack of portability.

LIMITED CONTRACTS

As mentioned earlier in this book, disability income had its beginnings in limited contracts, typically accident-only, which paid benefits only in the event of a travel accident. To this day there are a variety of contracts offering limited benefits to the public, normally through direct mail marketing approaches. Short benefit periods, accident-only, low indemnity payments, broad restrictions and exclusions, and low premiums are the characteristics of this coverage. Frequently, the coverage is still limited to disability resulting from travel.

Not infrequently, special-risk disability income contracts for "dread diseases," such as cancer and heart disease, are marketed.

The primary problem with this type of coverage is that it tends to mislead the public into purchasing coverage that is very restricted but has an attractive low premium. The coverage is cancellable and does not represent a full disability insurance program, any more than accident-only life insurance would cover an individual's entire life insurance need.

GOVERNMENTAL COVERAGE

The growth of various types of governmental coverage has been substantial since 1960 and has had a profound impact upon the disability insurance business.

Workers' Compensation

Workers' Compensation coverage was the first form of governmental disability and developed wide acceptance by the public. It is state administered and varies in benefit and length of coverage from one state jurisdiction to another. Generally speaking, those states with the largest metropolitan areas and with a high concentration of union workers have the more liberal Workers' Compensation programs. The level of benefits expanded during the 1960s and 1970s and represents an important cornerstone of benefits for the average working American.

Social Security

Federal Social Security disability benefits first appeared in the late 1950s and with subsequent changes in federal law expanded dramatically in the 1970s. As a result of this expansion, the federal government became the primary competitor for all disability income writers. As benefits under Social Security expanded, both individual and group actuarial assumptions required change. Group coverage is able to coordinate directly with either state or federal benefits; however, in several state jurisdictions individual disability is not afforded the same privilege. The result was the emergence of a serious overinsurance problem with individual disability income and Social Security during the 1970s.

The escalation of Social Security benefits during the 1970s occurred so rapidly that the ratio of benefits to income grew out of control until corrective legislation was passed in the late 1970s (see Figure 4–2). Claims experience escalated within the Social Security system, aggrevated by the mid 1970s recession as well as by the impact of the changing work ethic in the new age of entitlement.

FIGURE 4–2
Loss Ratio Changes

State Cash Sickness

Another area of governmental disability benefits can be referred to as state cash sickness. Since Social Security benefits normally do not become payable until after five months to one year of disability and since Workers' Compensation covers only on-the-job accidents, there is naturally a void of disability coverage during the first five months to one year for nonoccupational disabilities. Five states have attempted to close this gap through legislation enacted in the 1960s. The states of New York, New Jersey, Rhode Island, California, and Hawaii all provide varying levels of short-term disability coverage, payable for nonoccupational disabilities and generally coordinated with Social Security. The level of benefits is typically the same level as Workers' Compensation in those states and essentially eliminates the private disability income market for incomes less than $15,000 per year.

No-Fault Auto

The final piece of common governmental disability coverage is found in no-fault auto legislation, where the level of benefits varies substantially from one state to another. No-fault is normally payable regardless of what other private or governmental benefits may be payable, thereby creating an overinsurance risk.

Public Expectations

Perhaps one of the most important misunderstandings about all forms of governmental coverage is public expectation of the level of benefits. Much of the public believes that through Workers' Compensation and Social Security disability their disability needs are entirely taken care of, and governmental agencies have done little to correct this misconception. All governmental coverages do have areas in which benefits are limited or not paid, and indeed the basic fundamental of governmental coverage is that it should provide a "floor of coverage" only. A second problem with governmental coverage is the inconsistency of claims administration from one state jurisdiction to another. Programs in one state are considerably more liberal than in another under Workers' Compensation, and since federal Social Security benefits are administered at the state level, there is a wide difference in benefit administration from one state jurisdiction to another. Overinsurance exists between state and federal programs, particularly Workers' Compensation and Social Security, and naturally between governmental and private coverages. The effect is increased morbidity for both private and governmental programs.

The growth of disability income during the 60s and 70s through individual, group, and governmental programs resulted in a sharply increased awareness by the public of disability benefits. This awareness, undoubtedly affected by an enhanced entitlement ethic, resulted in increased morbidity under all programs. Actuarial assumptions that had proved sound for several decades were adjusted in the mid and late 1970s in an attempt to correct rising disability costs. At the same time individual product language and underwriting rules were tightened to prevent overinsurance and antiselection.

With some 42 sources of disability income available to the American public, coordination of benefits becomes essential. Individual underwriters have experimented since the mid 1970s with a variety of policies and benefits that coordinate with state and federal programs, in an attempt to avoid overinsurance with individual and group programs. The important fact for the reader to remember is that the climate and indeed the nature of the competition in the disability income business changed markedly in the 1960s and 1970s as group insurance, franchise, and finally the enormous growth of governmental programs were felt in the marketplace.

SALARY ALLOTMENT

Various types of business insurance began to emerge in the 1960s, and one of them was salary allotment, or salary savings plan. This approach is primarily a marketing mechanism to provide individual contracts to employees of small-business organizations, usually less than 25 lives. Although it is an employer-sponsored plan, frequently the employer does not contribute toward the premium but simply acts as a vehicle for collecting the premium.

The individual is the owner of the contract, signs the application, and in addition signs an agreement to allow the premium to be deducted from his or her salary either monthly or weekly. The employer accumulates the premium and, upon receiving a master bill from the insurer that lists all covered employees, remits the collected premium to the company. Salary allotment is an attractive vehicle to the employer, who can provide individual disability income coverage for employees, frequently at a discounted rate, without additional expense to the business. It is attractive to the employee since the salary deduction procedure enhances the ease of premium payment. It is attractive to the agent and the company because substantial additional commissions and premiums can be generated with the employer's endorsement.

Individual contracts approved on this basis in the early years of development were of the cancellable or guaranteed-renewable type; however, gradually non-cancellable contracts were also offered in salary allotment or salary savings programs. This marketing approach was particularly popular in the blue-collar occupations in the 1960s and early 1970s; however, with the growth of federal and state disability programs, the market began to diminish substantially. The significant growth in Social Security disability income benefits eliminated much of the need for short-term individual disability programs in the lower-income markets, and from the insurer's point of view, the limited coverage that could be written could not be done so profitably.

During the 1970s the same salary allotment or salary savings mechanism began to appear increasingly as a vehicle in the professional and independent business-owner marketplaces. The premium payment mechanism and the premium discount available under such plans were attractive to these markets and were attractive to the agent and the company because of the endorsement of the business owner. Whereas blue-collar salary allotment cases typically had very short elimination periods (0–7 days) and relatively short benefit periods (rarely in excess of two or three years), the characteristics of salary allotment programs in the professional and white-collar markets were quite different. Individual non-can or guaranteed-renewable disability income contracts were sold in this marketplace at the same amounts and with the same features that would be found on an individual sale. Large indemnity amounts and long benefit periods are characteristic of professional and white-collar salary allotment cases, and the number of lives insured under such plans rarely exceeds 15.

Guarantee to Issue

A more recent development in the professional and white-collar salary allotment market is the availability of limited "guarantee issue" or "guarantee to issue" programs. Many of the larger individual disability insurers are experimenting with limited guarantee issue offers to the more stable professional/white-collar markets where the number of lives insured exceeds at least 15. Under such programs selection techniques that encompass some group principles are employed. Typically, the insurer will request a census of the group to be considered and will make its guarantee offer based upon an analysis of the stability of the business, the average age, and the number of lives to be covered. The guarantee offer normally requires an elimination period of at least 90 days and a benefit period of not more than two or five years. The "guarantee to issue" phrase refers to the fact that the company retains the right to use exclusion endorsements and to charge extra premiums after it has completed its medical investigation of each applicant. Therefore, it is "guaranteeing to issue" a contract but not on a standard basis. As the size of the group increases and the average age becomes lower, the guaranteed offer becomes more liberal.

In large professional corporations and businesses involving 50 or more lives, there has been some experimenting in recent years with more liberal guarantees. In the more favorable cases such guarantees may include long-term benefits, even to age 65 and lifetime, and monthly indemnity amounts in excess of $3,000 per month if the applicants' incomes warrant such coverage. Occasionally in the most promising looking cases, the insurer may guarantee to issue without exclusion endorsements, usually when the elimination period is at least 180 days, but will still retain the right to use an extra premium. A very high percent of employee participation is necessary in order to avoid antiselection and the subsequent poor claims experience.

The attractiveness of writing an individual contract with its guarantees at a discounted premium will continue to be an important factor in the growth of this market.

BUSINESS OVERHEAD EXPENSE

A second form of disability business insurance is the business overhead expense contract, which also began to appear in the marketplace in the early 1960s and expanded rapidly in the 1970s but has not to this date reached its full potential. It is important to understand that business overhead expense insurance is not "income replacement" coverage since its intent is not to replace earned income when the insured is disabled. Its purpose is rather to provide a mechanism for paying the business overhead expenses that continue when the business owner is disabled.

Such business expenses include the reimbursement of actual expenses for utilities, rent, employee benefits, depreciation, and other normal fixed expenses. The need for such coverage is readily apparent to the professional risk whose income to the business ceases upon the professional's disability. The professional partnership will also have its income reduced upon the disability of one of the partners. However, in this case income will still be generated by the working partner, and therefore the actual expenses must be carefully analyzed at both underwriting and claim time. As the number of professionals in the organization increase, the need for overhead expense diminishes, and few companies will write overhead expense where there are more than four or five professionals involved in a particular business.

Retail businesses offer particular challenges for overhead expense since the disability of the owner may not significantly affect the income of the business, particularly during the short term. Employees of the firm will continue to generate income for the business, even though the owner/manager may be disabled. In such situations it is typical for the amount of overhead expense approved to be a reduced percentage of the total expenses, perhaps as low as 50 percent. Here again, the larger the business, the greater the number of employees, the less the need for overhead expense coverage.

Most business overhead contracts have a 30-day elimination period and a benefit period of between one year and 18 months. Indemnity amounts may be issued in quite large amounts, frequently at $5,000 per month and occasionally to $20,000 per month. Special applications are required, which itemize the normal business expenses for the individual, and the underwriter analyzes such expenses for their reasonableness.

It is important to understand that overhead expense policies, in contrast to individual disability income, are on a reimbursement basis. This means that at claim time the actual claim payment is based on the actual expenses incurred, rather than a flat monthly indemnity automatically being paid. In other words, a $5,000 per month overhead expense policy may pay less than this amount if the expenses at time of disability are less than this figure.

BUSINESS BUY-OUT

A more recent business insurance development is the business buy-out contract. Its need and purpose are similar to life insurance business buy-out insurance contracts, where the loss of one of the partners to the business operation places substantial burden on the remaining working partner.

Disability buy-out contracts are purchased to help fund a buy-out of the disabled partner when the disability is a particularly long-term one or is permanent. Since the need for a business buy-out only exists in the long-term or permanent disability situations, the elimination period on such contracts is normally at least one year and sometimes longer. The period during which benefits are paid may be anywhere from one to five years, and some insurers offer a lump sum buy-out after the elimination period has been satisfied.

Business buy-outs offer unusual challenges for the disability underwriter. Evaluating the worth of the firm becomes particularly important since overevaluation may prove to be a stimulus for one of the partners to elect "early retirement," funded by the disability buy-out contract. The ideal business buy-out contract would combine both the disability income and the life insurance buy-out need, where a buy-out might commence during a period of extended disability and be completed either at the end of the benefit period or on the death of the insured. With two separate contracts, one a life and one a disability buy-out, it is possible for buy-out funds to be paid during the period of disability and then paid again at time of death. Such a combination contract would also result in a lower net premium cost to the consumer.

Similar to life insurance, disability buy-out plans normally require a formal buy-out agreement between the partners. The business buy-out agreements define the role of the disability income contract, say when the buy-out will commence in the event of disability, and use language consistent with that of the insurance buy-out contract.

KEYPERSON

Keyperson life insurance has been a popular method of marketing life insurance for many years. However, disability income insurers have not adequately solved the problem of how to define and then safely insure the "keyperson" employee.

There is no quarrel with the basic assumption that particularly in small businesses, there are key employees who are critical to the continuing financial success of the business. However, the unique stability and motivation characteristics of the disability contract present complications. How much does the loss of the keyperson affect the income of the firm during the person's disability? How long does this effect last during the keyperson's disability? The insurer must consider the second question in setting the length of the benefit period. How can the insurer be certain that the key employee today will also be a key employee at time of claim? How does the insurer avoid the employer's temptation to fund "early retirement" for the older-age employee who was once a keyperson? The problems of approving non-cancellable or guaranteed-renewable individual disability insurance in such an environment are quite obvious, and consequently few companies offer true keyperson coverage to substantially reimburse the firm for the loss of the key employee.

However, there remain product development opportunities for experimenting with optionally renewable disability contracts to meet the unique keyperson need while at the same time protecting the insurer in situations in which the keyperson's worth to the employer may change.

The various types of business disability coverages (salary allotment, business overhead expense, business buy-out, and keyperson) are all relatively new product developments in the history of the industry. There exists in this area substantial opportunity for innovation and experimenting to meet the marketplace demand in a small-business marketplace that is rapidly growing.

Economy
and
Unemployment

5

The effects of the economy and the level of employment upon the disability income business are so direct and important that they demand the attention of a separate chapter. It is clear that in good economic times all insurance lines tend to prosper—life, medical care, disability, and casualty—and conversely in poor economic times each feels the effect of the down economy.

In life insurance, the principal effect of recessions has been in the area of poorer persistency and increased policy loans. This has not normally been of serious magnitude, although clearly the deeper the recession the more serious the problem. The recessionary period of 1980–83, coupled with high inflation and high interest rates, placed tremendous pressure on policy loans and surrenders. The resulting cash flow problems represented unique problems for the life insurance business that it had not experienced previously.

INCREASE IN CLAIM FREQUENCY

The cyclical economic impact upon the disability business has had a very consistent and well-established effect on its history. Similar to life insurance, persistency tends to deteriorate during poor economic times, but the most important impact is on morbidity itself. Simply stated, claims rates go down in good economic periods and up in poor economic periods. Furthermore, the deeper the recession, the more serious becomes the claim rate problem. First, and most seriously affected, are blue-collar risks, followed by white-collar workers, and then finally professional risks if the recession is long and deep enough. This result differs from that in the life insurance industry, in which the claim rate is affected very little by economic declines.

Remembering the fact that disability experience is closely related to motivation and stability, it is no wonder that claims experience deteriorates in poor economic periods. In normal economic times many individuals with serious and significant physical impairments continue to work. However, if the same people become unemployed during a recessionary period, their tendency to present a claim is greater. The person within 5 to 10 years of retirement may find the stimulus of a recession enough for him or her to make claim for total disability and essentially retire early. The emotional and psychological effects on the worker who is faced with unemployment may well be transmitted to real physiological problems. The added stress and fear of unemployment may play havoc with a normal, healthy digestive system or nervous system. It should be stressed, therefore, that the increase in disability claims that occurs during poor economic times is not so much the result of fraudulent circumstances but rather represents true legitimate claims for which the recession itself acted as the catalyst.

INCREASE IN LENGTH OF CLAIMS

In addition to the number of claims increasing during recessionary periods, the average length of claims also tends to increase. The individual who has been legitimately disabled and collecting under a policy may consciously or subconsciously extend the claim if there is no employment to return to or if income upon returning to work will be reduced because of the down economy. Again, the subjective is difficult to separate from the objective, and so company experience also shows an increase in the duration of claims; and the deeper the recession, the longer the average duration. The keys to disability income are motivation and stability, and in this instance economic conditions may well adversely affect normally sound levels of motivation and stability.

The effects of inflation on the disability business are very similar to those in life insurance in that expenses tend to increase substantially beyond the expense level assumed in the premium rates. Policies that have been on the books for several years with lower expense-rate assumptions still require administrative handling and therefore must be administered with a somewhat lower margin. We have not faced in the United States prolonged periods of high inflation. However, as we move into the 1980s, the effect of anticipated high levels of inflation are causing disability insurers, as well as life insurers, to examine their products, their methods of marketing, and various alternatives to improve expense rates.

PRODUCT LIBERALIZATION
AND RECESSIONS

The cyclical impact of the economy on the disability business has been further aggravated by several internal industry practices. During good economic times, when claims are lower than expected and profits somewhat higher, there is a natural tendency for disability insurers to begin to liberalize their product assumptions. The longer the good economic period lasts, the greater the temptation to relax underwriting, treat the claims somewhat more liberally, develop more liberal product language, and lower premiums. Competitive pressure begins to mount, and the liberalizations begin to surface and expand. The inevitable recession will come, however, and with it will come more serious financial consequences because of these liberalizations in product assumptions.

The recession of the mid 1970s was a good example of this phenomenon. From the mid 1960s to 1973, the disability insurance business experienced good profits, lower-than-anticipated claims, and phenomenal growth. The longer this cycle continued, the greater the competitive pressure to liberalize, and in fact all companies to some extent relaxed their product assumptions. The result was more serious losses during

FIGURE 5–1
Non-Can Disability Loss Ratios

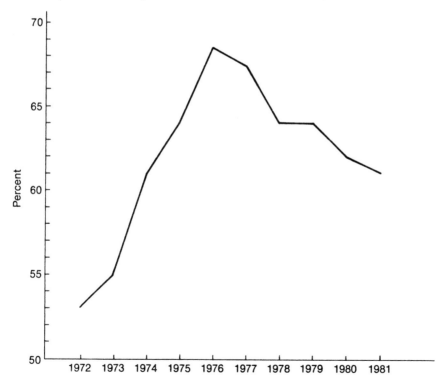

the mid 1970s for the disability business than in the previous four decades—much of the loss due to a deep recession but much of it exacerbated by the relaxing of product design assumptions (see Figure 5–1).

PREPARING FOR ADVERSE ECONOMIC SWINGS

How can the disability industry prepare for adverse economic swings? Can the disability industry adequately protect itself against such adverse swings? The answer to neither question is clear since so many variable factors are involved. However, the industry can do a much better job of preparing for adverse economic conditions and thereby avert a repetition of the magnitude of the losses that occurred during the mid 1970s. It cannot eliminate entirely the impact of economic swings since the assumptions in the disability product are so directly affected by inflation, unemployment, and recession. The more important question may be *Will we?* rather than *Can we?* The discipline required to resist overliberalization during good economic times, keeping in mind the inevitable recessionary effect, is a most difficult discipline in a competitive and changing marketplace.

Therefore, the first requirement in preparing for adverse economic cycles is to resist *over*liberalization!

Once the clouds of economic recession appear clearly on the horizon, there are conscious steps that the disability manager can take to limit the inevitable adverse impact. There are two areas to focus on: underwriting and claims.

It is never too late to take underwriting action, even when the recession is upon you. Obviously, if your underwriting has been overliberal leading up to the recession, then you are bound to be burned more than if your underwriting has been prudent. On the other hand, at the time when the recession clouds begin to mount, you are most likely to be subject to the effects of adverse selection from those people who, either consciously or subconsciously, fear for their own economic stability. As the recession approaches, it's time for the underwriter to be somewhat tighter on borderline cases. The individual whose income has fluctuated during the previous several years, or who has shown job instability, or who is in an occupation that will be clearly affected by a recession, or who shows other instability characteristics represents qualities that should be given more underwriting importance as the recession approaches.

Anyone who has underwritten either life or disability insurance for more than a year is well aware of the frequency of borderline situations—either borderline approval or borderline standard issue. In recessionary times the underwriter should consciously weigh instability characteristics more heavily and either charge an extra premium or reject the applicant entirely, depending upon the severity of the borderline situation.

The second area of emphasis is in claim handling and management. Since the insured is personally and actively involved in the claim and since the determination of disability is very often difficult to approve or disapprove, the pressure of recession carries with it both an increase in the frequency of claim and an increase in the duration of claim. The individual who in a stable employment situation would not be a disability candidate may in an unstable economic environment consciously or subconsciously elect disability. In order to adequately protect against those people who are attempting to use their disability contract as unemployment insurance, normal claims procedures must be strengthened and tightened as the recession commences. Increased investigation, more frequent review, and independent verification are all items that must be used more consciously during a recessionary period.

SOCIAL SECURITY AND RECESSION

The Social Security system is perhaps the clearest example of the adverse effects on a disability program that can result from overliberalization. The increase in benefits under the Social Security disability income program in the early 1970s established benefit levels not only above safe replacement ratios, but in some instances actually in excess of net and gross income (see Table 5–1). This set the stage for the serious financial problems that developed with the recession of the mid 1970s. As the recession deepened and unemployment increased, the frequency of claims within the Social Security disability program increased sharply. The level of benefits and replacement ratios were so high that expected rates of recovery were not reached since it was to

TABLE 5–1
Social Security Replacement Ratios: Disability
in 1980—Age 30

1978 gross earnings	Replacement ratios (MFB ÷ net income)		
	Prior to 1977 law	1979 law	1980 change
5,000	170%	90%	80%
10,000	150	90	73
20,000	100	67	55
25,000	82	55	45
30,000	70	46	38

MFB—Maximum Family Benefit.

the claimant's financial advantage to remain disabled. Legislative and regulatory corrective action in the late 1970s helped to ease the problems created by these high replacement ratios. Figure 5–2 shows the close relationship between Social Security benefit payments and unemployment levels during this period.

THE MID-1970s RECESSION

The private insurance industry itself, as has already been mentioned, suffered very severe economic losses during the mid 1970s. The prolonged period of profits and growth from the early 1960s through the mid 1970s increasingly resulted in product liberalizations, lower premiums, relaxed underwriting, and relaxed claim handling. This repre-

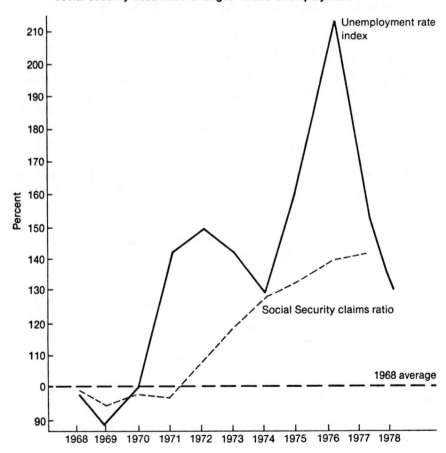

FIGURE 5–2
Social Security Loss Ratio Changes versus Unemployment

Source: Government unemployment data and annual Social Security data.

sented a perfect example of the fact that the longer the period of time between economic cycles, the more significant the liberalizations become. As a result, the disability industry suffered greater losses in the mid 1970s than it had in the previous 40 years.

Some companies in fact failed during this period, and other companies pulled out of the disability business; all disability companies to one extent or another restricted their marketing or withdrew from certain markets. The industry was forced to relearn some of the lessons of the 1930s. The erosion of traditional work-ethic patterns during the late 1960s, the overinsurance caused by governmental programs, and the overliberalizations of the industry itself all aggravated the normal adverse pressures that the disability business feels during a recession.

As a result of this period of adverse experience, the late 1970s through early 1980s was a period of readjustment and realignment within the disability business. Products, underwriting rules, and rates were all modified and adjusted to reflect the new environment the industry found itself in following this recession. As already mentioned earlier in this text, there is evidence that some disruption in historic work-ethic patterns began to emerge with dentists and physicians in the latter part of the 1980s. An oversupply of these professionals, increased government interference through regulation, and the threat of malpractice suits all combined to make these professions less desirable. The result may be that some professionals will elect early retirement based on an impairment that in the past would not have been enough to cause total disability.

The student of the disability business must remember the fundamental fact that the business is cyclical. Claims experience is directly related to the economy—in good times claims are low and profits are at good levels, but in poor economic times claims will increase and profits decrease. Complicating this statement is the natural phenomenon of the disability business that causes a liberalization in products, rates, and underwriting as a long period of sustained growth and profits develops. The longer the length of the good economic period, the greater the pressure to relax and liberalize, and consequently the greater the magnitude of loss when the recession finally emerges.

Contractual Provisions
and
Extra Benefits

6

Similar to life insurance, there has been a steady evolution and development of contractual provisions and extra benefits in the disability income product. Contractual provisions within the disability contract were affected by the Armstrong Investigation in the early 1900s and are guided by certain required Uniform Provisions, again similar to life insurance.

LIFE AND DISABILITY DIFFERENCES

There are, however, significant differences between life and disability income. First, the life insurance contract is generally more mature and more standard in its contractual provisions than is true in disability income. The disability income contract may be non-cancellable or cancellable; the definition of disability may be significantly different; and the length of benefit period, the elimination period, the treatment of partial disability, the exclusions may all vary from contract to contract. Thus is created an environment in which the basic contractual differences from one policy to another may be substantial. Most life insurance contractual differences relate to actuarial assumptions (i.e., term versus level premium, length of premium paying period, low versus high cash value, etc.). Disability contractual differences may not only result from actuarial considerations in rating, but also from different risk assumptions that result in different claim decisions at claim time.

There are some similarities in the extra benefits available in disability insurance and life insurance, such as waiver of premium and even accidental death benefits. However, there are clearly more differences than similarities. Generally speaking, the number of extra benefits available on disability income contracts is more numerous and varied. Some benefits call for increased indemnity when the claimant is hospitalized; others waive the elimination period if the claimant is hospitalized; some waive the requirement of total disability in certain situations; and others pay partial disability benefits.

It's important for the reader to remember that no two disability contracts are exactly alike, and indeed the variety of difference from one contract to another is much greater than that found in life insurance. Accordingly, it is not possible to discuss all the specific variations of basic disability contractual provisions and extra benefits, and therefore this chapter will concentrate on the major contract characteristics and extra benefits. It must be remembered that there are many varieties and modifications to each one of these provisions.

The disability income contract is regulated by the various state insurance departments through a set of specified language in the Uniform Provisions. The regulatory guidelines are very similar to those for life insurance, and the premium payment, contestability, and grace period language follow closely the pattern of life insurance contracts. The major contractual provisions are treated in the following section.

CONTRACTUAL PROVISIONS

1. *Insuring Clause*— Like all insurance contracts, the disability contract contains an insuring clause defining the general condition of insurance. It is here that the insured determines whether the contract is non-cancellable, guaranteed renewable, or cancellable. It states the length of the insuring period—normally to age 65, but in some instances for a longer period of time. Beyond age 65 the contract either terminates or is optionally continued so long as the insured continues to be employed full-time.

2. *Definition of Disability*— Since the purpose of the disability income contract is to insure against income loss from accident or sickness, a most fundamental part of the contract is the definition of disability. At first glance, one might think that a disability would be quite easy to define, but it is in fact a complex subject that has seen a variety of changes in language over many decades.

The definition of disability spells out when the insured will be considered totally disabled. In so doing, it distinguishes a total from a partial disability, a permanent from a temporary disability, an accident from a sickness disability. Although most disabilities are quite straightforward to determine, the subjective nature of many physical problems makes the determination of some disabilities more difficult. Disability is, quite simply, not as straightforward as death to determine. In addition, in the disability contract the insured in many instances has some control over both the onset and the continuation of the claim. Traditional definitions of disability in the contract have been based on whether or not claimants were able to perform duties for which they were "reasonably fitted by education, training, and experience" and also frequently took into consideration their "prior economic status." The objective with this type of definition was clearly to pay legitimate claims when an individual was unable to work but to avoid claims when an individual could reasonably work at a suitable occupation but chose not to. One practical sales problem with this definition has been the inability of the company to adequately satisfy the consumer's concern over how reasonably it would measure education, training, experience, and prior economic status in determining the eligibility for disability benefits.

As a result, in the late 1960s significant liberalizations occurred in the definition of disability, particularly the development of the "own occupation" definition, which provides for payment of claim benefits if an individual is unable to work in his or her regular occupational endeavor—even when the insured may be able to earn as much or more income in another occupation. This definition by the mid 1970s came under substantial criticism in some segments of the marketplace based on the fact that it provided benefits where no loss occurred.

As a result, in the mid 1970s a variety of *income* definitions began to emerge, and their development continued into the 1980s. Definitions of the words *income, partial,* and *residual* attempt through formulas in the contract language to indemnify the insured based upon the percentage of income lost because of disability.

3. *Indemnity Amount*— The amount of indemnity in the disability income contract may be stated on a daily, weekly, or monthly basis and is comparable to the face amount on a life insurance contract. Similarly, as the company attempts to make certain that the face amount of a life insurance application is consistent with the financial needs of the insured, in a disability income contract the company and the underwriter must determine whether the indemnity applied for bears a reasonable relationship to the applicant's current income. Indemnity amounts are most commonly stated on a monthly basis and may be as low as $50 per month and as much as several thousand dollars per month, but amounts always bear a relationship to the applicant's earned income.

4. *Benefit Period*— The benefit period in a disability income contract is a provision that is not found in a life insurance contract. It is the period of time that benefits under the disability contract are payable for a particular claim. Typically, an applicant may select a benefit period of 1 year, 2 years, 3 years, 5 years, 10 years, to age 65, or even lifetime. The longer the period that the applicant selects for benefits to be paid, the higher the premium. A short benefit period of two or three years is common for blue-collar occupations and lower income risks, and the

typical maximum benefit period for any lower-occupation risk would be five years. The long benefit periods—to age 65 and lifetime—are most frequently available to and chosen by the professional and high-middle- or high-income applicants. Lifetime accident coverage is frequently available to all occupations, even though the sickness benefit period may be for a shorter period. However, lifetime sickness benefits when available are normally restricted to only the highest quality of risks, and even then have more limitations than are found with the typical lifetime accident benefit.

5. *Elimination Period*— Another feature of the disability contract not found in life insurance is the elimination period. It is the period of time that must elapse during any disability before benefits commence. The logic behind the need for an elimination period is twofold: (1) Most people have some financial resources to call upon in case of emergency and therefore do not need immediate coverage; (2) the sooner the company provides benefits, the greater the cost of the coverage.

It is unusual for a contract to provide no elimination period and call for benefits to commence immediately upon disability. This is particularly true in our current "fringe benefit conscious" society, where most employers provide continuation of salary for some period of disability. Some disability policies are still written with no elimination period for accident but with at least seven days for sickness. Typical elimination periods today for both accident and sickness are 7 days, 15 days, 30 days, and 90 days. More and more companies are offering, and more and more applicants are electing, elimination periods of 180 days and 365 days, a reflection of the continued extension of disability benefits under employer salary-continuation programs.

In recent years there has been a steady and significant movement away from the short elimination period (less than 30 days), and some companies in fact no longer offer this option. The 30-day elimination period is today by far the most frequently offered period and the most commonly selected by applicants.

6. *Recurrent Disability*— Another clause found in the disability contract, but not in the life insurance contract, concerns recurrent disability. The language in this clause defines how the company will treat disabilities that recur for the same accident or sickness. The specific purpose of the clause is to state how long a period of time must elapse between disabilities for the same physical impairment in order to be considered an entirely separate disability. This is an important distinction for two reasons. First, if an individual has suffered a disability for several months and then attempts to return to work for a few days and is unable to do so, without language defining recurrent disability the company might unreasonably require that another elimination period be fulfilled before resuming benefits. On the other extreme, if an individual with a contract that paid benefits for two years had been totally disabled and collected benefits for that maximum period of time, without language defining

recurrent disability, the claimant could return to work for as short a period of time as one day and then recycle the entire two-year benefit period. The recurrent clause attempts to clarify these situations, and normally any disability that recurs within six months following the original disability is deemed to be a continuation of that original disability.

7. *Waiver of Premium*— The waiver of premium benefit under disability contracts is very similar to that for life insurance, normally waiving the payment of any premium that becomes due after 90 days of total disability. In addition, more and more disability contracts provide for a refund of any premium that became due during that 90-day period, and others prorate and refund premiums back to the first day of disability.

8. *Residual Disability*— In recent years contract provisions have been extended to pay some portion of the total disability benefits during periods of partial disability. The amount of residual benefits is based upon the percentage of lost income, and benefits are normally payable for the entire benefit period of the contract. Their purpose is to encourage the disabled claimant to return to work, even if on a limited basis, while at the same time paying limited benefits if the claimant is unable to earn at the same level that he or she was able to earn prior to disability.

9. *Preexisting Conditions*— Another provision found in the disability contract is that relating to preexisting conditions, and here the language is similar to that found in life insurance contracts. Very simply, normal disability income contractual language provides for a contestable period of two years and at the same time states that benefits are not payable for disabilities that manifest themselves prior to the issuance of the contract. Similar to life insurance, a preexisting condition cannot be challenged if it was disclosed on the application or by the medical examination.

Since the number of physical conditions that may disable an individual is much greater than the number of those that have an impact upon mortality, the detail of medical history and physical condition on both the disability income application and medical examination are of critical importance in the underwriting process. To the extent that they are minimized, the preexisting condition language or contestable language may not be adequate to cover the insurer's additional risk.

10. *Exclusions*— Most disability contracts today carry exclusions for only "act or accident of war." In the not too distant past, however, additional exclusions were common for disabilities resulting from attempted suicide, foreign residence or travel, self-inflicted injury, etc.

11. *Claim Procedures*— There are standard provisions in the disability contract governing notice of claim, payment of claim, and claim procedures that are designed to protect both the insured's and the insurer's interests.

12. *Payment of Premium*— Similar to life insurance contracts, there is specific contractual language relating to premium payment and grace

periods. The grace period of 30 days is typical of that found in life insurance contracts, and the procedures for late premium payment and reinstatement are also similar to those in life insurance.

13. *Relation of Earnings*— An optional provision found in some disability contracts is one that allows the insurer to reduce the level of indemnity payment if the insured at time of claim is found to carry more disability insurance than his or her income would justify. In such instances the contractual language allows the insurer to reduce the indemnity but requires the insurer to also reduce the premium and in fact refund premium in certain instances. This optional provision was frequently found in disability contracts with longer benefit periods prior to 1965, but competitive pressure resulted in its disappearance from most contracts by the early 1970s.

There has periodically been interest demonstrated in developing new "relation to earning" language that would help to control and limit overinsurance. The current relation to earnings clause is cumbersome and was developed prior to the time that high amounts of governmental benefits were available to most Americans. Many insurers today believe that all individual disability contracts should coordinate with governmental programs, although several states have legislation or regulation that prohibits direct offsetting of benefits in individual plans. Group disability insurers are able under legislation and regulation to coordinate directly with other coverage; however, this continues to be a problem in the individual disability contract.

14. *Nonoccupational Clause*— Some contracts directly coordinate with Workers' Compensation benefits and contain a clause that simply states the benefits will not be payable if the individual is eligible for Workers' Compensation benefits.

15. *Presumptive Disability*— Many disability contracts, especially those sold in the professional and white-collar markets, include language that waives the requirement of total disability under certain circumstances. For example, if the insured suffers loss of sight or loss of hearing, he or she is presumed to be totally disabled, and the benefits under the contract are payable for either the length of the benefit period or for lifetime, without the requirement that the claimant in fact be no longer earning income. In addition to the above two circumstances, it is frequent for presumptive disability clauses to also include loss of speech and loss of two limbs.

16. *Qualification Period*— The qualification period is only applicable with residual benefit payments. It is simply a required period of total disability that must have occurred prior to the time that an individual will be considered to be residually or partially disabled. The intent of this qualification period is to make certain that an individual collecting residual benefits is in fact suffering from a long-term and severe disability, rather than simply electing to slow down or become semiretired without

any significant disability problem. Qualification periods may be for 30, 60, 90 or 180 days, and some companies offer policies without a required qualification period.

OPTIONAL EXTRA BENEFITS

In addition to the basic contractual provisions, there are a large number of optional extra benefit provisions found in some disability contracts, and here again the most common of these provisions are briefly described:

1. *Reduced Elimination Period If Hospital-Confined*— This optional benefit waives the normal elimination period under the contract if the individual is hospitalized. For example, if the basic contract contains a 30-day elimination period before benefits normally start, this period is waived, and benefits begin on the first day if the individual becomes hospitalized and while he or she is hospitalized. The obvious intent is to recognize the fact that the claimant incurs additional expense with hospitalization.

2. *Hospital Confinement Benefit*— This benefit, regardless of when an individual is hospitalized, pays an additional monthly indemnity along with the basic monthly indemnity while the insured is hospital-confined.

3. *Accidental Death and Dismemberment*— Similar to life insurance accidental death coverage, this benefit provides a flat face amount payment for accidental death and also for dismemberment. Dismemberment may be defined differently in different contracts but normally pays a portion of the face accidental death amount if the insured loses a limb or sight. The amount of accidental death and dismemberment is normally a multiple of the base monthly indemnity.

4. *Future-Income Option*— Similar to life insurance, this is a guaranteed insurability benefit that provides for periodic increases in the basic indemnity without evidence of insurability. Normally the options are available every two or three years up to age 45 or 50. Although the additional benefits are guaranteed regardless of changes in physical condition, the insured must show evidence that his or her income warrants the additional coverage.

5. *Return of Premium*— This is a special provision, available in some contracts, that provides for a refund of the entire or some part of the premium based upon favorable claims activity over a specified period of time. If the claim activity has been heavy, then no return of premium is made. Some contracts provide for a return of the premium periodically based on favorable experience, while others determine the premium return at age 65.

6. *Cost of Living*— This is a benefit that has emerged in recent years that attempts to adjust the basic indemnity to recognize cost-of-living changes. Some contracts base the increase in indemnity upon a flat percentage after the individual has been disabled for a year, and

others tie the increase to some external factor, such as the change in the consumer price index. It should be emphasized that the cost-of-living factor is applied only at claim time; upon recovery the benefits under the contract revert to the original contractual level.

7. *Medical Reimbursement Rider*— This benefit was found more frequently in contracts issued prior to the 1980s but is still sold in some instances on an accident-only basis. It attempts to indemnify the applicant for medical expenses incurred for specific accidents, or in some cases sicknesses, where hospitalization is not required.

8. *Partial Disability*— Partial disability benefits have existed in disability contracts as an option for many years. Typically they pay 50 percent of the basic disability benefit during any period of partial disability and where partial disability is carefully and specifically defined in the contract. Such benefits are normally paid for a limited period of time, typically six months. The primary difference between partial and residual benefits is that the former pays a flat indemnity, without regard to the actual income loss, whereas the residual benefit attempts to relate the level of benefit payment to the actual income loss.

9. *Business Overhead Expense*— Business overhead expense coverage is normally found as a separate contract, but in some instances it may also be found as an additional benefit rider on a basic disability income contract. It should be emphasized that business overhead expense coverage is not "income replacement" but is rather designed and intended to cover the business expenses of an individual that will continue when he or she is disabled and under circumstances in which no income is coming in to cover those expenses. If the normal level of business income continues to be generated during disability, then there is no need for business overhead coverage. This coverage is normally approved only on a reimbursement basis, which means that the benefit payments are only made if the insured can demonstrate that he or she has incurred the expense.

The foregoing discussion identifies the primary contractual provisions and extra benefits but in no way attempts to identify all of those that may be found in disability contracts or indeed all of those that may be developed in the future.

The following pages reproduce part of the Uniform Individual Accident and Sickness Policy Provision Law as found in Section 3216 of the New York Insurance Laws.

(d) Each policy of accident and health insurance delivered or issued for delivery to any person in this state shall contain the provisions specified herein in the words in which the same appear in this subsection, except that the insurer may, at its option, substitute for one or more of such provisions corresponding provisions of different wording approved by the superintendent which are not less favorable in any respect to the insured or the beneficiary. Each provision contained in the policy shall be preceded by the applicable caption herein or, at the insurer's option, by such appropriate captions or subcaptions as the superintendent may approve.

(1) Each policy shall, except with respect to designation by numbers or letters as used below, contain the following provisions:

(A) ENTIRE CONTRACT; CHANGES: This policy, including the endorsements and the attached papers, if any, constitutes the entire contract of insurance. No change in this policy shall be valid until approved by an executive officer of the insurer and unless such approval be endorsed hereon or attached hereto. No agent has authority to change this policy or to waive any of its provisions.

(B) TIME LIMIT ON CERTAIN DEFENSES:

(i) After two years from the date of issue of this policy no misstatements, except fraudulent misstatements, made by the applicant in the application for such policy shall be used to void the policy or to deny a claim for loss incurred or disability (as defined in the policy) commencing after the expiration of such two year period.

(The foregoing policy provision shall not be so construed as to affect any legal requirement for avoidance of a policy or denial of a claim during such initial two year period, nor to limit the application of subparagraphs (A) through (E), inclusive, of this paragraph in the event of misstatement with respect to age or occupation or other insurance.)

(A policy which the insured has the right to continue in force subject to its terms by the timely payment of premium until at least age fifty or, in the case of a policy issued after age forty-four, for at least five years from its date of issue, may contain in lieu of the foregoing the following provision (from which the clause in parentheses may be omitted at the insurer's option) under the caption "INCONTESTABLE":

"After this policy has been in force for a period of two years during the lifetime of the insured (excluding any period during which the insured is disabled), it shall become incontestable as to the statements contained in the application.)"

(ii) No claim for loss incurred or disability (as defined in the policy) commencing after two years from the date of issue of this policy shall be reduced or denied on the ground that a disease or physical condition not excluded from coverage by name or specific description effective on the date of loss had existed prior to the effective date of coverage of this policy.

(C) GRACE PERIOD: A grace period of . . . . (insert a number not less than "7" for weekly premium policies, "10" for monthly premium policies and "31" for all other policies) days will be granted for the payment of each premium falling due after the first premium, during which grace period the policy shall continue in force.

(A policy in which the insurer reserves the right to refuse renewal shall have, at the beginning of the above provision, the following clause:

"Unless not less than thirty days prior to the renewal date the insurer has delivered to the insured or has mailed to his last address as shown by the records of the insurer written notice of its intention not to renew this policy beyond the period for which the premium has been accepted,"

Furthermore, such a policy, except an accident only policy, shall also provide in substance, in a provision thereof, or in an endorsement thereon or in a rider attached thereto, that the insurer may refuse renewal of the policy only as of the renewal date occurring on, or nearest its first anniversary, or as of an anniversary of such renewal date, or at the option of the insurer as of the renewal date occurring on or nearest the anniversary of its date of last reinstatement.)

(D) REINSTATEMENT: If any renewal premium be not paid within the time granted the insured for payment, a subsequent acceptance of the premium by the insurer or by an agent duly authorized by the insurer to accept such premium, without requiring in connection therewith an application for reinstatement, shall reinstate the policy; provided, however, that if the insurer or such agent requires an application for reinstatement and issues a conditional receipt for the premium tendered, the policy will be reinstated upon approval of such application by the insurer or, lacking such approval, upon the forty-fifth day following the date of such conditional receipt unless the insurer has previously notified the insured in writing of its disapproval of such application. The reinstated policy shall cover only loss resulting from such accidental injury as may be sustained after the date of reinstatement and loss due to such sickness as may begin more than ten days after such date. In all other respects the insured and insurer shall have the same rights thereunder as they had under the policy immediately before the due date of the defaulted premium, subject to any provisions endorsed hereon or attached hereto in connection with the reinstatement. Any premium accepted in connection with a reinstatement shall be applied to a period for which premium has not been previously paid, but not to any period more than sixty days prior to the date of reinstatement.

(The last sentence of the above provision may be omitted from any policy which the insured has the right to continue in force subject to its terms by the timely payment of premiums until at least age fifty or, in the case of a policy issued after age forty-four, for at least five years from its date of issue.)

(E) NOTICE OF CLAIM: Written notice of claim must be given to the insurer within twenty days after the occurrence of commencement of any loss covered by the policy, or as soon thereafter as is reasonably possible. Notice given by or on behalf of the insured or the beneficiary to the insurer at . . . . . . (insert the location of such office as the insurer may designate for the purpose), or to any authorized agent of the insurer, with information sufficient to identify the insured, shall be deemed notice to the insurer. (In a policy providing a loss-of-time benefit which may be payable for at least two years, an insurer may at its option insert the following between the first and second sentences of the above provision:

"Subject to the qualifications set forth below, if the insured suffers loss of time on account of disability for which indemnity may be payable for at least two years, he shall, at least once in every six months after having given notice of claim, give to the insurer notice of continuance of said disability, except in the event of legal incapacity. The period of six months following any filing of proof by the insured or any payment by the insurer on account of such claim or any denial of liability in whole or in part by the insurer shall be excluded in applying this provision. Delay in the giving of such notice shall not impair the insured's right to any indemnity which would otherwise have accrued during the period of six months preceding the date on which such notice is actually given.)"

(F) CLAIM FORMS: The insurer, upon receipt of a notice of claim, will furnish to the claimant such forms as are usually furnished by it for filing proofs of loss. If such forms are not furnished within fifteen days after the giving of such notice the claimant shall be deemed to have complied with the requirements of this policy as to proof of loss upon submitting, within the time fixed in the policy for filing proofs of loss, written proof covering the occurrence, the character and extent of the loss for which claim is made.

(G) PROOFS OF LOSS: Written proof of loss must be furnished to the insurer at its said office in case of claim for loss for which this policy provides any periodic payment contingent upon continuing loss within ninety days after the termination of the period for which the insurer is liable and in case of claim for any other loss within ninety days after the date of such loss. Failure to furnish such proof within the time required shall not invalidate nor reduce any claim if it was not reasonably possible to give proof within such time, provided such proof is furnished as soon as reasonably possible and in no event, except in the absence of legal capacity, later than one year from the time proof is otherwise required.

(H) TIME OF PAYMENT OF CLAIMS: Indemnities payable under this policy for any loss other than loss for which this policy provides any periodic payment will be paid immediately upon receipt of due written proof of such loss. Subject to due written proof of loss, all accrued indemnities for loss for which this policy provides periodic payment will be paid . . . . . (insert period for payment which must not be less frequently than monthly) and any balance remaining unpaid upon the termination of liability will be paid immediately upon receipt of due written proof.

(I) PAYMENT OF CLAIMS: Any indemnity for loss of life will be payable in accordance with the beneficiary designation and the provisions respecting such payment which may be prescribed herein and effective at the time of payment. If no such designation or provision is then effective, such indemnity shall be payable to the estate of the insured. Any other accrued indemnities unpaid at the insured's death may, at the option of the insurer, be paid either to such beneficiary or to such estate. All other indemnities will be payable to the insured. (The following provisions, or either of them, may be included with the foregoing provision at the option of the insurer: If any indemnity of this policy shall be payable to the estate of the insured, or to an insured or beneficiary who is a minor or otherwise not competent to give a valid release, the insurer may pay such indemnity, up to an amount not exceeding $. . . . . (insert an amount which shall not exceed one thousand dollars), to any relative by blood or connection by marriage of the insured or beneficiary who is deemed by the insurer to be equitably entitled thereto. Any payment made by the insurer in good faith pursuant to this provision shall fully discharge the insurer to the extent of such payment.

Subject to any written direction of the insured in the application or otherwise all or a portion of any indemnities provided by this policy on account of hospital, nursing, medical, or surgical services may, at the insurer's option and unless the insured requests otherwise in writing not later than the time of filing proofs of such loss, be paid directly to the hospital or person rendering such services; but it is not required that the service be rendered by a particular hospital or person.)

(J) PHYSICAL EXAMINATIONS AND AUTOPSY: The insurer at its own expense shall have the right and opportunity to examine the person of the insured when and as often as it may reasonably require during the pendency of a claim hereunder and to make an autopsy in case of death where it is not forbidden by law.

(K) LEGAL ACTIONS: No action at law or in equity shall be brought to recover on this policy prior to the expiration of sixty days after written proof of loss has been furnished in accordance with the requirements of this policy. No such action shall be brought after the expiration of three years after the time written proof of loss is required to be furnished.

(L) CHANGE OF BENEFICIARY: Unless the insured makes an irrevocable designation of beneficiary, the right to change of beneficiary is reserved to the insured and the consent of the beneficiary or beneficiaries shall not be requisite to surrender or assignment of this policy or to any change of beneficiary or beneficiaries, or to any other changes in this policy.

(The first clause of this provision, relating to the irrevocable designation of beneficiary, may be omitted at the insurer's option.)

(M) "CONVERSION PRIVILEGE" (under this caption) a provision which shall set forth in substance the conversion privileges and related provisions required of certain policies by paragraph five of subsection (c) of this section.

(2) Other provisions. No such policy delivered or issued for delivery to any person in this state shall contain provisions respecting the matters set forth below unless such provisions are in the words (not including the designation by number or letter) in which the same appear in this paragraph except that the insurer may, at its option, use in lieu of any such provision a corresponding provision of different wording approved by the superintendent which is not less favorable in any respect to the insured or the beneficiary. Any such provision contained in the policy shall be preceded individually by the appropriate caption appearing herein or, at the option of the insurer, by such appropriate individual or group captions or subcaptions as the superintendent may approve.

(A) CHANGE OF OCCUPATION: If the insured be injured or contract sickness after having changed his occupation to one classified by the insurer as more hazardous than that stated in this policy or while doing for compensation anything pertaining to an occupation so classified, the insurer will pay only such portion of the indemnities provided in this policy as the premium paid would have purchased at the rates and within the limits fixed by the insurer for such more hazardous occupation. If the insured changes his occupation to one classified by the insurer as less hazardous than that stated in this policy, the insurer, upon receipt of proof of such change of occupation, will reduce the premium rate accordingly, and will return the excess pro-rata unearned premium from the date of change of occupation or from the policy anniversary date immediately preceding receipt of such proof, whichever is the more recent. In applying this provision, the classification of occupational risk and the premium rates shall be such as have been last filed by the insurer prior to the occurrence of the loss for which the insurer is liable or prior to date of proof of change in occupation with the state official having supervision of insurance in the state where the insured resided at the time this policy was issued; but if such filing was not required, then the classification of occupational risk and the premium rates shall be those last made effective by the insurer in such state prior to the occurrence of the loss or prior to the date of proof of change in occupation.

(B) MISSTATEMENT OF AGE: If the insured's age has been misstated, all amounts payable under this policy shall be such as the premium paid would have purchased at the correct age.

(C) OTHER INSURANCE IN THIS INSURER: If an accident or sickness or accident and health policy or policies previously issued by the insurer to the insured be in force concurrently herewith,

"making the aggregate indemnity for . . . . . . (insert type of coverage or coverages) in excess of $. . . . (insert maximum limit of indemnity or indemnities) the excess insurance shall be void and all premiums paid for such excess shall be returned to the insured or to his estate,"

or, in lieu thereof:

"Insurance effective at any one time on the insured under a like policy or policies in this insurer is limited to the one such policy elected by the insured, his beneficiary or his estate, as the case may be, and the insurer will return all premiums paid for all other such policies."

(D) INSURANCE WITH OTHER INSURERS: If there be other valid coverage, not with this insurer, providing benefits for the same loss on a provision of service basis or on an expense incurred basis and of which this insurer has not been given written notice prior to the occurrence or commencement of loss, the only liability under any expense incurred coverage of this policy shall be for such proportion of the loss as the amount which would otherwise have been payable hereunder plus the total of the like amounts under all such other valid coverages for the same loss of which this insurer had notice bears to the total like amounts under all valid coverages for such loss, and for the return of such portion of the premiums paid as shall exceed the pro-rata portion for the amount so determined. For the purpose of applying this provision when other coverage is on a provision of service basis, the "like amount" of such other coverage shall be taken as the amount which the services rendered would have cost in the absence of such coverage.

(If the foregoing policy provision is included in a policy which also contains the next following policy provision there shall be added to the caption of the foregoing provision the phrase ". . . EXPENSE INCURRED BENEFITS." The insurer may, at its option, include in this provision a definition of "other valid coverage," approved as to form by the superintendent, which definition shall be limited in subject matter to coverage provided by organizations subject to regulation by insurance law or by insurance authorities of this or any other state of the United States or any province of Canada, and by hospital or medical service organizations, and to any other coverage the inclusion of which may be approved by the superintendent. In the absence of such definition such term shall not include group insurance, automobile medical payments insurance, or coverage provided by hospital or medical service organizations or by union welfare plans or employer or employee benefit organizations. For the purpose of applying the foregoing provision with respect to any insured, any amount of benefit provided for such insured pursuant to any compulsory benefit statute (including any workers' compensation or employer's liability statute) whether provided by a governmental agency or otherwise shall in all cases be deemed to be "other valid coverage" of which the insurer has had notice. In applying the foregoing policy provision no third party liability coverage shall be included as "other valid coverage.")

(E) INSURANCE WITH OTHER INSURERS: If there be other valid coverage, not with this insurer, providing benefits for the same loss on other than an expense incurred basis and of which this insurer has not been given written notice prior to the occurrence or commencement of loss, the only liability for such benefits under this policy shall be for such proportion of the indemnities otherwise provided hereunder for such loss as the like indemnities of which the insurer had notice (including the indemnities under this policy) bear to the total amount of all like indemnities for such loss, and for the return of such portion of the premium paid as shall exceed the pro-rata portion of the indemnities thus determined.

(If the foregoing policy provision is included in a policy which also contains the next preceding policy provision there shall be added to the caption of the foregoing provision the phrase ". . . OTHER BENEFITS." The insurer may, at its option, include in this provision a definition of "other valid coverage," approved as to form by the superintendent, which definition shall be limited in subject matter to coverage provided by organizations subject to regulation by insurance law or by insurance authorities of this or any other state of the United States or any province of Canada, and to any other coverage the inclusion of which may be approved by the superintendent. In the absence of such definition such term shall not include group insurance, or benefits provided by union welfare plans or by employer or employee benefit organizations. For the purpose of applying the foregoing policy provision with respect to any insured, any amount of benefit provided for such insured pursuant to any compulsory benefit statute (including any workers' compensation or employer's liability statute) whether provided by a governmental agency or otherwise shall in all cases be deemed to be "other valid coverage" of which the insurer has had notice. In applying the foregoing policy provision no third party liability coverage shall be included as "other valid coverage.")

(F) RELATION OF EARNINGS TO INSURANCE: If the total monthly amount of loss of time benefits promised for the same loss under all valid loss of time coverage upon the insured, whether payable on a weekly or monthly basis, shall exceed the monthly earnings of the insured at the time disability commenced or his average monthly earnings for the period of two years immediately preceding a disability for which claim is made, whichever is the greater, the insurer will be liable for only such proportionate amount of such benefits under this policy as the amount of such monthly earnings or such average monthly earnings of the insured bears to the total amount of monthly benefits for the same loss under all such coverage upon the insured at the time such disability commences and for the return of such part of the premiums paid during such two years as shall exceed the pro-rata amount of the premiums for the benefits actually paid hereunder; but this shall not operate to reduce the total monthly amount of benefits payable under all such coverage upon the insured below the sum of two hundred dollars or the sum of the monthly benefits specified in such coverages, whichever is the lesser, nor shall it operate to reduce benefits other than those payable for loss of time.

(The foregoing policy provision may be inserted only in a policy which the insured has the right to continue in force subject to its terms by the timely payment of premiums until at least age fifty or, in the case of a policy issued after age forty-four, for at least five years from its date of issue. The insurer may, at its option, include in this provision a definition of "valid loss of time coverage," approved as to form by the superintendent, which definition shall be limited in subject matter to coverage provided by governmental agencies or by organizations subject to regulation by the insurance law or by insurance authorities of this or any other state of the United States or any province of Canada, or to any other coverage the inclusion of which may be approved by the superintendent or any combination of such coverages. In the absence of such definition such term shall not include any coverage provided for such insured pursuant to any compulsory benefit statute (including any workers' compensation or employer's liability statute), or benefits provided by union welfare plans or by employer or employee benefit organizations.)

(G) UNPAID PREMIUM: Upon the payment of a claim under this policy, any premium then due and unpaid or covered by any note or written order may be deducted therefrom.

(H) CANCELLATION: Within the first ninety days after the date of issue, the insurer may cancel this policy by written notice delivered to the insured, or mailed to his last address as shown by the records of the insurer, stating when, not less than ten days thereafter, such cancellation shall be effective. In the event of cancellation, the insurer will return promptly the pro-rata unearned portion of any premium paid. Cancellation shall be without prejudice to any claim originating prior to the effective date of cancellation.

(Nothing in this subsection shall be construed to prohibit an insurer from granting to the insured the right to cancel a policy at any time and to receive in such event a refund of the unearned portion of any premium paid, computed by the use of the short-rate table last filed with the state official having supervision of insurance in the state where the insured resided when the policy was issued).

(I) CONFORMITY WITH STATE STATUTES: Any provision of this policy which, on its effective date, is in conflict with the statutes of the state in which the insured resides on such date is hereby amended to conform to the minimum requirements of such statutes.

(J) ILLEGAL OCCUPATION: The insurer shall not be liable for any loss to which a contributing cause was the insured's commission of or attempt to commit a felony or to which a contributing cause was the insured's being engaged in an illegal occupation.

(K) INTOXICANTS AND NARCOTICS: The insurer shall not be liable for any loss sustained or contracted in consequence of the insured's being intoxicated or under the influence of any narcotic unless administered on the advice of a physician.

(3) If any provision of this subsection is in whole or in part inapplicable to or inconsistent with the coverage provided by a particular form of policy the insurer, with the approval of the superintendent, shall omit from such policy any inapplicable provision or part of a provision, and shall modify any inconsistent provision or part of the provision in such manner as to make the provision as contained in the policy consistent with the coverage provided by the policy.

(4) The provisions which are the subject of paragraphs one and two of this subsection, or any corresponding provisions which are used in lieu thereof in accordance with such paragraphs, shall be printed in the consecutive order of the provisions in such paragraphs or, at the option of the insurer, any such provision may appear as a unit in any part of the policy, with other provisions to which it may be logically related, provided the resulting policy shall not be in whole or in part unintelligible, uncertain, ambiguous, abstruse, or likely to mislead a person to whom the policy is offered, delivered or issued.

(5) The word "insured," as used in this section, shall not be construed as preventing a person other than the insured with a proper insurable interest from making application for and owning a policy covering the insured or from being entitled under such a policy to any indemnities, benefits and rights provided therein.

(6) The superintendent may make such reasonable rules and regulations concerning the procedure for the filing or submission of policies subject to this section as are necessary, proper or advisable to the administration of this section. This provision shall not abridge any other authority granted the superintendent by law.

Overinsurance

7

LIFE VERSUS DISABILITY FACTORS

In life insurance it is important for the home office underwriter to determine that there is an insurable interest on the part of the beneficiary, while at the same time making certain that the face amount applied for bears a reasonable relationship to the expected financial loss to the beneficiary if the insured should die. Some factor of the applicant's earnings or net worth is generally the basis for determining the amount of life insurance that is safe for the company to insure. However, this face amount frequently carries with it a great degree of judgment, depending upon individual circumstances and characteristics. There is substantial evidence in all lines of insurance—life, casualty, hospitalization, and disability income—that claims experience is adversely affected when the amount of insurance in force exceeds the amount of reasonable loss expected. Indeed, evidence indicates that the greater the degree of overinsurance in relation to the value of the loss, the more adverse the claims experience.

In disability income the relationship between the applied for indemnity and the applicant's earned income is much more direct; and it is much more important to establish the earned income with some accuracy than is true for life insurance. Claim studies indicate quite clearly that the higher the percent of earned income insured, the greater the frequency of disability and the greater the chance that the ultimate length of the disability will be extended. There is, therefore, a much more definite cause-and-effect relationship between overinsurance and disability income claims than between overinsurance and life insurance claims. Indeed, it is probably more accurate to compare the importance of overinsurance in disability income to that for casualty insurance coverages. Consumers readily accept the fact that they can insure neither their homes nor their automobiles for a greater value than actual market worth, and, similarly, in disability income, the consumer should not expect to receive an indemnity at time of disability in excess of actual income loss. To do so violates a most fundamental principle of all insurance contracts.

DETERMINING INSURABLE INCOME

Whereas it is not possible to determine a precise value of the life of an individual for life insurance purposes, it is normally somewhat easier to quantify one's potential income loss. However, this potential loss is not a precise figure, since one's income does not remain static and does not increase according to some logical schedule. Self-employed people tend to have greater fluctuations in income than do other workers. Individuals in unstable jobs may have their incomes reduced or may lose their jobs. Individuals on commission income may suffer substantial variations during economic recession. Indeed, the stability of an applicant's income is one of the most important factors for the underwriter to determine.

Furthermore, it must be remembered that not all income is insurable for disability purposes, but only that income that will cease when disability commences. Income from investments, savings, and rental properties cannot be considered insurable income for disability purposes since the income will not cease upon disability. It is common to normally refer to income that is insurable as earned income in contrast to unearned income, which does not depend on the daily personal attention or physical activity of the insured. Although there may be some difficulty in precisely determining the difference between earned and unearned income in some instances, earned income is generally that portion of a person's income that is derived from personal employment activity.

Once we determine the earned income amount, however, we cannot simply insure 100 percent of this gross figure since it is not all spendable income. We must first exclude that portion of earned income that is tax deductible as a business expense, since it does not fall in the category of income for personal use but is rather business expense income that may be insured in a different way. A further step must be taken to exclude that portion of an individual's income that represents federal and state income taxes since this also is not spendable income. That figure arrived at after removing business expenses and taxes can be referred to as net earned income, or perhaps more clearly take-home

TABLE 7–1
Group Long-Term Disability Experience 1969–73

Percent of gross income insured	Ratio of actual/expected claims
50% or less	.88
more than 50%	1.09
more than 60%	1.42
more than 70%	2.19

Transactions, Society of Actuaries, "1975 Reports of Mortality and Morbidity Experience," p. 266.

pay. This true spendable income is the item the disability underwriter must focus on to determine how much to insure.

HOW MUCH TO INSURE

Assuming the income figure arrived at is a stable one, after examining the applicant's employment history and past earnings record, disability underwriters will not traditionally insure the entire amount. Industry studies indicate that the greater the percentage of earned income insured, the higher the morbidity. There is, very simply, a direct relationship between how much of one's income is insured and how often he or she will be disabled and how long that disability will last.

This phenomenon is an extremely important underwriting consideration requiring careful management attention in setting underwriting rules that determine the amount of indemnity at various levels of income. Group long-term disability studies by the Society of Actuaries display and support this phenomenon. Table 7–1 is based upon earned income *before* taxes, and therefore the percent of income insured must be lower than if the earned income figure had been reduced to net earned income.

Although similar figures have not been developed for individual disability income, general industry studies indicate that the same pattern exists.

NET EARNED INCOME

The key to determining what percent of net earned income to insure is to remember that it is not the same fixed percent for all incomes. Generally, "replacement ratios," the percent of income to indemnity, are higher at the lower incomes and gradually reduce as the income increases. The primary reason for this is that it is assumed that lower-income individuals spend all of their income or most of it, but as incomes

TABLE 7–2

Annual earned income	Net annual earned income *	Replacement ratio
$ 16,000	$ 14,000	90%
20,000	17,000	90
30,000	24,000	90
40,000	32,000	89
50,000	39,000	89
75,000	56,000	83
100,000	72,000	80
150,000	103,000	71
200,000	134,000	68
250,000	168,000	62

* Annual earned income less federal withholding taxes, state withholding taxes, and FICA taxes for worker with four dependents equals net annual earned income.
Source of data: The Paul Revere Life Insurance Company.

increase the percent of discretionary income also increases. There is less need to insure discretionary income, and, consequently, the replacement ratios decrease sharply as one approaches high-income earners.

Generally, 80 percent of net earned income is the highest replacement ratio that should be employed, and this only at the lower incomes. However, it is not unusual for some companies to insure as high as 90 percent of net earned income for incomes below $50,000. Replacement ratios decrease from that point to a low level of some 50–60 percent of net earned income at figures of $200,000 and above.

Table 7–2 represents the replacement ratios at various net earned incomes that The Paul Revere Life Insurance Company recommended for its reinsurance clients in the late 1980s.

Before using the income chart to determine the amount of individual disability income that can be approved for an applicant, the underwriter must take into consideration other disability income coverage that is available to the applicant. This is an extremely important underwriting step that requires knowledge of the various types of disability income programs available and frequently involves additional investigation and questioning of the applicant. The Health Insurance Association of America in 1979 conducted a study in which it identified some 42 different programs in the United States where disability benefits of some kind were available. These programs included a large variety of governmental benefits along with group insurance, salary continuation, franchise, association, and of course other individual programs. The total of all disability income benefits already available to the applicant must be subtracted from the maximum allowable indemnity before the underwriter can determine how much room there is to approve additional individual disability coverage.

OVERINSURANCE WITH GOVERNMENT PROGRAMS

During the 1970s the normal level of concern about overinsurance in the disability business was heightened considerably by the expansion of various governmental disability benefits. Disability income benefits under Social Security expanded substantially in the late 1960s and early 1970s. When these governmental benefits were paid to claimants on top of their own personal disability coverage, situations were frequently created in which total claim benefits not only exceeded take-home pay, but actually exceeded gross income. Inflation escalators built into the 1972 Social Security legislation caused disability benefits under this program to expand at almost twice the rate of inflation, until this error was corrected in 1977. In addition, the replacement ratios under the Social Security disability program exceeded those levels that the private industry considered prudent. This problem continues to exist today, particularly at income levels under $20,000. Throughout the serious recession of the mid 1970s, therefore, morbidity experience showed adverse trends for both the Social Security program and private insurers. Clearly the large amount of disability benefits available through Social Security, particularly for incomes of less than $20,000, added unusual overinsurance strains in a depressed economic period when increased claims could normally be expected.

In addition, during the late 1960s and early 1970s significant expansion occurred in state disability programs, both Workers' Compensation and state cash sickness coverages. Workers' Compensation benefit levels generally increased sharply although not at uniform levels in each state. These increases also aggravated claims experience during the mid 1970s recession. Five states currently have cash sickness benefits to complement Workers' Compensation: California, New Jersey, New York, Rhode Island, and Hawaii. The benefit levels vary greatly from one state to another, but California stands head and shoulders above the others in the amount of benefits. It is no accident, therefore, that industry experience with individual disability income has tended to be more adverse in California than in the rest of the country as a whole. Some companies since the mid 1970s have taken the step of having a separate premium structure for the state of California, and other companies have withdrawn from that state entirely.

GROUP INSURANCE PROGRAMS

During the 1960s and 1970s group disability programs, both weekly income and long-term disability, appeared in the marketplace with greater and greater frequency. The individual disability income writer consequently became more concerned with the existence of group insurance as the decade of the 1970s went on. Many companies until

TABLE 7–3
Disability Income in 1980—Age 30 Replacement Ratios (MFB and net income)

1978 gross earnings	*Prior to 1977 law*	*1979 law*	*1980 law*
$ 5,000	170%	90%	80%
10,000	150	90	73
20,000	100	67	55
25,000	82	55	45
30,000	70	46	38

1970 ignored group disability benefits entirely. However, by the mid 1970s, prudent home office underwriters began to realize that they had to consider the actual amount of group insurance benefits or else run a serious risk of overinsurance adversely affecting their own claims.

By the end of the 1970s, therefore, with very substantial growth in federal Social Security benefits, state cash sickness, Workers' Compensation, and group insurance, individual writers of disability income were forced to consider much more precisely the level of existing coverage available to an applicant from all of these sources. To do otherwise frequently resulted in serious overinsurance and ultimate serious claim problems.

Table 7–3 indicates the replacement ratios under the Social Security disability income program at three different times. The replacement ratio is the maximum family benefit payable under Social Security divided by net income (gross earned income less business expenses and less taxes). Replacement ratios prior to the 1977 change in the law affecting disability benefits under Social Security were unreasonably high. As the chart indicates, it was possible to receive disability benefits at or exceeding net income at income ranges of $20,000 and less. Although the 1977 law reduced these ratios, compared with safe industry replacement ratios, they were still high for incomes less than $20,000. The final 1980 change improved the situation somewhat further, but replacement ratios are still dangerously high in the Social Security system for incomes less than $15,000. When this level of benefits is added on to private disability coverage, the obvious overinsurance difficulty becomes evident.

MOTIVATION

The overinsurance problem is not an easily quantifiable one. The individual's motivation, amount of unearned income, marital status, age, general health, and the economic climate all combine in various ways to influence whether or not the replacement ratio in a given instance is too liberal or too conservative. Some people are motivated in their working environment so strongly that they will not elect or extend disability, even if the level of disability benefits exceeds their earned income. Other individuals will elect disability or extend disability even when there is a substantial gap between the replacement ratio and their actual income. Examples of the latter might be the insured who is approaching retirement and decides to "retire" on a disability contract and turn the business over to a son or daughter, someone who, because of recently inheriting a substantial amount of net worth, is not as dependent upon earned income and therefore may elect disability, and the young person who is not stable in a job and whose low level of financial commitments are such that he or she can live off of the disability benefits. No accurate and precise method of measuring and carefully quantifying the level of motivation and the work ethic of a particular applicant has yet been devised. The claim experience of a particular group of applicants is very much dependent upon their level of motivation.

MOTOMANOMETER

For some years now I've been working at home on a device that will help solve this dilemma for the disability underwriter, and after several false attempts I'm close to perfecting this selection tool that I call a motomanometer. It's in some ways similar to the blood pressure measuring device, the sphygmomanometer. I've taken a gauge from an old automobile, a piece of rubber hose, and an old bicycle pump and combined them. My plans are to mass produce the device and give one to each of our agents to be used in place of a medical application. They'll be instructed to wrap the hose around a potential insured's leg, pump the hose with the bicycle pump until the applicant gives a cry of pain, and at that point quickly record the reading on the gauge. Based upon this reading we will have a measure of the individual's tolerance to pain and anticipated level of motivation; then we'll set the premium accordingly (see Figure 7–1).

The important point to remember from this facetious discussion is that motivation in disability income cannot be underestimated in impor-

FIGURE 7–1
Motomanometer

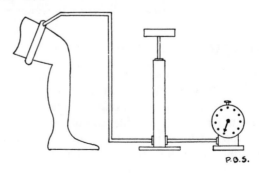

P.O.S.

tance. Since we are insuring individuals who are all motivated differently, the underwriter's judgment of a wide number of variable factors becomes critical. Two people with the same physical impairment often provide entirely different claims experience. One succumbs to the impairment and accepts disability, and the other is motivated quite differently and learns to live and work with the impairment. Not only do different individuals act differently under similar circumstances, but to the extent that the work ethic standard in our society changes, basic actuarial assumptions must also change. We have experienced such a change since the mid 1960s, and indeed actuarial assumptions that had been standard in the disability industry for several decades had to be adjusted. The impact of a change in basic work ethic standards and the relationship of worker to employer were key factors in the need to change these assumptions.

CLAIM HANDLING

The overinsurance problem is frequently not identified until claim time. Either the applicant (1) failed to indicate on the application other disability coverages carried, (2) overstated income, or (3) purchased additional disability coverage since the original purchase. This overinsurance problem at claim time is one frequently addressed during the contestable period and one necessarily requiring alertness on the part of the claim examiner. The person who is overinsured and/or gave inadequate or inaccurate information on the application represents a substantial claim risk for the life of the policy and should be identified during the contestable period if at all possible. There are several instances of deliberate overinsurance in which an individual "loaded up" on individual disability contracts in anticipation of filing a claim after the contestable period, thereby creating a circumstance in which the claimant was eligible for benefits far in excess of the insurable interest.

In summary, the problem of overinsurance is much more directly related to claims experience in disability insurance than in life insurance. The greater the percent of income insured, the greater the actual morbidity that will result. The less stable the individual, the less motivated the individual, the greater the risk that the normal replacement ratio will prove to be too liberal. Private insurers today must carefully consider the level of coverage available to an applicant from all sources—including federal, state, and group insurance programs—before deciding what private insurance benefits should be approved. To overinsure an applicant may not create problems during good economic times but may cause very severe claim problems during recessionary periods.

In recent years there has been growing concern in the area of overinsurance, and clearly the foregoing problems of the broad availability of both public and private disability benefits have heightened industry concern. More underwriting investigation is now focused on overinsurance; more claim investigation during the contestable period is encouraged; and in 1980 the Health Insurance Association of America through its disability income committee worked with the Medical Index Bureau to establish an underwriting/claim index to specifically address this problem.

Sales
and
Marketing

8

DISCIPLINES

The insurance disciplines found in the disability income product line are very similar to those found in life insurance. Sales and marketing, underwriting, claims, administration, and actuarial are all common functional designations, even though the specific activities may be somewhat different. The purpose of the next several chapters will be to discuss these various disciplines, emphasizing the differences in their functions for disability income and for life insurance.

One obvious area of substantial difference is in the claim function. In life insurance there is only one death claim for each policy, except for waiver of premium; however, in disability income it is common to have a dozen or more disability claims during the lifetime of the contract. Consequently, the position of the disability income claim examiner is equal in professional status to that of any other insurance professional and indeed requires substantial knowledge of medicine, particularly the expected duration of different disabilities. The claim examiner's function represents the area of greatest difference in the two insurance disciplines. (The chapter on the claim function will deal with this subject in more depth.)

One important factor is that the success of any company's disability income operation is directly related to the commitment it makes to its success. Life insurance companies too frequently give too little management attention to their disability income product line. Frequently it is established only as an accommodation to the field force in order to discourage agents from brokering with other companies, and no commitment is made for financial resources or for people resources to assure success.

The volatile nature of the disability income product is such that an accommodation approach by management runs a great risk of not only low sales, but also financial failure. The nature of disability income is such that management action and redirection is frequently required and required quickly. Unless the disability line is being managed closely, a problem may grow to a crisis before the necessary action has been taken. The most important discipline in managing disability income is to make certain that management commits the necessary resources to ensure the product's success.

DISTRIBUTION

The distribution system for selling disability income insurance is identical to that for life insurance. Most disability income is sold either through normal life insurance career agency systems or through special brokerage outlets for companies specializing in disability income products. In either event, the salesperson is normally the same one who sells other forms of individual coverages—life, annuities, and medical care. Disability income is simply one other product line to complete one's portfolio of financial services. Indeed, without the disability income product, the sales portfolio is quite incomplete.

There are three primary risks to an individual's income. One is loss of income as a result of death, and life insurance is designed to meet that need. A second is the loss of income that occurs when an individual retires, and annuities and pension plans are designed to satisfy this individual need. The third is the possibility of income loss as a result of disability, and, of course, disability income is specifically designed for this purpose.

Most salespeople sell the disability income product as a second product line, with their primary line being life insurance—of course, this behavior naturally follows the pattern and the emphasis of their company and their training. Indeed, many well-qualified life insurance estate planners and advanced sales specialists have not developed confidence in the selling of disability income and may consequently miss many disability sales and not fill the entire needs of their clients.

Many companies and salespeople who specialize in disability income approach it with an almost missionary zeal. They will argue convincingly that the disability income need should precede all other insurance needs, because a person whose income ceases because of disability lacks the financial ability to fulfill other insurance purchases. Furthermore, it can be argued that, whereas life insurance benefits are used to sustain the purchasing power of a spouse and the children of a family, at time of disability the disabled person is an additional financial burden. Finally, statistics clearly indicate that the odds of death during an individual's working years are much less than the odds of a significant long-term disability, one lasting more than 90 days.

MARKETS

Although the markets where disability income is sold are generally the same as for individual life insurance, there are some differences. First of all, in the past two decades employee benefit programs including salary continuation and long-term disability plans have become more and more common. Therefore, the need for individual disability income in such circumstances is quite limited, particularly in the lower-income markets. Even though group disability programs are neither portable nor carry conversion privileges, to approve individual disability income on top of group plans would cause serious overinsurance with its associated problems.

The growth of governmental disability programs, primarily Social Security and Workers' Compensation, has encroached upon some disability markets that were active and large 10 and more years ago. Life insurance is still sold in substantial quantities at almost all income levels, whereas disability income needs are essentially taken care of by Social Security for incomes of less than $20,000. There is some room for short-term disability coverage—six months or one year, before Social Security benefits commence. However, in the five states (New York, New Jersey, Rhode Island, California, and Hawaii) that provide state cash sickness coverage, there is no demonstrated need whatsoever below $20,000 of earned income.

The primary individual disability market, therefore, exists with those people with incomes over $20,000 who are self-employed or employed by firms who have no salary continuation or LTD group coverage.

Up through the early 1970s the majority of individual disability income policyholders and the majority of disability income coverage in force was in the middle- and lower-income markets, since the majority of the American population was found in these areas. With the encroachment of the federal government, those traditional markets essentially dried up. As a result increased emphasis was placed upon the self-employed business and professional markets, the upper-middle and high-income segments of our population. Up through the middle 1960s, maximum monthly indemnities rarely exceeded $1,000 per month, with consequently limited and inadequate protection for the high-income professional or self-employed risk. As the industry concentrated more on these markets, the demand for higher indemnities became greater. As a result, in the past 15 years issue limits have increased markedly to a point today where $6,000 to $10,000 per month of disability income is common, and several companies will regularly approve amounts up to $20,000 per month.

In order to meet the needs of the self-employed and professional markets, new product approaches began to emerge. The design of disability income products to specifically meet the need of the self-employed began to occur in the late 1960s and early 1970s. Products to cover business overhead expenses at time of disability, disability buy-and-sell products, and keyperson disability coverages all have emerged during this period. In many ways these business products, particularly keyperson coverage, are still in their development stage and will increasingly change as the market changes and demands new approaches. The disability income market is a growing one, a changing one, one affected by the world in which we live, but clearly one that requires the salesperson and the company to respond to its dynamic environment.

COMPETITION

The competitive environment in the individual disability income sale also has its similarities and differences with life insurance. The method of sale, the fact-finding, the proposal service, the general sales approach are very much the same. The need must be clearly identified before the sale can be made. Various types of sales makers and specially designed proposals are used in disability income, similar to life insurance; and they vary according to the type of need. The salesperson must be alert and familiar with the various types and forms of disability income products so as to properly evaluate both the prospect's needs for the amount of indemnity necessary and the restrictions and limitations that exist in the prospect's existing disability program.

One very clear difference in the competitive arena in disability insurance is the heavy emphasis on contract and contractual language. Most companies offer approximately the same level of indemnity for the same amount of earned income; most companies' underwriting is quite similar; most companies' premium structure is similar; and most contractual language is quite similar. However, to the extent that differences occur in any of these areas, they quite naturally represent points for competition to emphasize. Historically the greatest emphasis has been on differences in contractual language. The definition of disability has been the primary area of "language competition" for almost two decades, and this competition has resulted in continual extension and experimentation with various types of disability language over that period of time. Language competition also occurs over waiver-of-premium provisions, recurrent disability provisions, partial disability language, cost-of-living benefits, and a variety of other language areas. Without question this emphasis on "language competition" has been excessively emphasized.

Perhaps the most important factor in selecting an insurance product from the consumer's point of view should be the record of the company in paying its claims and paying them fairly. Since we are dealing here with a more subjective question that cannot be adequately described in contract language, it is not an important competitive factor during the sales process.

Again, the competition, particularly in the higher-income markets, is aggressive, knowledgeable, capable, and continually changing as it adjusts to the market, which itself continually changes and adjusts. The most important fundamental fact to remember is that disability income is much more product sensitive than is life insurance.

TRAINING AND FIELD UNDERWRITING

The training of the disability income salesperson is of critical importance to the process. Not only must he or she be trained in the product, the competitor's products, and how to compete and sell successfully, but the salesperson must also be trained in the proper field selection techniques. Field selection is clearly more important in disability income than in life insurance since, as emphasized in previous chapters, the motivation and stability of the risk are paramount.

Through the design of applications, the use of inspection reports, and other underwriting tools, home office underwriters use every tool available to measure the quality of the risk applying for insurance. However, the salesperson in the field is in the unique position of knowing or being able to develop more information than the underwriter. The face-to-face contact is an advantage the field salesperson has that indeed is important in the selection process. Salespeople must be taught that not only is field evaluation important to the company, but, in fact, the reputations they develop as good or bad field selectors will affect the underwriting of other cases.

There is a potential for many claims on a disability product during its lifetime. Since claims frequently occur in the early years following issuance, it is possible to evaluate more quickly the quality of field selection of a particular agent in disability income than it is in life insurance. Indeed, home office underwriters have tools at their disposal that allow them to draw conclusions and make judgments about the quality of the field underwriting of a particular agent or agency. Two factors that are of paramount underwriting importance are the earned income and occupation of the applicant. Since the disability income contract insures earned income, it is important that the proper earned income be determined in order for the applicant to be insured for the right amount. To overinsure increases the frequency and the length of claims! Disability income premiums are broken into anywhere from three to five different schedules that are based upon occupation class. Therefore, the determination of the correct occupation and, consequently, the occupation class is a critical step in determining the rate. There is frequently a natural temptation for the salesperson to somewhat overstate the earned income in order to increase the indemnity applied for. Similarly there is a tendency to understate the risk of the occupation so as to obtain a more favorable occupation class and a more favorable premium. It doesn't take long for the home office underwriter to recognize those agents who are abusing the selection process, and it's important under such circumstances for the underwriting department to take action.

The most common action in such cases is, of course, to pull the salesperson up short and strongly emphasize the importance of field underwriting. In the early months of an agent's training, this is often necessary and is successful in helping the agent recognize the importance of the selection role. For the continual abuser, more definitive action must be taken in order to protect the interests of the company. Sometimes this involves restricting them from certain markets, requiring them to go through special evaluation procedures, such as ordering inspection reports on all of their business. Finally, the most serious abuser must be terminated as an agent.

The degree of success in field selection can be directly measured in the claim results that ultimately emerge on a block of business. The proper training to support the proper field selection is therefore important and clearly carries with it more field selection emphasis than in life insurance.

SUBSTANDARD AND MODIFIED CASES

The salesperson who has been trained and has sold life insurance for some period of time may find some other areas that are different and perhaps irritating in the disability income product process. One of the most common areas of misunderstanding is in the treatment of rejections and substandard risks. In life insurance it's common for some 1 to 3 percent of all applicants to be rejected and for some 3 to 5 percent of all applicants to be charged an extra premium as a substandard risk. In disability income insurance the ratios are substantially different. It is common for the rejection ratio to run in the 6 to 10 percent range and for the percentage of substandard risks to run in the 14 to 20 percent range. In life insurance then some 4 to 8 percent of all risks are either declined or substandard, whereas in disability income insurance the ratios are typically from 20 to 30 percent. The increased frequency of substandard decisions on disability income is an annoyance to the established life salesperson, who frequently fears that the substandard decision on disability income may affect his or her ability to place the life insurance contract.

There is an additional irritant to the salesperson that takes place in the disability underwriting process. In addition to the rejections and the substandard risks is another group of cases that are changed from the way they were originally submitted. The most common changes occur in the indemnity amount (based upon home office underwriting income information) and the occupation class (based upon the home office evaluation of the applicant's occupation). The percentage of cases in which changes other than rejections and substandard decisions are made runs from 10 to 15 percent of all cases submitted. If we add all of these percentages together, we are looking at a situation in which from 30 to 45 percent of all business submitted may involve some sort of change.

It's therefore important that, in addition to the normal sales training, salespeople are also trained in how to place the substandard or "changed" contract. Here again, the accuracy and reliability of the salesperson's field underwriting in a major way determines the percent of cases that must be changed upon issuance.

Although it is common for experienced life insurance salespeople to fear this increased percent of changed cases and its impact upon established life insurance clients, in practice experienced disability salespeople find that it is not a serious problem. As a matter of fact, when approached properly, the delivery of a substandard or changed policy with the proper explanation may solidify with the client the fact that the salesperson and the company have accurately evaluated and serviced the client's own personal needs. The percent of not-takens on disability income should be very little changed from what it is in life insurance in spite of the high percentage of changed cases. The experienced and trained field salesperson senses at application time those cases that may present underwriting problems and sells the impairment or extra premium at that time.

Finally, one additional piece of the substandard environment in disability income is the introduction of the exclusion endorsement or rider. In life insurance the treatment of substandard risks is almost exclusively by extra premium. In disability income the substandard risk, depending upon the nature of the impairment, may only be able to be approved with an exclusion endorsement eliminating coverage for a particular impairment. The problem for the agent in placing such a contract is obvious, since the impairment excluded is normally the one that the applicant is most concerned about disabling him or her. Proper training on how to place this type of case will ease the agent's problem, with particular emphasis on the importance of home office offers to consider removing the exclusion endorsement in the future.

PROGRAMMING THE NEED

Training disability salespeople requires—in addition to normal sales techniques, product familiarity, and underwriting approaches—technical skills in the area of programming. In life insurance we call this process "estate planning" or "financial planning," evaluating an applicant's specific life insurance needs based upon the client's personal situation and other coverage that the client already carries. In disability income client need is determined by the amount of the client's earned income. The field underwriter must then evaluate what other disability income benefits are available. This includes Social Security, state cash sickness, Workers' Compensation, and employer salary continuation and LTD programs. Once this information is developed and programmed, the salesperson is in a position to determine how to design a disability contract to fill the remaining disability need. Since most companies are careful to avoid overinsurance, this evaluation is important not only in meeting the client's needs, but also in satisfying home office underwriting requirements.

COMMISSIONS

Commission levels in disability income follow patterns somewhat similar to life insurance, particularly in first-year commissions. Since companies are competing for an agent's time in the sale of disability income, it is natural that the level of compensation be similar to that of life insurance. Typical first-year commissions run from 40 to 55 percent, very often varying by occupation class—the more favorable the occupation class, the higher the first-year commission. Renewal commissions tend to be highest from the second through the fifth year, frequently 20 percent in the second and third years and 10 percent in the fourth and fifth years. Beyond five years, however, the typical commission is 5 percent, somewhat lower than normally found in life insurance. Override commission patterns are also similar to life insurance for general agents and managers. Also similar to life insurance, many companies that specialize in disability income offer additional commission incentives for production or persistency or both. As mentioned previously, the pattern of persistency closely follows the pattern of claims experience, and therefore persistency rewards may well be of greater value in disability than in life insurance. Some companies include a persistency rater on their applications and will not accept business that fails to meet a certain score. Although the factors are closely related to the persistency factors found in life insurance evaluations, they in fact measure variables that are measuring an applicant's stability.

In summary, sales and marketing of disability income is very similar to life insurance, but important differences primarily stem from the importance of stability and motivation in evaluating the disability income risk. The agent's important role in field selection and the ability of the home office to measure the quality of the agent's results early are important factors in the salesperson's disability sales success.

The Disability Application

9

As is the case with any insurance product, the application performs a critical role. It is a legal document, becomes a part of the contract, and must be approved by the various state jurisdictions before it can be used. It contains a variety of information from general identification to a description of the type of insurance coverage desired (see Figure 9–1). In between these two functions is more detailed information regarding occupation, income, medical history, physical condition, and avocations.

When completed properly, the application represents the bridge between the field and the home office, between the applicant and the company. When incomplete or inaccurate, it fails to bridge the gap and results in the process ceasing or being delayed before a contract is approved. As mentioned in the previous chapter, the agent is a vital link in this process. The agent's care in completing the application, skill and training in developing correct information, and reputation in the home office based upon prior reliability all come together in determining the confidence the home office places in the information on a particular application.

SIMILARITIES TO LIFE APPLICATIONS

The disability application has many similarities to one for life insurance, and as a matter of fact, many companies have one application used for both purposes. The state insurance department regulations

82

Chapter 9

FIGURE 9–1

APPLICATION   WORCESTER, MA 01608

THE PAUL REVERE LIFE INSURANCE COMPANY	THE PAUL REVERE PROTECTIVE LIFE INSURANCE COMPANY	THE PAUL REVERE VARIABLE ANNUITY INSURANCE COMPANY
For ☐ Life ☐ Health Insurance	For ☐ Life ☐ Health Insurance	For ☐ Life ☐ Health Insurance

PART I: **A** PROPOSED INSURED   N⁰ **46555**

1. Print Name as it is to appear on policy. Include professional designation.	Last	First and Middle

2. Sex: M ☐   F ☐   3. Birthdate: Mo   Day   Yr   4. Age (nearest)

5. Birthplace (State)   6. Social Security Number

7. Residence: Street _____ Apt # _____

City _____ State _____ Zip _____ Phone No (___) _____

Give prior address if at above address less than 2 years. } Street _____ Apt # _____
City _____ State _____

B PROPOSED INSURED'S OCCUPATION

1. Occupation _____ % Traveling ____ % Supervision ____

2. Exact duties _____

3. Employer _____

4. Business Address: Street _____ City _____
State _____ Zip _____ Phone No (___) _____

5. Nature of Employer's business _____

6. Length of current employment _____ Yrs. 7. If self-employed, number of full-time employees _____

8. Do you have any part-time or other full-time jobs, or any additional duties? Yes ☐ No ☐ If "Yes", describe:

C FAMILY MEMBERS TO BE COVERED AND PREMIUM PAYER FOR WHOM INSURANCE IS APPLIED

Full name and relationship	Birthdate	Hgt	Wgt	Full name and relationship	Birthdate	Hgt	Wgt

D ADDITIONAL INFORMATION

Any person refers to the Proposed Insured, any Family Member or Premium Payer listed in Section C above.

1. Has any person within the past two years engaged in: motorcycle riding, scuba diving below 40 feet, parachuting, karate, judo, gliding, motor vehicle or motorboat racing, rodeo activities, or any similar sport or avocation? Yes ☐ No ☐ If "Yes", give details below.

2. Has any person ever piloted a plane or have any intention of piloting a plane within the next six months? Yes ☐ No ☐ If "Yes", forward Aviation Supplement.

3. Has any person received, requested, or been refused disability, hospital, or medical benefits or a pension for any sickness or injury within the past five years? Yes ☐ No ☐ If "Yes", give details below.

4. Has any person had life, disability or hospital insurance rated up, modified, rejected, cancelled, or renewal or reinstatement not approved within the past five years? Yes ☐ No ☐ If "Yes", give details below.

5. Has the Proposed Insured smoked cigarettes in the past 24 months? Yes ☐ No ☐

6. Has any person within the past two years been convicted of a moving violation, or had a license restricted or revoked? Yes ☐ No ☐ If "Yes", show Driver's License Number _____ and give details below.

App 50   80-1

If applying for Business Overhead Expense coverage, complete Section E.

E OVERHEAD EXPENSE INFORMATION

1. How is your business organized? Sole Owner ☐   Corporation ☐   Partnership ☐   Other _____

2. Are your office expenses shared with anyone else?   Yes ☐   No ☐   If "Yes", your share_____ %

3. Complete if applying for $1,000 or more of coverage. Use your actual current average monthly expenses. If expenses are shared, include only your portion. Exclude any payments to yourself or to any other member of your profession.

Rent	$_____	Depreciation $_____	Liability Insurance $_____
Electricity	$_____	Salaries	$_____	Property Taxes	$_____
Heat and Water $_____	Telephone	$_____	Mortgage Interest $_____

Other normal and customary fixed office expenses $_____ (Give *full* details below if over 10% of total)

_____
_____
_____

PART 2: MEDICAL HISTORY – To Be Completed Whenever:

   1. A medical exam is <u>not</u> required for the Proposed Insured, or
   2. Premium Payer, Family Plan, or Children's Plan is applied for

A PROPOSED INSURED

1. Name (Print in full) _____

2. Present Height _____ Weight_____

3. Has weight changed within the past year?   Yes ☐   No ☐   If "Yes", indicate pounds gained_____

or pounds lost_____ Cause?_____

4. Name(s) and address(es) of personal physician(s) or health care facility(ies). If none, write "none". _____

_____
_____

5. Date and reason for last consultation. _____

6. Is Proposed Insured presently under observation or treatment or taking medication? Yes ☐ No ☐ If "Yes", give details.

_____
_____

B FAMILY HISTORY

1.	Age if Living	Age at Death	Cause of Death
Father			
Mother			
Brothers & Sisters			

2. Has any member of the Proposed Insured's family ever had a stroke or diabetes, cancer, high blood pressure, heart or kidney disease, mental illness, or committed suicide?   Yes ☐   No ☐   If "Yes", give details.

_____
_____
_____
_____

C MEDICAL DETAILS

For these questions, any person refers to the Proposed Insured and any other person listed in Section C of Part 1.	Proposed Insured		Fam Mem Prem Payer	
	Yes	No	Yes	No
1. Has any person *within the past five years*:				
a. Been examined by or consulted a physician or other practitioner?	☐	☐	☐	☐
b. Been under observation or treatment in any hospital, sanitarium, or institution?	☐	☐	☐	☐
c. Had an X-ray, EKG, blood or urine test, or other lab tests?	☐	☐	☐	☐
2. Has any person *ever*:				
a. Except as legally prescribed by a physician, used: cocaine, barbiturates, heroin, or any narcotic drug?	☐	☐	☐	☐
b. Sought or received advice for, or treatment of, or been arrested for the use of alcohol, marijuana or drugs?	☐	☐	☐	☐
c. Been rejected for or given medical discharge from military, naval, or air service?	☐	☐	☐	☐
3. Is any person pregnant? If "Yes", what is due date? _____	☐	☐	☐	☐
4. Has any person *ever* had any known indication of or been treated for:				
a. Any disease or impairment of eyes, ears, nose or speech?	☐	☐	☐	☐
b. Any type of back or spinal trouble, including sprain or strain?	☐	☐	☐	☐
c. Chest pain, heart murmur, high blood pressure, or any disease of the heart, blood vessels, or blood?	☐	☐	☐	☐
d. Peptic ulcer, indigestion, or any disease of the stomach, intestines, gall bladder, or liver?	☐	☐	☐	☐
e. Tuberculosis, asthma, pleurisy, or any disease of the chest or lungs?	☐	☐	☐	☐
f. Kidney stone, albumin, pus, blood or sugar in urine, or any disease of the kidneys, bladder, or genital organs?	☐	☐	☐	☐
g. Headaches, fainting spells, epilepsy, paralysis, nervousness, mental disorder, or any disease of the brain or nervous system?	☐	☐	☐	☐
h. Rheumatic fever, syphilis, gout, arthritis, thyroid disease, diabetes, cancer, or tumor?	☐	☐	☐	☐
i. Allergies or any disease of the skin?	☐	☐	☐	☐
j. Any disease of the reproductive organs or breast?	☐	☐	☐	☐
k. Any amputation or deformity, hernia or rupture, hemorrhoids or varicose veins?	☐	☐	☐	☐
5. Has any person had any surgical operation, treatment, special diet, or any illness, ailment, abnormality, or injury, not mentioned above. *within the past five years*?	☐	☐	☐	☐

6. Give details to any of the "Yes" answers to questions C-1 through C-5.

Question Number	Person's Name	Diagnosis	Date of Each Occurrence	Duration	Current Status	Names & Addresses of Doctors & Medical Facilities

PART I (continued) **:**   If applying for Health Insurance, complete Sections F through H.

F EXISTING AND PENDING HEALTH COVERAGE

1. Describe all coverage in force. Include disability, hospital, and overhead expense coverage under individual, franchise, association, group, and government plans. If none, write "none".

Company or Source	Issue Date	Amount of ADB	Amount of Hosp	Amount of BOE	Monthly Indemnity	Elim Pd	Ben Pd	To be Cont Yes	To be Cont No	Effec Date of Discont
a.								☐	☐	
b.								☐	☐	
c.								☐	☐	
d.								☐	☐	
e.								☐	☐	

2. Has Proposed Insured applied for health insurance within the past six months with any other company?
Yes ☐ No ☐ If "Yes", give details in F-1 above.

3. Is Proposed Insured eligible for: State Cash Sickness? Yes ☐ No ☐   Worker's Compensation? Yes ☐ No ☐

4. Is policy applied for intended to replace or change any existing insurance? Yes ☐ No ☐   If "Yes", give details in F-1 above. Forward appropriate replacement forms, if required.

G HEALTH COVERAGE APPLIED FOR

1. List below any coverage with Paul Revere to continue, be made over, or lapsed. (Use abbrev.—Cont , M/O, or Lapse)

Pol #_____ #_____ #_____

2. Policy(ies) Applied For	Form #		Basic Indemnity	Additional Indemnity	Additional Indemnity	SSII Form #_____
Disability Income		Indemnity	$	$	$	$
		Elim Period				
		Ben Period	A S	A S	A S	A S
		Qual Period		/////	/////	/////
Overhead Expense		Indemnity	$	/////	/////	/////
		Elim Period			/////	/////
		Ben Period			/////	/////
Hospital Income		Indemnity	$	/////	/////	/////

3. Additional Benefits Applied For

Form #	Benefit Name	Amount	Form #	Benefit Name	Amount	Form #	Benefit Name	Amount

H FINANCIAL INFORMATION

Earned income is the total of your annual salary or wages, commissions, fees, or earned income, *reduced by* your regular business expenses, but *before* all other deductions.

1. My earned income: At the current annual rate is $_____ For prior year was $_____

2. Do you have a salary continuation program? Yes ☐ No ☐ How much? $_____ How long?_____

3. Does your unearned income exceed $5,000 per year? Yes ☐ No ☐   If "Yes", give sources and amounts.

_____

4. My net worth (assets minus liabilities) if more than $500,000 is $_____

If applying for Life Insurance, complete Sections I through K.

I | EXISTING AND PENDING LIFE COVERAGE

1. Describe all coverage in force. Include individual and group. If none, write "none".

Company	Issue Date	Type	Amount	ADB	To be Cont Yes	No	Effec Date of Discont
a.					☐	☐	
b.					☐	☐	
c.					☐	☐	
d.					☐	☐	
e.					☐	☐	

2. Has Proposed Insured applied for life insurance within the past six months with any other company?   Yes ☐   No ☐
If "Yes", give details in I-1 above.

3. Is policy applied for intended to replace or change any existing insurance or annuity?   Yes ☐ No ☐   If "Yes", give details. Forward proper replacement forms. _____

J | LIFE COVERAGE APPLIED FOR

1. Plan of Insurance   2. Amount (basic policy)   3. Waiver of Premium:
6 Months ☐ 3 Months ☐ None ☐
4. Automatic Premium Loan (if avail.)   Yes ☐   No ☐

5. Additional Benefits Applied For (Specify Benefit Name, Amount, Duration, etc.):

6. My earned income (less business expenses) at the current annual rate exceeds $

7. Complete if Proposed Insured is under age 15 or if Premium Payer Benefit is applied for.

Name of Applicant or Premium Payer	Relationship to Proposed Insured
Address	With whom does Proposed Insured make his home?
Occupation and Duties	

Life insurance in force on Premium Payer and other Family Members:
Prem Payer / Fam Mem   Age   Amount   Prem Payer / Fam Mem   Age   Amount

8. Complete if special selection life plan applied for.

If Proposed Insured is not eligible for a special selection life plan, another plan of insurance will be offered if Proposed Insured qualifies. Indicate alternate plan desired:

If Owner is other than Proposed Insured, or if Proposed Insured is under Age 18, complete Section K.

K | OWNERSHIP

Proposed Owner	Address
Contingent Owner	Address

L BENEFICIARIES

If applying for Life Insurance or Health ADB, complete Section L.

Principal(s) (Print full name)	Relationship	Birthdate
equally, or survivor(s) , if any		
Contingent(s)	Relationship	Birthdate
equally, or survivor(s) , if any		

M PREMIUM INFORMATION

1. If either of the following questions is answered "Yes" or left blank, no agent or broker is authorized to accept money and no Receipt and Conditional Insuring Agreement shall be given. *Has any person proposed for coverage:*

  a. Within the past two years been treated for heart trouble, stroke or cancer (other than of the skin), or had such treatment recommended? **Yes ☐ No ☐** **b.** Within the past 90 days been admitted to a hospital or other medical facility, or been advised to be admitted? **Yes ☐ No ☐**

2. If collected, this Initial Deposit is in exchange for Receipt and Conditional Insuring Agreement: (Check at least one) *Collected:* ☐ $_____ for proposed life insurance ☐ $_____ for proposed health insurance ☐ None.

3. Paid by: Proposed Insured ☐ Employer ☐ Other _____ Notices to: Residence ☐ Business ☐

4. Check Pay Method/Mode ➡

	Ann	S A	Qtr	Mo	5. If Pre-Auth Check	6. List other PAC Pol #s
☐ Regular Premium Notice			See Rate Book		*circle* deposit date	#_____ #_____
☐ ESP (Case #)					1st 10th 15th	#_____ #_____
☐ Pre-Authorized Check					20th 28th	#_____ #_____

N CORRECTIONS AND AMENDMENTS (For Home Office Use Only)

It is understood and agreed as follows:

(1) I have read the statements and answers recorded in Parts 1 and 2 above. They are, to the best of my knowledge and belief, true and complete and correctly recorded. They will become part of this Application and any policy(ies) issued on it.

(2) I will discontinue any policy(ies) shown to be discontinued in answer to questions F-1 and I-1 of Part 1 on or before the date(s) indicated. The Company will rely on such answers in determining the amount, if any, of insurance it will issue.

(3) No agent or broker has authority to waive the answer to any question, to determine insurability, to waive any of the Company's rights or requirements, or to make or alter any contract or policy.

(4) The Company has the right to require medical exams and tests to determine insurability.

(5) The insurance applied for will not take effect unless the issuance and delivery of the policy and payment of the first premium occur while the health of the Proposed Insured and any other person to be insured under the policy remains as stated in the Application. The only exception to this is provided in the Receipt and Conditional Insuring Agreement detached herefrom and issued if the premium is paid in advance, in accordance with section M above.

(6) The Company is authorized to obtain an investigative consumer report on me.

(7) Acceptance by the Proposed Owner of any policy issued on this Application will ratify any changes listed under "Corrections and Amendments".

Signed at _____   Date_____ 19____

I certify that I have truly and accurately recorded on this Application the information supplied by the Applicant. To the best of my knowledge, replacement of existing life insurance or annuities ☐ is ☐ is not involved. I have listed all such policies in question I-3 of Part 1.

X _____
Proposed Insured

X _____
Spouse (required for family plans)

X _____
☐ Premium Payer, or ☐ Proposed Owner, or ☐ Applicant (if other than Proposed Insured or if Proposed Insured is under age 15).

Witness_____
Agent or Broker

on applications are also very similar for both life and disability. Although the application is primarily used by the underwriter for evaluation, its design requires the participation of other home office professionals, including sales, claim, administrative, legal, and actuarial personnel.

The underwriter has the most input into the application design, including the areas of general identification information, income, occupation, medical history, and coverage applied for. However, the claim examiner also has a keen interest in making certain that the information requested in the application is specific and accurate enough to protect the company's interests at claim time. The actuary, in developing the product, has made certain assumptions, very often involving occupation and income, and is anxious to make certain that adequate information is developed in these areas. The law department must make certain that the design complies with the various state insurance regulations and that it does not violate any other state or federal statutes—for example, those dealing with a person's privacy. The home office administrator is anxious to make certain not only that the design takes into consideration information that will be necessary in the servicing of the approved contract, but also that the layout of the application allows administrative ease in processing information for company records and systems. Finally, after every other discipline has had its opportunity to put its own information into the design of the application, the marketing department must determine and make suggestions as to how it will fit into the sales process without being a detriment or a deterrent to the sale.

The primary difference between the types of information necessary for life insurance and for disability income is in the depth and detail of certain types of information. There are four areas in which this difference is particularly noticeable: occupation description, income information, certain medical impairments, and general stability. Since the disability contract has varying premium rates based upon the applicant's occupation, it is naturally quite vital to be able to accurately place an applicant in the proper occupation grouping. This is not always as easy as it might sound, and the entire subject of occupation classification and the occupation schedule will be discussed in Chapter 12. We will look at the other three areas of information in this chapter, particularly how they differ from life insurance.

INCOME DETERMINATION

The accurate determination of an applicant's income is more critical in disability insurance since (similar to a casualty contract) the insurer is providing protection against the loss of income, which has a specific value. To overstate the income and, consequently, to overinsure it will result in increased morbidity. Industry studies indicate that the greater the percent of income insured, the greater the morbidity. Since this relationship can be definitely established, the accurate determination of income is an essential step for the underwriter.

The application is the start of this process, and most application forms require a statement of income, which is followed by the applicant's signature. The relationship of that income figure to the amount applied for, the stability pattern of that income, and whether or not the income appears reasonable based upon the individual's occupation are factors that must be considered by the underwriter in determining whether to attempt to develop more detailed income information.

Earned Income

It is important to understand that the only type of income that can be considered as properly insurable is "earned income." This is simply that income that is generated from an individual's own efforts in his or her profession, business, or trade. It is that income figure that is derived after deducting business expenses. The figure does not include such unearned income items as dividends, interest, rental income, and pensions.

Perhaps the most objective measure to determine what income can be insured is to ask the following question: Will the income stop when the individual is disabled? If it will stop, it's insurable; if it won't, then there is nothing to insure!

What percent of an individual's earned income is proper and safe to insure? This is not an easy question to answer since some individuals are so motivated in their careers that the percent of income available to them at time of disability will neither be an incentive to elect disability nor to remain disabled. On the other hand, some other people with little motivation in their careers may elect or prolong disability even though it affects their income substantially. A study by the Society of Actuaries of group disability experience indicates that once the percent of earned income insured exceeds 50 percent, then the morbidity rate tends to escalate at an increasing pace. Although this phenomenon cannot be precisely tracked for every individual at a given income and percent insured, the trend does become evident as shown in Table 9–1.

There has been a tendency for income charts to have become more sophisticated in the past decade in an attempt to more accurately reflect the percent insured. One of the most common methods for developing a schedule of indemnities that may be written at given incomes requires breaking the income down to what we may call net take-home pay. This step simply requires taking the gross earned income figure (after business expenses) and reducing it further by the amount of federal withholding tax, state withholding tax, and social security tax, assuming the applicant to be married and to have two children. The resulting figure is referred to as net take-home pay or spendable income. This

TABLE 9–1
Group Long-Term Disability Experience 1969–1973

Percent of gross income insured	Ratio of actual/expected claims
50% or less	.88
More than 50%	1.09
More than 60%	1.42
More than 70%	2.19

Source: *Transactions, Society of Actuaries,* 1975, "Reports of Mortality and Morbidity Experience," p. 266.

is the income that will not be available to the applicant when he or she becomes disabled. Since individual disability income benefits are not taxable, it is proper to relate the level of indemnity to this take-home figure.

Furthermore, it is sound and common practice to insure a greater percent of net take-home pay at the lower earned-income amounts and to gradually reduce that percent as the earned income grows. The primary reason for this approach is that the lower-income individual has very little discretionary income and consequently needs a greater percent of earned income protected at the time of disability. On the other hand, the high-income earner has a greater percent of discretionary income. If all of this discretionary income were insured, the applicant might elect, consciously or subconsciously, to extend the disability, since he or she could live comfortably without the luxuries.

The maximum percent of take-home pay to insure is normally 75 to 90 percent. Some companies insure at a somewhat higher level and others at a lower level. It is important, however, to have this corridor between the amount insured and the net take-home pay in order to have an incentive for the applicant or claimant to return to work.

The schedule in Table 9–2 indicates for different income levels the monthly indemnity amount typically insured and the percent of net take-home pay the amount represents. You will notice that as the earned income and net take-home pay increase, the percent insured, or replacement ratio, decreases from a high of 90 percent to a low of 50 percent. Although a student examining different companies' income charts would find some variance in the percentages, this pattern would generally be followed.

Also shown in Table 9–2 is the fact that coverage stops at $300,000 of income. Throughout the history of the disability business, there has always been present in disability limits a maximum income amount beyond which the company would not insure, regardless of the applicant's

TABLE 9–2

Annual earned income	Net monthly earned income *	Maximum monthly indemnity	Replacement ratio
$ 16,000	$ 1,162	$ 1,050	90%
20,000	1,409	1,300	90
30,000	2,029	1,850	90
40,000	2,639	2,350	89
60,000	3,786	3,300	89
80,000	4,817	4,100	83
100,000	5,984	4,800	80
160,000	9,127	6,450	71
200,000	11,198	7,600	68
300,000	16,852	10,000	59
400,000	22,506	11,900	53

* Annual earned income less federal withholding taxes, state withholding taxes, and FICA taxes for a worker with four exemptions equals net annual earned income.

income. The underlying philosophy is that there is a level of earned income that is at such a high level that the applicant will also have significant amounts of unearned income upon which to depend at time of disability. Just where this level falls is a point of great discussion in the industry, and indeed it varies substantially depending upon the stability of the applicant. In recent years some of the larger disability companies have removed their maximum issue limit cap. Theoretically, therefore, a policy would have no maximum limit except the amount determined by an individual's own annual earned income. In practice, very few disability contracts have been approved for amounts greater than $20,000 per month.

Net Worth and Unearned Income

Some companies today will not issue any disability income to an individual whose net worth exceeds $1 million; for others it is $2 million; and some have no limits whatsoever. The question of net worth and unearned income is one that is being evaluated and modified regularly. Perhaps the key element is not so much the level of net worth or unearned income but the stability and motivation of the insured. The person who is actively involved in his or her business and has been personally responsible for the net worth growth is more likely to be properly motivated when faced with a disability. The individual who has inherited the net worth and unearned income and whose participation has little effect on the continuation of this unearned income is a poor risk for any type of disability coverage. The relationship of a person's earned income to unearned income is a measure of how dependent he or she is upon the income derived from the business or profession. Here, as in so

TABLE 9–3
Unearned Income

Earned income	Net worth	and/or	Unearned income	Maximum indemnity	
$100,000	$1,000,000		$ 35,000	$ 3,950	L/65
	4,000,000		75,000	2,300	Short term
	6,000,000		200,000	0	
200,000	1,000,000		35,000	7,400	L/65
	4,000,000		75,000	5,700	Short term
	6,000,000		200,000	0	
300,000	1,000,000		35,000	10,000	L/65
	4,000,000		75,000	8,750	Short term
	6,000,000		200,000	0	

many other instances in the disability product, common sense on the part of the underwriter is critical. The wide variety of circumstances that may be present from one individual to the next when examining the earned income, unearned income, and net worth question requires true individual selection with flexible guidelines, and not narrow underwriting rules and restrictions.

Table 9–3 is an unearned-income chart that may be used as a guideline. It's important to recognize that individual circumstances may require being more lenient or more strict than the chart indicates.

The business overhead expense contract does not insure either earned or unearned income. Its purpose is to insure that portion of gross business income that is used to pay business expenses. This subject was discussed in more detail in Chapter 4.

Needless to say, therefore, accurate determination of income and the stability pattern of that income is of vital importance in the disability underwriting process. Underwriters will frequently use supplementary applications to develop more detailed income information. On occasion the company may ask for specific signed income statements from the applicant, and may also request certain income tax forms. In addition, of course, outside inspection services as well as direct contacts over the telephone with the applicants to discuss questions surrounding the income pattern are common in the underwriting process. However, the process starts with the application itself, and the agent is the key to developing reliable and dependable income information.

MEDICAL HISTORY QUESTIONS

Another item in the disability application where differences exist between life and disability insurance is the area of medical history. The next chapter will discuss in more detail the underwriting process and the differences with life insurance. However, in the area of the application itself, let's look briefly at some of the key differences as far as medical history. The disability application must be designed in such a way that it develops information for impairments that may be very serious for disability but not have a significant mortality effect for life insurance. There are several such impairments, and their degree of importance is not the same. Muscular-skeletal problems are clearly the most numerous—back problems, knee problems, arthritis, and so on are all items of concern to the disability income underwriter. Since 15 percent of all disability income claims involve back impairments, it is not an accident that some 15 percent of all disability applications have substandard ratings or riders involving back conditions. One complicating factor with back conditions is that neither the existence nor the severity of the impairment can always be accurately determined by the physician. Therefore, it is not uncommon for the disability insurer to be presented with a back claim where there is no clear physical evidence that a back problem actually exists.

A second area of impairments that is more important in disability insurance has to do with the nervous system. Here again we are confronted with a subjective subject. Such general nervous disorders as psychoneurosis, nervous stomach, and anxiety are common disability impairments whose existence and severity are difficult to prove.

It is critical that the field salesperson be trained in the importance of securing information on these conditions when completing an application for disability insurance. The application itself normally includes more questions in the area of musculoskeletal problems and general disorders than would be true of a life insurance application.

APPLICANT'S STABILITY

A final area that is increasingly given more attention in disability applications is the stability of the applicant. Since stability and motivation are such critical elements in the disability claim process, any attempt to develop reliable measures of these factors is important. Because we are dealing here with elements that are very subjective, very little concrete progress has been made with such evaluation. Indeed even if such a tested and proven psychological test could be given to disability insurance applicants to determine their stability and motivation, the results would only be reliable at the time the application was taken. An individual's stability and motivation may and will change through time, depending upon changes in job circumstance, family circumstance, and age.

Nevertheless some companies are beginning to experiment with basic measures of stability. Some companies include on the application a section referred to as a persistency rater (even though its primary purpose is to measure stability). Experience studies have shown a close relationship between persistency and morbidity, and the elements mea-

FIGURE 9–2

INDIVIDUAL PERSISTENCY RATER
Circle the proper score for each persistency factor Total the circled numbers and enter in the space provided This indicates the likelihood of a policy remaining in force beyond the first year

DI and Life

CLASS	AGE		MODE		INCOME	
B 0	18 25	0	Monthly ESP	0	$15,000 17 999	0
A 1	26 30	1	Monthly PAC or		18,000 22 999	1
2A 2	31 35	2	Semiannual	2	23,000 29 999	2
3A 3	36-60	3	Annual	3	30,000 and above	3
4A 5						

CURRENT POLICYHOLDER		YEARS IN CURRENT JOB	
Existing P R policyholder		Less than 18 months	0
over one year	2	18 36 months	1
		Over three years	2

Life Only

POLICY TYPE		FACE AMOUNT	
Level Term	0	Less than $50,000	0
Other	1	$50,000 and over	1

Total Score	DI [ ]	Life [ ]

POOR	FAIR	GOOD TO EXCELLENT
0	7 10	20

sured at application time are important for both the expectation of claim and the expectation of lapse. Figure 9–2 shows material that might be used on a disability application to measure stability. Agents using the rater shown in Figure 9–2 are told that if a potential applicant scores less than a five, the application is not to be submitted.

The key elements in the rater are age, marital status, occupation class, stability of employment, and whether or not one is a homeowner or a previous policyholder. Industry studies indicate that these factors have a direct impact on both persistency and claims experience. The applicant who is over age 30, married, a professional, more than three years in an occupation, a homeowner, and a present policyholder combines together the most positive stability characteristics. There are many other stability elements, but studies indicate these are the most important. New agents should be trained on the importance of such raters.

OTHER APPLICATION FORMS

There are other application forms common to disability income. Similar to life insurance there is a trial or preliminary application process, where a potential applicant may submit an unsigned application that the underwriter may examine briefly to determine whether there is a possibility of acceptance. Usually this type of trial application process is used with highly impaired applicants or those in hazardous avocations or vocations.

Disability insurance also uses reinstatement applications similar to those used in life insurance. The reinstatement application is an abbreviated form, and its primary purpose is to generate information to determine whether there has been significant change in the applicant's medical history.

Policy changes are also frequent in the disability income business, and most companies use an abbreviated application to find any serious changes in medical history when evaluating the requested policy change.

OTHER APPLICATION FACTORS

Similar to life insurance the disability application will also address questions in the area of hazardous avocations. If the application carries significant disability risk with it, the underwriter may exclude coverage for this activity.

A final area of importance on the disability application has to do with foreign-born applicants or individuals who may live outside the United States or Canada. In the first instance, the development of prior medical history is frequently a problem, similar to life insurance, but there is an additional problem. When we insure for disability income a person who is a resident of the United States or Canada but later returns to his or her native country, we cannot follow our same practices in claim administration. Similarly, to insure an individual at a specific percent of income may be proper and safe in this country, but in certain parts of the world the income we would pay at time of disability in American dollars would be substantially out of proportion to the insured's earned income in his or her native land.

It's important, therefore, that we determine at application time whether or not the foreign-born national is a permanent resident of this country. If there is a question, frequently the problem can be solved by placing an exclusion endorsement eliminating coverage outside of the United States or Canada.

The disability application, therefore, is the starting point for the insurance process. The salesperson is an important cog in the selection process and must understand clearly the importance of certain types of information in disability income versus life insurance. The areas of occupation information, earned income determination, stability and motivation, and medical history are areas in which the degree and nature of information may be considerably different and of greater importance than for life insurance.

Underwriting Tools

10

SIMILARITIES TO LIFE INSURANCE

There are a great many similarities between life and disability income underwriting: The application follows a similar pattern; the underwriting tools used are frequently identical; the training of the underwriter follows a similar pattern. The similarities between life and disability income underwriting are particularly close when examining non-cancellable disability income. Since both life insurance and non-can disability involve commitments on the part of the insurer for many years into the future, the evaluation of the risk at underwriting time takes on significant importance.

The structure of the typical non-can disability income underwriting department is similar to that found in any life underwriting department. The experience levels and training of assistant underwriters, underwriters, and senior underwriters follows a similar pattern, and compensation patterns are also similar. The volume of work handled by the experienced underwriter, the depth of underwriting investigation, the cost of that investigation, the length of the underwriting process, are all very similar.

DIFFERENCES FROM LIFE INSURANCE

There are, however, significant differences, both general and specific, in the underwriting process. The general difference centers around the fact that the life underwriting process tends to be somewhat more objective. There is a large volume of mortality data on which the life industry has developed underwriting manuals over several decades in an attempt to relate the underwriting decision to the physical history or condition. Life underwriting still demands substantial judgment on the part of the trained underwriter, particularly in the more complex impaired cases. Nevertheless, mortality data in such areas as height and weight, blood pressure, diabetes, and smoking is based upon substantial accumulations of data.

In contrast, in the disability income business there is only a fraction of reliable data available by impairment. Underwriting manuals consequently are not as objective and as reliably based upon factual data. As more and more disability income data is accumulated, more reliable morbidity analysis becomes possible; however, there is a substantial gap between the two product lines that does exist currently.

Naturally, the fact that the determination of death is usually much more objective than the determination of disability complicates this objective/subjective comparison even further. The factors of motivation and stability clearly enter into the subjective evaluation of the disability income applicant to a greater extent than is true of life insurance since the disability income policyholder simply has more control over the submission of a claim than is true of life insurance.

In addition to the general difference between the two lines that has just been discussed, there are specific differences in the underwriting process that are quite easy to understand. Some impairments are not significant for mortality, such as muscular-skeletal disorders of the back or joints; however, they are very important in the disability income underwriting process. Similarly, some impairments that are substandard for life insurance are clearly uninsurable for disability income. The individual who is severely impaired but who is acceptable for life insurance on a rated basis may well not be a candidate at all for disability income since the person's impairment is so severe that he or she is in fact totally disabled.

UNDERWRITER TRAINING

As mentioned above, the training of the disability underwriter follows closely the pattern of training of the life insurance underwriter. The trainee is assigned to an experienced underwriter to learn the basic insurance language and underwriting procedures and then gradually, through on-the-job experience, is exposed to varying types of situations. For several months all decisions must be reviewed by a more experienced underwriter, and then gradually the trainee's approval limits are increased as his or her experience and knowledge grows. Similar to life insurance, it would probably be true to state that the underwriter is 80 percent trained after two years of experience, and then the last 20 percent occurs in the following three- to five-year period.

As with life insurance, it is common to encourage the home office underwriter to participate in a variety of industry courses to broaden exposure to the entire insurance process. Participation in the series of Life Office Management Association (LOMA) courses is usually encouraged early in an underwriter's career, as is the study of the education courses offered by the Health Insurance Association of America and the Registered Health Underwriter (RHU) program of the Disability Income Training Council. Similarly it is common to encourage underwriters to expose themselves to the Joint Life Underwriting Committee courses and the Chartered Life Underwriter (CLU) program.

DEPARTMENT STRUCTURE

One question that company management in a company writing both product lines must address is whether or not the two underwriting departments should be combined and the underwriters trained to underwrite both products. This combining has been done successfully by some companies, but there are some considerations that are particularly important in successfully combining the two departments:

1. Neither the life nor the disability underwriting department in the merger should end up dominating the other either in management personnel or in rules and procedures. It is important that the procedures of both underwriting departments be objectively analyzed and the best ones retained in the merger. This is particularly difficult when one department dominates the other in the number of personnel.

2. In order for the quality of underwriting to remain at a high level, the combination underwriter must be exposed frequently to both types of cases. If the volume of one line or the other is small in comparison with the larger line, then the combination underwriter in such a situation may not be exposed frequently enough to the smaller product line cases to develop into a true professional underwriter. As a guideline, I believe that if one line is less than 25 percent of the other, then there may not be enough exposure of the smaller product line to make the combination underwriting step a prudent one.

3. It makes much more sense to consider combining the life and disability underwriting departments if the disability product line is noncancellable or guaranteed renewable. If, on the other hand, the disability income line has a large volume of optionally renewable or hospital/medical business, then the techniques and level of underwriting is such that the combination step may not be a prudent one.

4. There are economies to be gained. Obviously, a duplication of management is avoided. In addition, frequently an application for both life and disability income may be pending simultaneously. If so, the trained combination underwriter can evaluate both applications, thus

avoiding the complexity, delay, and extra expense involved in having two separate departments or people process the applications.

In the final analysis the decision as to whether or not to develop a combination department and combination underwriters must rest with the particular needs and characteristics of each company. The primary caution is not to proceed if the resulting structure will end up with one department entirely dominating the other.

MEDICAL EXAMINATIONS

The tools in the underwriting process are indeed similar, but frequently their use and emphasis are different. As mentioned in the previous chapter, the application is indeed the most important tool. It is designed by the insurer to specifically elicit information that is essential in the selection process, and the degree of its value is dependent to a great extent on the quality and care the field underwriter or salesperson takes in completing it. There are some application questions that are different than in life insurance. They fall into four categories: (1) questions to elicit specific information to determine earned income, (2) questions to determine the specific occupation and duties of the applicant, (3) questions to determine the applicant's stability, and (4) medical questions to develop physical history that is of particular importance in underwriting disability income. The latter item refers primarily to muscular-skeletal-type impairments.

Circumstances Requiring a Medical Examination

Medical examinations are frequently required in disability income, particularly in non-cancellable and guaranteed-renewable contracts, and their requirement is based upon age, amount applied for, and length of benefit period. Similar to life insurance, the greater the risk the company is asked to assume, the greater the likelihood a medical examination will be required. Table 10–1 is a typical medical examination chart for disability income. Nonmedical limits have been expanded substantially since the mid 1960s as the disability industry has gained more confidence in its selection techniques and has evaluated the results of medical exami-

TABLE 10–1
Medical Requirements

Ages	ParaMed exam* (per month)	ParaMed + EKG* (per month)
18–50	$4,000	$11,000
51–60	2,500	11,000

* ParaMed includes blood and urine specimens.

nations. Similar to life insurance, as the cost of medical examinations has increased, the medical rules have been liberalized.

Since we measure the size of disability income contracts by the monthly indemnity, we sometimes mask the true liability of a particular contract and the risk involved. For example, an individual applying for $2,500 per month of disability income at age 35 and with a to-age-65 benefit period represents a potential claim liability of close to $1 million if the policyholder were to be disabled at age 35 and if the claim were to run to age 65. With issue limits in excess of $10,000 per month and with lifetime coverage it is not uncommon at the younger ages for a company's liability to exceed $3 million. With this sort of potential claim payment, not only are medical examinations necessary, but frequently so are electrocardiograms, X rays, and special blood tests.

The medical examination questions are usually identical to those used for life insurance. The physical history part of the medical examination becomes a part of the insurance contract in disability income, again similar to life insurance.

Medical Examiner's Familiarity with Underwriting Considerations

One practical problem for the disability underwriter is that the physician completing the medical examination is usually unfamiliar with the underwriting considerations that are important in evaluating a risk for disability income. As a result, important physical history may be omitted or given minimal attention. Not infrequently, the medical examiner either consciously or subconsciously thinks in terms of how the applicant's history affects mortality, rather than morbidity.

Paramedical examinations have become more and more frequently used in disability underwriting, similar to their growth in life insurance. To a great extent they may be more valuable than the average medical examination done by a physician, since the paramedical technician tends to give more detailed information without making judgments as to its importance. It is the feeling of many disability underwriters as well as some life underwriters that the paramedical examination would be preferred in the majority of instances where medical examinations are required, except for those cases requiring the specific skills of an internist.

Even though both the examination and the physical history portions of the medical examination are important for both life and disability income underwriting, I believe that the physical examination part is more important for life insurance and that the physical history section is more important for disability income.

ATTENDING PHYSICIAN'S STATEMENTS

Attending physician's statements are particularly important for disability income, and some companies' statistics indicate that more APSs are requested for disability income than for life insurance. On the other hand, more medical examinations are normally requested in life underwriting—the reason being that the disability underwriter is particularly concerned about the details of the physical history and its impact upon disability, whereas the life underwriter is able to draw firm conclusions from the result of the physical examination itself. The decision to order or not to order the attending physician's statement in disability income is based upon the amount of total risk involved and upon the answers to the specific health questions on the application. It is common to write the physician for details when answers to questions on the application state that the applicant has had a recent physical or an annual physical or has a personal physician. The recency of a physical impairment is of particular importance in disability income since the exclusion endorsement or extra premium may be avoided if enough time has elapsed. Although the same circumstance exists in life insurance, the increased frequency of the substandard decision in disability income increases the frequency of the need for the attending physician's statement and the need for the details of a particular physical history.

In order to elicit from the attending physician the specific information desired, it is quite common for the disability underwriter to request that in replying "particular attention be given to any possible history of (a specific impairment)." Such an approach tends to avoid the problem of the physician assuming that the request for information is for life insurance and making erroneous judgments of the importance of the history.

Hospital records are also requested in the disability underwriting process, similar to life insurance, but to nowhere near the frequency of attending physician's statements.

Another source of information is the recently established Disability Income Record System information from the Medical Index Bureau. The primary purpose of the DIRS/MIB is to alert the company to possible overinsurance situations, rather than specific information on physical history.

OTHER MEDICAL INFORMATION

Electrocardiograms are usually not routinely required in the disability income underwriting process. However, the underwriter may request them because of information developed during the underwriting process. Similarly, chest X rays are not automatically required at any specific indemnity but are requested when the history available or physical condition indicates that additional information is necessary to make a proper evaluation.

The emergence of the AIDS epidemic in recent years has caused companies to review their medical exam and blood profile rules and requirements. Blood tests have been expanded by most companies to determine the existence of the AIDS virus or antibodies.

Urine specimens are also a part of the underwriting process, and similar to life insurance, the same type of abnormal readings frequently requires additional specimens, supplementary information, and a subsequent classification of substandard.

Diabetes questionnaires, usually identical to the life insurance questionnaire, are required when a history or a suspicion of diabetes exists.

Blood pressure questionnaires, again similar or identical to the life insurance questionnaire, are requested in similar situations as are found in life insurance.

INSPECTION REPORTS AND INFORMATION

Inspection reports are common in the disability business and are used primarily to verify income and occupation information. Similar to life insurance, their use has been replaced in recent years more and more by home office investigation over the telephone. Disability income underwriters have found that the proper training of telephone specialists can elicit not only a high quality of income and occupation information, but also a variety of additional information affecting stability, health history, and avocation. Inspection reports continue to be ordered for the large-indemnity and high-risk cases; and similar to life insurance, more extensive reports may be ordered for the true "jumbo" risk case.

ADDITIONAL INCOME INFORMATION

Because income information is so important to the disability underwriter, additional information about income is frequently requested on a supplementary application form. Circumstances in which the income has not shown a stable pattern or has been difficult to verify through inspection sources may require more detailed information as shown in Figure 10–1. The basic purpose of the financial supplement is to probe deeper into the income question to make certain the indemnity requested bears the proper relationship to the income being insured. Since net worth and unearned income may affect the disability claim, questions about net worth and unearned income are frequently used to elicit more detailed information. The type of form used varies from one company to another, and indeed the measurement of this information from one company to another may vary, but the form shown in Figure 10–1 is typical of those used.

In large-indemnity, high-income, high-net worth or high-unearned income situations, the underwriter may also require or request the applicant's tax return or information from the applicant's accountant.

FIGURE 10–1

FINANCIAL SUPPLEMENT   WORCESTER, MA 01608

☐ THE PAUL REVERE LIFE   ☐ THE PAUL REVERE PROTECTIVE   ☐ THE PAUL REVERE VARIABLE
  INSURANCE COMPANY   LIFE INSURANCE COMPANY   ANNUITY INSURANCE COMPANY

1. NAME	Last		2.	Birthdate
	First / Middle			Mo Day Yr

3. What were your earnings from your occupation or profession as reported on your federal tax return — form 1040?

	Annual Rate		
	Current Year	Last Year	2 Years Ago
a. Salary, Wages, Fees and/or Commissions			
b. Pension and Profit Sharing Plan Contributions			
c. Bonus			
d. Earnings from any other occupations (state occupation and give details in **6.** below)			
e. TOTAL EARNINGS (a + b + c + d)			
f. Deductible Business Expenses			
g. NET EARNINGS (e − f)			

4. What was your other income for the last calendar year as reported on your federal tax return — form 1040?
   $ _____ (give details below)

Dividends	$ _____	Rental Income (gross less cash
Interest	$ _____	spent but before depreciation) $ _____
Net Realized Capital Gains	$ _____	Other (give details in **6.** below) $ _____

5. Estimate your net worth (gross worth less any mortgages, loans and other debts).
   $ _____ (give details below)

Cash Savings, Stocks, Bonds	$ _____	Real Estate — Residence only $ _____
Interest in my Business		Other Real Estate $ _____
(exclude goodwill)	$ _____	Other (give details in **6.**
Personal Property	$ _____	below) $ _____

6. Remarks: Show here any details to your answers to the questions above.

_____

_____

_____

It is understood and agreed as follows:
(1) I have read the statements and answers made above. They are, to the best of my knowledge and belief, true and complete and correctly recorded. The Company will rely on them to determine the amount, if any, of disability income insurance it will issue.
(2) This Supplement will become a part of my application for insurance and any policy issued on it.

Signed at _____   Date _____ 19____

Witness _____   X _____
              Agent or Broker   Applicant

This form may be completed in private, but your signature must be witnessed by an Agent or Broker. Place it in an envelope addressed to the Vice President, Underwriting Department, The Paul Revere Companies, Worcester, MA 01608.

App 60   80-1

UNDERWRITING USE OF COMPANY DATA

It has been emphasized throughout this book that field underwriting selection is of particular importance in disability income, and indeed the disability income home office underwriter places significant value on the reputation of the field underwriter on the borderline case. Those disability insurers that have developed a large block of business are in a position to evaluate that business annually, and this evaluation in some instances involves an evaluation of the veteran agent's block of business. The results of this evaluation are available to the underwriter, and, if the problems found are serious enough, specific restrictions may be placed on all of an agent's business. Similar to the claims data, persistency information is also available by agent and is an important piece of information in determining the overall quality of an agent's business.

Therefore, the company's claims and persistency experience data in disability income by occupation, geographical area, type of contract, producing agent, and experience of the agent should be evaluated annually. Furthermore they should become a part of the disability income underwriter's knowledge of the block of business he or she is underwriting.

COMMUNICATIONS

Open and effective communication between the claim and underwriting departments in a disability income operation are most critical. The claim department is in a position to determine trends and identify problems more quickly than such things become evident through morbidity or persistency studies. It is important for the claim examiner to be alert to such situations and to, in turn, inform the underwriting department. Similarly, it's important for the underwriting department to listen carefully to the claim examiner's input and to modify its procedures or be alert to potential problem situations. This type of communication is not always easy and open, since the underwriting department may believe that the claim department is second-guessing the quality of their underwriting. On the other hand, the claim examiner only sees those cases where a claim has occurred and never is exposed to those policyholders with identical physical histories who have never submitted a claim. Overreaction must be avoided in both departments, but each must listen carefully to the other.

Identical to life insurance, the effectiveness of the home office underwriter's job is enhanced if communication with the field force is effective and sound. The smoothness of the process, the confidence in each other, and the reliability of the information are all enhanced by good communications. The existence of effective communications must never be taken for granted but must constantly be encouraged and promoted by underwriting management.

In summary, there are great similarities between the life and disability underwriting processes. The department structure is similar, and under the right circumstances, it may be advisable to combine both departments and cross-train the underwriters. The underwriting tools, medical examinations, attending physician's statements, and supplementary reports are very similar between the two lines of insurance, although some information is more important in life insurance than in disability, and vice versa. Both lines of insurance require substantial judgment on the part of the underwriter; but the volume and reliability of mortality data is such that life insurance is somewhat more objective, whereas disability income continues to be somewhat more subjective in the underwriting process.

Substandard Underwriting

11

The subject and study of impaired-risk underwriting in disability income insurance is one that demonstrates dynamic change over the past quarter century. New and different products with new and different risks, contracts having longer elimination periods and longer benefit periods, advances in treating medical impairments, some improvement in the availability of experience by various impairments are all factors that have had an impact upon the trends and the underwriting of disability insurance during this period. The purpose of this chapter is to identify the principal characteristics and guidelines in impaired-risk disability underwriting. I intend to give only limited attention to specific underwriting decisions, except as examples of trends.

COMPARISON WITH LIFE INSURANCE

A comparison of disability income and life insurance underwriting reveals several areas of difference. First and most evident in the initial observation is the importance of some impairments and the lack of importance of other impairments. The nature of the disability income product requires that many physical conditions and physical impairments (1) demand more attention than in life insurance and (2) frequently result in a substandard underwriting decision because of the potential for long-term disability. These same impairments may have little effect on life insurance because they have no adverse affect on mortality expectancy whatsoever. Such types of impairments are frequently structural in nature, impairments affecting the muscular-skeletal system of the body. Back conditions are clearly the most common impairments in this category and are frequently used as examples of the difference in disability and life insurance underwriting approaches. Back claims are indeed a common cause of disability claims, and some company studies indicate that they represent some 15 percent of all disability income claims. It's not surprising, therefore, that the percentage of impaired-risk cases resulting from back conditions also runs in the same neighborhood of 15 percent. Clearly, a back condition has very little impact upon life insurance and mortality, unless that back condition involves damage or injury to the spinal cord itself.

The nature and degree of back problems for the disability underwriter run the breadth of severity from minor sprains and strains to herniated and ruptured discs. Some show good potential for full recovery, whereas other back conditions are chronic in nature and likewise present chronic claim risks.

Disorders of the knee joint (the joint in the human body most susceptible to injury) are also commonly of concern to the disability underwriter. Other joint problems, such as arthritis, bursitis, and tendonitis, may require substandard underwriting in disability insurance, but they are of little concern to the life insurance underwriter unless the severity raises questions about the impact on the waiver-of-premium benefit.

Disorders to the nervous system represent another area that presents unique problems to the disability underwriter. A medical history of nonlife-threatening impairments—such as nervous tension, simple neurosis, anxiety state, nervous stomach, or various types of nervous problems—represent physical history that is both difficult to quantify and difficult for the underwriter to handle. Whereas the life underwriter would be concerned with only the more serious nervous and psychological problems, the disability underwriter must be concerned about any that may result in a disability.

Remembering the importance of stability and motivation in the incidence and length of disability claims, the more subjective the impairment, the greater the opportunity for misrepresenting or extending a claim. Impairments of the nervous system, and to a great extent musculoskeletal impairments, carry with them a substantial subjective characteristic. How bad does the back ache? How serious is the nervous problem? Does the knee disorder truly prevent the claimant from pursuing his or her normal occupation? All disability claim examiners face such questions daily and recognize clearly the difficulty in obtaining medical certification as to the degree of disability.

Hypochondriacs may live to complain about various physical problems well beyond average life expectancy, but they will use their disability income policies frequently.

TYPES OF SUBSTANDARD DECISIONS

One major difference between life and disability income underwriting is that there is very often more than one underwriting approach to handling the impairment. In life insurance the impaired risk is either rejected or receives a rated contract. The severity of the impairment determines the severity of the extra premium charge. In disability insurance the impaired risk, depending upon the nature and severity of the condition, can be handled with an extra premium, a full-exclusion endorsement, a limited-exclusion endorsement, a longer elimination period, a shorter benefit period, or some combination of all these approaches. All of these underwriting options will be discussed in this chapter, but it should be remembered that these options give both the underwriter and the salesperson some flexibility. The underwriter may well be able to charge a high extra premium in place of the exclusion endorsement in some situations, or conversely to use an exclusion endorsement in place of a normal extra premium for that applicant where the premium charge is critical. It is particularly helpful to the underwriter if salespeople will indicate at application time which substandard approach they believe to be more salable in a given circumstance, in order to avoid subsequent discussions and possible reissue.

The number of substandard risks in disability insurance differs substantially from that in life insurance. The percentage of applications rated in life insurance ranges from 3 to 5 percent, whereas the percentage of applicants with either ratings or exclusion endorsements in disability insurance ranges from 15 to 20 percent. Similarly, the percentage of life insurance rejections ranges in the 1 to 3 percent area, and in disability insurance it ranges from 6 to 10 percent. In addition, some 12 to 15 percent of all disability applications are approved with some other significant change, such as a smaller indemnity than applied for, a lower occupation class than asked for, or some change in the elimination period or benefit period. The nonmedical changes in life insurance, however, represent only 2 to 3 percent of all applications received.

Some 4 to 10 percent, therefore, of all life insurance applications are either rejected, rated, or carry some change in the initial application. On the other hand, from 30 to 45 percent of disability applications carry such changes. This particular difference is very difficult for trained life insurance salespeople to adjust to. They are fearful of upsetting established life insurance clients by presenting them with limited or substandard disability contracts. There is a technique and a skill involved in placing the ridered or rated disability contract, and the skill is not as well developed in the life insurance salesperson.

SCARCITY OF RELIABLE DATA

The final important difference between life and health substandard underwriting is the lack of reliable claim experience studies on impaired disability risks. Both the smaller volumes and the subjective nature of disability impairments have made reliable studies very difficult to come by. In more recent years some of the larger disability income writers have developed experience studies on those impairments that generate substantial premium volume—such as back conditions, high blood pressure, and obesity.

Because of the subjective nature of many disability claims, the underwriting tends to be somewhat more of an art than a science in comparison with life insurance. Consequently, the underwriting manuals themselves tend to give ranges of suggested action for impaired risks, rather than more objective and precise standards.

RATEUPS AND EXTRA PREMIUMS

During the past 25 years, there has been more and more frequent use of the extra premium in place of the exclusion endorsement to handle the impaired applicant. Much of this trend results from greater confidence in handling particular impairments as more claim experience has become available. However, another significant factor has been the change in the nature of the benefits applied for, particularly the trend toward longer elimination periods. Historically, the extra premium charge was more common for the less severe impairments; and the longer the elimination period, the less serious the impairment was to the underwriter. *Minor* nervous disorders, digestive problems, muscular problems, and so on have historically been treated in this manner. Not too many years ago, it was quite common to routinely charge an extra premium to any individual who had lost the sight of an eye or had severely impaired vision in one eye. Experience studies indicated that extra premiums were not necessary except in the most extreme cases. The handling of overweight risks has also become more liberal in disability insurance in recent years as experience has become available. Perhaps the most significant and substantial area of underwriting relaxation has come in the treatment of high blood pressure. Similar to trends and patterns in the life insurance underwriting of this impairment over the past 10 to 20 years, disability income underwriting has also become more liberal. Some 20 years ago individuals with blood pressure in excess of 150/100 were considered uninsurable, but today applicants with readings substantially higher who are under regular treatment are taken on a substandard and rated basis.

In the 1960s some one third of all impaired disability risks were handled with an extra premium, and the remainder carried exclusion riders. Since that time there has been a gradual reversal of those ratios to the point that in most companies today more than two thirds of the substandard risks are handled with an extra premium. This is a clear indication of increased confidence on the part of the disability underwriter and indeed is more in the policyholder's interest—since with an extra premium the policyholder has coverage for all impairments, instead of having an exclusion rider that eliminates coverage for the condition the policyholder is most concerned about. It is not infrequent to handle some impairments that the underwriter expects may be of short duration by combining an extra premium with a longer elimination period. The individual who has recurrent bouts of minor digestive problems might be such an example.

The underwriter should always keep in mind when approving the rated disability policy that reconsideration of the rating may be possible in the future. Because of the high percentage of impaired-risk policies issued in disability income, it is important for the underwriter to offer to reconsider the underwriting decision after a certain period of time has elapsed. Similar to life insurance such reconsideration is normally subject to medical evidence that there has been no recurrence or worsening of the condition.

The amount or degree of the extra premium charge in disability insurance also differs from life insurance. It is not infrequent for the extra premium in disability contracts to be only 10 percent of the basic premium of the contract, and indeed most extra premium charges for disability insurance range in the 10 to 50 percent area. It must be remembered that the purpose of the extra premium is not to generate enough additional premium to cover all anticipated claims for the specific impairment on the particular substandard contract underwritten, but rather the total of all substandard premiums for all risks with similar impairments should be adequate to cover the increased morbidity. Occasionally, the extra premium charge on a disability contract may extend beyond 50 percent and even up to 200 percent of the basic premium; however, charges above 100 percent are quite rare.

EXCLUSION RIDERS

The exclusion endorsement or exclusion rider is a negative approach to handling the impaired risk. In a real sense it represents an admission of defeat for the underwriter! It is an indication that the underwriter cannot adequately determine the degree of the risk involved and consequently chooses to exclude any form of coverage for the particular impairment. The exclusion rider is the most traditional method of treating disability impaired risks. Unfortunately, to exclude coverage entirely for an impairment fails to meet the applicant's concern for the one physical problem that is uppermost in his or her mind. Consequently, as mentioned previously, there has been an increasing trend in recent years toward less use of the full exclusion endorsement and greater use of limited exclusions and extra premiums.

The full-exclusion endorsement is worded in such a way that it will pay no benefits for any disability resulting from the impairment. For example, typical wording for an exclusion endorsement for peptic ulcer might read, "This contract excludes coverage for any loss due to or resulting from peptic ulcer." Many impairments do not require a full or complete endorsement since the nature of the impairment normally is confined to a short period of time. For example, the applicant with a history of kidney stones will usually experience a relatively short disability unless abdominal surgery is required. Therefore, a limited-exclusion rider for this impairment might be worded in such a way that it excluded coverage for kidney stones for only the first 30, 60, or perhaps 90 days of the disability. Beyond that point the odds of the claim continuing are much less, and the company is willing to assume the risk of paying a claim in those few situations in which the claim is extended beyond the period excluded. Frequently, the limited exclusion endorsement and a small extra premium charge are used together in order to provide for the extra morbidity for those risks who will have claims extending beyond the excluded period. This same limited-rider approach can be employed on more serious conditions, such as peptic ulcers. However, the period excluded would be longer, and the extra premium would tend to be larger.

A second type of limited rider not only lengthens the elimination period for a particular impairment, but also reduces the benefit period. This exclusion rider is frequently called a "qualified condition rider." For example, individuals with chronic back conditions, because of frequent possibility of recurrence, may be underwritten with an exclusion endorsement that will not pay benefits during the first 90 or perhaps 180 days of a disability and then will limit benefits for one, two, or perhaps three years following that period. Such a rider could be placed on a basic contract that had a 30-day elimination period and a benefit period to age 65, but it could confine any claims for the specific excluded impairment to, say, a 90-day elimination period and a two-year benefit period. The clear advantage of using such limited riders is that they both provide the company protection against the more serious impairments and also provide some coverage for the policyholder.

One basic difference from one company to another is in the actual wording of exclusion endorsements or riders. Most companies follow a pattern of keeping the exclusion rider language as narrow and specific as possible in order to provide as much reasonable coverage for the policyholder as possible. However, some companies consciously use a broader exclusion endorsement in order to avoid the possibility of any claims that might be related to or result from the known impairment. The person who was found to have a peptic ulcer upon initial underwriting may submit a claim subsequently for a hiatus hernia, which has similar symptoms. The more narrow and specific approach to this sort of situation would be for the insurance company to initially exclude coverage for any loss resulting from peptic ulcer. With such an exclusion rider, the company would be liable for the hiatus hernia claim. The broad exclusion approach would exclude any coverage resulting from

disease or disorder of the stomach or digestive tract. In this instance
the hiatus hernia claim would be excluded. Most underwriters make
every attempt to keep the wording of the endorsement as narrow as
possible in order to provide as much coverage for the policyholder as
possible. For a company to follow a pattern of generally using broad
endorsements is not in the public interest.

The most equitable way of handling the serious impairment that
must be excluded but carries with it the potential of associated impairments is to use an extra premium along with the exclusion endorsement.
Some company studies have indicated that for many impairments, because of the chance of misdiagnosis, a full exclusion endorsement simply
proves inadequate, and an extra premium is also necessary to cover
the added risk. Studies on risks who have been diagnosed as having
peptic ulcer have shown that even with a full exclusion endorsement,
the morbidity for such risks runs higher than expected. They tend to
have a higher incidence of other digestive disorders and a higher incidence of coronary disease. The solution is to use an extra premium
along with the exclusion endorsement.

The underwriter should keep in mind that, similar to extra premiums, some exclusion endorsements can be removed after a period of
time subject to no evidence of recurrence. Time does tend to heal many
wounds, and to offer consideration for removing the exclusion endorsement after a reasonable period of time with no recurrence is not only
in the policyholder's interest, but also makes it somewhat easier for
the salesperson to place the contract. Not infrequently, upon reconsideration of the exclusion endorsement, it can be replaced with an extra
premium charge.

ELIMINATION-PERIOD IMPACT

Up through the mid 1970s, a large proportion of non-cancellable
disability business was written with first-day accident coverage and a
seven-day elimination period for sickness disorders. The more common
elimination period today is for 30 days—occasionally 15 days, but frequently 60, 90, or 180 days. The longer the elimination period, the
less need there is for many exclusion endorsements, and the lower the
extra premium charge necessary. Many impairments that require some
sort of exclusion endorsement or require an extra premium charge with
an elimination period less than 90 days can be taken standard with a
90-day or longer elimination period. The use of elimination periods in
substandard underwriting has become more prevalent in the past 10
years, and the salespeople in the field are alert to the fact that by applying
for a longer elimination period they may avoid having to place a substandard policy.

In addition to impaired-risk underwriting for physical problems,
a small percentage of applications are also handled on an impaired-

risk basis because of habits and vocational or avocational hazards. The applicant with a slight or moderate history of excessive alcohol abuse, the individual with a significant bad-driving record, and the person with a history of mild or moderate marijuana use are all examples of applicants whose additional morbidity risk may be adequately handled with an extra premium charge or an extra premium along with a longer elimination period. Avocations that carry with them potential for serious physical injury are appropriately handled with exclusion endorsements. Sky diving, deep-sea diving, and motor vehicle racing are examples of such avocational hazards that may appropriately be underwritten with an exclusion endorsement. Depending upon the nature of the avocation risk and the frequency of participation, the underwriting treatment may range from a full-exclusion endorsement, to a slight extra premium, to a combination of an extra premium and a longer elimination period.

REJECTIONS

As already mentioned, the frequency of application rejection is much greater in non-can disability income than in life insurance. Rejection rates between 6 and 10 percent are common, although there has been a tendency for these rates to diminish during the past decade. Some impairments that in the past were considered totally uninsurable are now taken on a highly substandard basis. The underwriting of hypertension has become more liberal, allowing companies to insure risks today that were uninsurable 15 years ago. The combination use of full-exclusion endorsements, limited-exclusion endorsements, and large extra premiums allows the underwriter to approve a substandard policy in today's disability underwriting environment.

A much more competitive marketplace atmosphere has resulted in companies stretching their underwriting decision to an extent that was not as common in the past. This competition has generally been a positive development for the industry since without such keen competitive pressure the tendency to experiment, innovate, and test new areas would have grown at a much slower pace. Because of the subjective nature of disability claims, it is unlikely that the percent of rejected business will ever approach the levels now experienced in life insurance. Disability income rejection rates, however, will continue to diminish as new techniques are developed, as experience emerges from morbidity studies, and as the industry continues to mature and gain more confidence.

DISABILITY WASTAGE

Incomplete and filed disability applications run similar patterns as in life insurance and generally for the same reasons. The more common reason for filing an incomplete application is because of a lack of medical information—either the medical exam or attending physician's statement.

The rate of not-taken policies also follows patterns similar to life insurance. One might expect that with a higher percentage of substandard decisions, the not-taken rate would run considerably higher than in life insurance. However, if anything, the opposite has been true. Although the not-taken rate on impaired risks is greater than on standard risks, the total not-taken rate shows little difference. The reason may be that at the time of application the agent often prepares the disability applicant for the substandard decision, and this improves considerably the odds of placing the contract. In addition, the extra premium amounts charged in life insurance tend to be considerably higher than in disability income, and, of course, some disability income contracts carry no change in premium but handle the impairment with the exclusion endorsement. It may be that the tendency for the impaired risk to be asked to pay proportionately greater premium in life insurance than in disability contributes significantly to the higher life insurance not-taken ratio.

UNDERWRITING MANUALS

Perhaps one of the most obvious places to observe the considerable difference in the volume of reliable data in disability income versus life insurance is in the underwriting manual itself. First of all, there are very few published impaired-risk manuals in the disability income business, whereas in life insurance every reinsurer and many of the larger companies have their own manuals that are based upon their own experience studies. The fact is that the scarcity of large volumes of impaired-risk information limits the industry's ability to quantify and statistically report an expansive underwriting manual. Many of the underwriting approaches have grown and evolved over a period of time based upon underwriting judgment and common sense tempered by whatever statistical data is available.

A second characteristic of the disability income impaired-risk manual is that, of necessity, it is more subjective since the nature of the risk itself is so subjective. The recommended decision for a particular impairment varies not only by the severity of the impairment, its recentness, and the number of attacks, but also by the occupation of the applicant and the type of contract he or she is applying for. The underwriting manual, therefore, serves as a guideline rather than a specific and more quantifiable approach.

The medical department and staff physicians are as important in the disability income underwriting process as in life insurance. Obviously, the same differences in approach that affect the disability underwriter versus the life underwriter also carry through to the medical department function. Considerable judgment is required in physician analysis of the more complex disability income impairments, as is the case for their life insurance counterparts. An additional element of judgment is the importance of stability and motivation in evaluating the risk. Indeed, the stability and motivation judgment is often more important to the underwriting decision than is the severity of the physical impairment, even in the more extreme cases.

In summary, disability income underwriting of substandard risks, like life insurance, has characteristics that make it an art as well as a science. The subjective impact of a variety of factors offers more creative alternatives to the disability underwriter. This fact coupled with the lack of significant morbidity data causes one to conclude that disability income substandard underwriting has the greater emphasis on art.

Occupation Schedule

12

The occupation of the disability income risk plays a much more critical role than in life insurance. In underwriting and selection for life insurance, the primary occupation concern is whether or not there are unusual physical hazards associated with the occupation that may increase mortality. If so, the life policy carries a rating, or in the most severe cases, the risk may be rejected. If waiver of premium is requested on the life application, then more consideration may be given as to how the applicant's specific physical history may result in or prolong waiver of premium benefits. It is in this area of "waiver of premium underwriting" that occupation evaluation for life insurance comes closest to that for disability income.

CLASSIFICATION

The physical requirements of an occupation are of primary importance in disability income. Very simply stated, a laborer requiring the regular physical use of his or her body may be totally disabled, whereas an employee with the same impairment but whose occupation primarily requires mental skills may be able to continue to work. Or even though both individuals are disabled with the same impairment, the laborer may be disabled longer because of the physical demands of his or her occupation. There are varying degrees of physical requirements—from heavy physical labor, to more moderate physical demands, to light physical requirements, to the more cerebral occupations. There are even gradations in the latter group—the store clerk who is required to move around the store, the office clerk whose duties are performed at a desk but require the use of the hands, the individual whose occupation is purely cerebral. Early occupation schedules recognized the fact that stability, motivation, and the work ethic were factors that might increase or decrease the normal physical requirement risk. Dentists and electricians both require the use of their hands; but early in the disability business, companies recognized that education and income tended to improve morbidity.

Traditional occupation schedules were primarily based upon the hazard of the occupation and the physical requirements associated with it. Occupation schedules in the 1920s and 1930s normally had three or four different classifications, although in some instances gradings and rate differentials numbered many more. Although it is impossible to precisely describe the group of risks that appeared in each of the four common categories without examining the formal occupation schedule, the groupings might be generally described as follows:

Class 1: The most favorable occupation class and consequently the lowest premium included professional risks—all white-collar employees and those clerical employees who had minor physical demands associated with their occupation.

Class 2: This grouping included supervisory personnel in factories, retail clerks in stores selling medium- or heavy-weight articles (hardware), most outside-sales occupations, and other occupations that required special education but carried some physical requirements (surveyors, construction engineers, etc.).

Class 3: This grouping primarily included such skilled trades personnel as electricians, plumbers, and carpenters as well as manufacturing occupations that carried no special hazards.

Class 4: The lowest classification was reserved for those occupations that either required only manual work or carried unusual hazards. People involved in heavy construction of roads, buildings, bridges, and so on were typical of this grouping. Drivers of heavy trucks were usually found in this classification.

There were, of course, some occupations that were entirely uninsurable because of the nature of the risk. Steeplejacks, construction steelworkers, and crop dusters are examples of such occupations. Another grouping of occupations, usually at the lowest occupation class, was considered for insurance but with an extra premium charge. This group was normally made up of occupations that carried some special hazard beyond the regular occupation class but did not have the premium volume to warrant a separate occupation classification. Some mine workers, fishing boat crew members, structural steelworkers, and so on were treated in this manner.

In addition to the physical risk and its impact upon occupation class, other occupations were deemed uninsurable based upon the feeling that a high moral or stability risk was associated with the particular occupation. Actors, actresses, musicians, bartenders, and racetrack personnel all fell into this category.

TREND TOWARD MEASURING STABILITY

The occupation schedule followed the pattern described above pretty much through the 1930s and 1940s and well into the 1950s. As companies gained more experience, however, and as competition increased, several factors emerged that caused insurers to examine further their method of classification. The stability of an individual in her/his occupation was increasingly recognized as an important factor. The longer the employee worked in the same occupation, the more dependable the employee became, the more favorable his/her work ethic, and consequently the better the expected morbidity. Similarly, the owner and the employee, both subject to the same physical hazards in their occupations, presented different morbidity results to the insurers. Owners have more of a personal stake in the performance of their business and consequently will push themselves to work, whereas the employee might claim a day of disability. Similarly, and for the same reasons, owners are more apt to return to work sooner following a disability than are employees. The same pattern is true of managers versus employees. Therefore, the characteristics of the occupation class schedule gradually began to change in the late 1950s, and continued to change through the 1960s and 1970s. Risks who were unstable in their employment, even though in an occupation having minimal physical risk, might be deemed uninsurable because of the risk of future claim instability. Instability breeds unemployment, and unemployment or the threat of it tends to increase the odds of disability.

Owners and managers, because of their improved level of motivation, were given a higher occupation class than their employees. This initial recognition took place in the skilled-trade occupations in the lower two classification groupings.

This trend of more accurately recognizing the work-ethic effect was gradually extended to the upper occupation classes. Clerical employees, who had been generally classified the same as professional risks, were found to generate a much poorer experience, in spite of the fact that the physical hazards of the occupation were no different. Indeed, in the case of such professional occupations as dentists, the physical requirements are clearly more demanding than for many clerical occupations. Nevertheless, professional and white-collar occupations clearly had the most favorable morbidity. As a result, retail clerks, typists, and general clerical employees were reclassified one or two grades lower. The employer/employee phenomenon is clearly one factor affecting this occupation distinction. Similar to the owner of a construction trade business who is motivated differently than are employees at time of claim, the owner of a retail store is motivated differently than are employees. During this period from the mid or late 1950s, significant and substantial changes began to take place in the nature of the occupation schedule.

INCOME AND STABILITY

Another important factor is involved in distinguishing between the employer and employee and the owner and worker. The income of the employee may well be as good a measure of the expected level of morbidity as any other factor. There seems to be some close relationship between the levels of morbidity for occupations with quite different physical hazards as long as the income in those occupations is similar. The clerical employee and the more physically involved worker in the building trades industry experience similar morbidity when their incomes are generally similar. Conversely, the clerical employee experiences quite different morbidity than does the owner of the business if the physical hazards are no different but there is a great income difference. The greater importance of income and stability in measuring occupation class versus physical requirements has increased during the past 20 years as a result of a change in the basic level of work ethic and the attitude of the employer toward the employee. Employees do not place the same value on their jobs today in the way they did prior to the 1960s. There is a greater expectation of entitlement and a general questioning of authority in any form. All of these factors pull together to emphasize the point that the responsibility of an individual in his/her occupation, the stability in that occupation, the level of income, and the general motivation to go to work are more important measures of occupation class than is the physical risk of the occupation itself.

The more transient occupations—those requiring little skill—generally incur poorer morbidity for the same stability reasons mentioned above. Perhaps the industry should adopt a classification method that recognizes even greater stability in one's occupation depending upon the skilled nature of the work and the income level.

The business of underwriting selection is still imperfect even with the substantial changes that have taken place in disability underwriting over the past several decades. There are always exceptions to the norm! Some individual risks classified in a lower occupation class will pay a higher premium, even though they have a much higher level of motivation and work ethic than is the case in the group in which they are placed. Similarly, some individuals classified in the highest occupation class because of their occupation and income are not as well motivated as their group as a whole and present higher morbidity risk. If there were only some way of accurately measuring the motivation of an applicant for disability insurance, regardless of his or her occupation, we might well have a measure that was more important in rating and selection than even physical history itself. Is there a psychological test that would fulfill the requirements? If so will the individual who scores favorably on such a test today exhibit the same favorable work-ethic and motivation characteristics throughout his or her working lifetime?

Barring any such reliable measuring device, the disability insurer continues to group his risks by occupation class, with some modification based upon stability and income.

By the mid 1980s some early indications began to appear that professionals' morbidity was changing. Industry experience with both physicians and dentists began to deteriorate. It is probable that three factors are affecting this trend. First, an excess of professionals (particularly dentists) in some areas tended to flatten out income and consequently the motivation to work. Second, the trend toward more professionals working in group practices, rather than as solo practitioners, results in professionals behaving more like employees than employers. And finally, malpractice threats and costs encouraged some professionals to retire early on their disabilty policies. How serious a deterioration occurs in professional morbidity will take several years to develop and determine.

LENGTH OF EMPLOYMENT

The length of time an individual has been in his/her present employment is an important element in measuring stability. The new employee is more likely to be laid off than the veteran, is more apt to fail in the new job, and is more apt to find the new job not to his or her liking. Recognizing that there is a very close relationship between unemployment and morbidity, length of employment then takes on great importance. A large number of additional variables enter this equation, most of them related directly to common sense.

The employee who has been on the job less than six months but who has shown job stability for the previous 10 years is a much different risk than is the individual on the job for only six months where this job represents the fourth one in two years. The individual in a skilled or professional position for only six months represents a more favorable risk than does an employee in the same circumstance in an unskilled position. No single time period can be established as far as minimum length of employment, but rather the specific circumstances of each case must be examined. Occupation class, income level, number of jobs in the past three years, age of the applicant, skilled nature of the work, and education level are all factors that must be examined together in order for the underwriter to make an accurate commonsense judgment.

ACCURATE DESCRIPTION OF OCCUPATION

The agent is in the most favorable position to accurately determine the occupation of an applicant. If the agent develops the proper information at application time, including a description of the occupation, length of employment, and any special circumstances, the proper judgment can be made by the home office underwriter. Applications too often contain limited information—a general description of the occupation—and consequently more detail is needed. Inspection reports have traditionally been the source of secondary information used to properly determine occupation class, and they have been of great value in quantifying the specific duties, risks, and stability of applicants in their occupations. In more recent years companies have performed their own telephone investigations to more accurately quantify the occupation classification as well as to develop other underwriting information.

In either event the home office underwriter must have an accurate description of an applicant's duties in order to make the proper classification. Properly training agents to develop such information will substantially improve the speed of underwriting as well as the quality and accuracy of the underwriting process.

Even though at times the home office underwriter will lack some of the information necessary to make the correct classification decision, at some point the underwriter must make a decision based upon this less-than-complete information. Frequently, the underwriter's approach is to approve the contract at the occupation class that appears to be the correct one and then ask the agent to obtain additional information before placing the policy. The underwriter might ask the agent to obtain, before placing the policy, a signed statement from the applicant that the occupational duties do not include specified activities that would cause the applicant to be classified lower. Conversely, the underwriter might tell the agent that if the applicant will sign a statement that the occupation does not involve certain specified duties, then the company will be willing to reclassify the applicant more favorably. It is important for the home office underwriter to retain the flexibility and openness of reconsideration of occupation class when additional information is available.

On the other hand, the underwriter must be careful not to accept all information without questioning. Human nature will tend to cause both the applicant and the agent to understate the risk of an occupation class and overstate those characteristics that would warrant a higher classification. Without proper investigation and substantiation, the underwriter will be faced with a circumstance in which an individual who was classified at one class because of the stated supervisory and managerial duties shows up later as a claimant who lists his/her duties then to be of a more manual nature.

PHYSICAL IMPAIRMENTS AND OCCUPATION

Physical impairments identified at time of underwriting will impact the underwriting decision in one occupation class or occupation differently than in another. This is true because some types of physical impairments will either cause or prolong disability in one occupation but will have either no impact or a lesser impact in another occupation. The most obvious group of such situations involves structural impairments and their effect on the more manual occupations. A bad back history should be of greater concern for the manual worker than for the clerical employee. The chronic knee injury is a much different risk for the mail carrier than for the bank clerk. Slightly impaired hearing is a substantial problem for the pilot but perhaps no problem at all for the construction worker. The dentist with psoriasis of the hands may become totally disabled, whereas the disease represents minimal risk in most other occupations.

A good dosage of common sense is the best quality the disability underwriter can have in measuring the impact of a particular physical impairment on a specific occupation. After the judgment is made, then the underwriter's approach to handling the problem involves the same alternatives that might be used with any impairment.

Depending upon the risk in the occupation, some applicants will have a full-exclusion endorsement for the same impairment for which another applicant will have a limited-exclusion endorsement or none at all. The percentage of back riders is greater in the lower occupation classes since the incidence of history is greater in this grouping and since the claims experience itself shows a greater preponderance of back injuries. Longer elimination periods and extra premiums are naturally other tools the underwriter may use in distinguishing between the specific hazards of an impairment and its effect on one occupation versus another.

OCCUPATION SCHEDULE CHANGES

There is a need for continual reevaluation of the occupation classification in use by a company. Changes in the nature of an occupation, analysis of experience trends, and new occupations—all must be considered on a regular basis. The level of the occupation class is also a key element in competing in the marketplace. It not only determines the rate charged to the applicant, but also frequently the availability of more liberal contracts or extra benefits. There will be situations in which, although a company's experience indicates an occupation class should be lowered, in doing so the company will be placed at a competitive disadvantage. The importance of addressing the weight given to the business decision versus the underwriting decision in such a circumstance is not an easy one. Such judgments must be made not only on a case-by-case basis, but also when determining whether or not an entire occupation grouping should be moved up or down. Not infrequently the actuaries wish to move the group in one direction, and the marketing department wishes to move it in another; the underwriter is found weighing the balance. Making exceptions to sound underwriting and actuarial rules should be the exception and not the rule. The underwriter must choose carefully those few cases where a business decision overrides normally prudent underwriting judgment.

Finally, the underwriter should offer to reconsider a more favorable classification of a risk if circumstances warrant it. The person who at underwriting time had been in an occupation only a short period and had therefore been classified in a previous more hazardous occupation should be offered reconsideration to a higher occupation class after a reasonable period of time has elapsed. Sometimes such an offer to reconsider in the future is enough to allow the salesperson to place the case at the more hazardous occupation class; at the same time, the company avoids the risk of an overoptimistic classification that may present claims problems in the future.

In conclusion, the disability income occupation schedule has gone through great modification in the past two decades. The trend has generally been away from purely job-hazard classification toward a greater evaluation of stability, motivation, and responsibility in one occupation versus another. Length of employment, skill of the occupation, and income all must be measured in determining the proper occupation class. The underwriter must take great care to properly classify the applicant, and the quality field underwriter can make this process much quicker, more reliable, and more accurate.

Administration

13

DIFFERENCES BETWEEN LIFE AND DISABILITY

The similarities between life and disability income continue in the area of administration. It is only natural that two products that have so many similarities in marketing and underwriting are also administered in very similar ways. What differences there are tend to come from basic differences in the design of the product that require special attention. For example, the use of the exclusion endorsement is unique to disability income and requires special procedures.

There are more variable factors that determine the premium rate for a disability contract and more numerous policy changes. The greatest difference is found in the substantial and significant administrative effort in the handling of claims.

Conversely disability income does not need to address the complexity of cash value pages in the contract, nor frequent beneficiary changes, nor frequent and numerous value inquiries on in-force business.

Aside from the above areas of difference, the functions and procedures in the administration of disability income are very similar to those found in life insurance. While examining more closely the specific functions involved, this chapter will concentrate on factors that cause a somewhat different emphasis in disability income administration than in life insurance.

124

FIELD OFFICE ADMINISTRATION

Depending upon the structure of a company's sales organization, the nature of functions and responsibilities assigned to field offices varies considerably from one company to another. This is true of life insurance as well as disability income. Most companies, however, do require certain specific new-business–processing functions to be performed in the field. The initial application is forwarded by the salesperson to the local office, whether life or disability income, and is processed there before being forwarded to the home office. It is a natural responsibility of the field office to perform initial screening of each application to determine whether it is fully and accurately completed, and meets the general guidelines and requirements established by the home office. Proper screening in the field office not only speeds the new-business process in the home office, but also improves the quality, reliability, and confidence that the home office places in a particular field office.

One area that requires considerably different emphasis and importance in disability income than in life insurance is the depth or detail of the application screening itself. Since the salesperson is so important in the field selection of the applicant for disability income, field office administration also fills an important role in making certain the applicant meets established underwriting requirements that appear in field manuals. For example: Is the applicant's occupation clearly described? Does the occupation class selected coincide with the description of duties? Is the amount of indemnity applied for consistent with the earned income given on the application? Do the elimination period, benefit period, policy form, and a variety of extra benefits meet the requirements described in field manuals? The large number of variables present in disability contracts of necessity require more attention in the field offices.

In addition to the above, disability field offices request information similar to that requested on life applications: the ordering of attending physician's statements, medical examinations, and inspection reports, and the completion of special reports based upon the nature of the coverage requested. Field offices for both life and disability perform a number of record-keeping and control functions in the areas of production, business pending, business to be placed, premium collection records, bank accounting and balancing, and other routine control functions.

Field offices may have responsibility for some part of the premium collection procedure, although more and more companies today control collections from their home offices and have premium payments made directly to the home office. However, some companies under the general agency system continue to have premium payments actually made directly to field offices. Closely connected with the premium collection activity is the servicing of existing policyholders. Much of this activity is coordinated in the field offices, with inquiries either directed to the home office or the producing agent, whichever is the more appropriate. A most important responsibility, again similar to life insurance, is the servicing of orphan policyholders and the assignment of servicing to an active agent.

NEW-BUSINESS REGISTRATION

When the application is received from the field office, a variety of administrative functions is performed before the application is forwarded to the underwriter for evaluation and approval. Further application screening is performed, including verifying that the producing agent is properly licensed in the state in which the application is written. Many companies authorize their new-business departments to return applications that are inaccurate or incomplete to the field. The home office verifies that all the questions are answered, that the benefits applied for are consistent with the occupation of the applicant, that the policy is accurately described, that the identification of the applicant is complete—this verification function is similar to the screening of a life insurance application.

In addition to the screening and preunderwriting functions, a most important responsibility in the registration activity is the formal establishment of the home office record of the pending application. Information is taken from the application and a record made of the applicant, the producing agent, and the coverage applied for. In almost all companies today this activity involves direct computer input in substantial detail to provide for follow-up during the pending process and enough detail data to automatically print the policy from the computer record when it is ultimately approved. The accuracy and detail of this initial computer record is most important, since underwriting correspondence, the issue process itself, and the ultimate master file record are in a major way based upon this input.

Other functions performed in the registration process further prepare the file before it goes to the underwriter. Similar to life insurance, home office records must be checked to determine whether or not the applicant has a record of previous coverage with the company and to record this information in the underwriting file that is being prepared. Many disability income companies participate in the Disability Income Record System (DIRS), which is similar to Medical Index Bureau (MIB) information in life insurance. During the registration process information is requested from DIRS.

A final function in preparation for delivering the file to the underwriter takes place in either new-business registry or in underwriting services. It involves obtaining the prior application file if company records indicate there are such files—a procedure similar to that in life insurance. It is common for disability income underwriters to look not only at prior disability files, but also at prior life insurance files. A unique function to disability income at this stage in the process is obtaining records of previous claims that may have an impact upon the underwriting of the new application. Some companies allow the file to first go to the underwriter, who determines whether or not to look at the detail of claim records. Other companies may automatically ask their service personnel to pull any claim record within a specified period of time.

The new applications are finally ready for sorting and assignment to underwriters to proceed with the job of selection (this process has already been discussed). During the underwriting process an important clerical or administration function is underwriting support. This support involves preparation of forms, letters, and a variety of requests from the underwriter to develop information in order for the underwriter to make the proper decision. This information may be requested from the agent, physicians, hospitals, inspection companies, and other sources. Finally, this administrative function controls and records the activities involved in the underwriting decision. It follows up on physicians, medical examiners, and information from agency offices, and it records when this information is received. In an automated environment it has responsibility for a periodic report to the field office indicating the status of pending applications.

POLICY ISSUE

Once the underwriter has made the final decision on the application, it is forwarded to the policy-issue area, where the function and procedure followed is almost identical to that in life insurance. Increasingly, companies are automatically initiating the final-issue process in the underwriting department, where the underwriter at a terminal screen keys in the detailed final decision, and from this information the policy is automatically prepared.

However, many companies still employ a semiautomated or a full-manual system in their policy-issue sections, particularly in disability income. It is important to remember that the high percentage of changed applications in the underwriting process places an unusual burden on the policy-issue function. As was mentioned in the underwriting section, close to 40 percent of disability applications are changed in some way in the underwriting process; 6 to 10 percent are rejected; 15 to 20 percent carry either exclusion endorsements or extra premiums; some 10 percent have occupation-class changes; and another 10 percent have required a modification in the benefits applied for.

This high percentage of changes naturally necessitates substantial corrections to the record that was established when the application was initially registered. If the underwriter is controlling the final decision, he or she must make the changes in the record. If the final underwriting decision is forwarded to a clerical or administrative area to trigger the policy-issue process, then it is at this location that the detail of the underwriter's decision must be coded and loaded into the system. In any event, it is important to understand and accept the fact that the percentage of changed applications is much higher in disability than life insurance and consequently requires additional administrative or clerical steps in the process.

In some life insurance companies the policy is actually prepared during the registration phase and then held until the application is approved. The high percentage of policy approvals on a standard basis allows such a procedure to be followed. This type of procedure to speed the ultimate policy-issue process is not possible in disability income because of the high percentage of changes.

As a result of the high percentage of changes in the coverage applied for, changes in the occupation class, and normal errors on the application, making corrections and amendments is a more tedious process in disability than is normally found in life insurance; but the basic process is similar.

Disability income is also subject to the same degree of special state forms and amendments that must be attached in certain required circumstances. The cost of special manual and automated procedures necessary to accurately and properly reflect the variety of different forms and amendments from different states causes the same cost pressures in disability income that is found in life insurance.

The premium calculation function, the billing information, and the commission process are today almost without exception automated procedures. Not too many years ago, the disability premium, with all of its variables and complexities, was calculated by hand and naturally experienced a high error rate.

The final underwriting information loaded in during the policy-issue process—either manually or directly by the underwriter—completes the policy master record, which controls the contract throughout its lifetime. The accuracy of this record is critical to the proper administration of the contract. Similar to life insurance, it not only controls the billing and collection cycle, but also the payment of commissions. In addition, policy valuation records are built from this master record, and if constructed properly, it is the source of all future management information reports.

One natural and important requirement of the master record in disability income is its use by the claim department. If the master record is constructed properly, it should contain all of the identification information about the applicant, all of the policy information, all of the coverage information, and all of the underwriting and selection information that will be of importance to the claim examiner. Without adequate master file information for the claim department, the claim process is slowed down while the claim examiner searches many different sources to build a file.

The final activity in the policy-issue process is assembling the contract. The schedule page, or detailed policy-descriptive information, is normally computer prepared in today's disability income and life insurance environment. This page is then inserted in the proper policy form. More and more frequently companies are printing the entire contract on the computer and also assembling it in an automated environment. There seems little question that by the end of the 1980s in most insurance administrative environments the schedule page and the contract itself will be printed, prepared, and assembled in field offices, based upon data input in the home office. The significant saving of time and expense accompanying this sort of system is important enough for the industry to focus its energies to move in that direction.

REISSUES AND REPLACEMENTS

There are a couple of special activities in the new-business process that should be addressed because of their importance in disability income. The first is the frequent number of policy reissues that occur after the initial contract is prepared and issued. The large number of variables in the disability contract and the high percentage of changed applications during the selection process result in many more field requests after initial issue for some change in the contract. It may be a reconsideration of the underwriting decision, it may be a change in elimination period, benefit period, indemnity, or an extra benefit—all requests with the primary objective of preparing a final contract that will be acceptable to the consumer.

A second area of heavy activity in the disability income process is the number of policies that are rewritten or replaced by new applications. It is frequent for an existing policyholder to replace a current policy when applying for additional benefits rather than simply to request a second policy in addition to the first. Part of this tendency results from the fact that there may have been improvements in the contract since the original policy was approved. In any event, in disability income one in-force policy is frequently replaced with a new one. This immediately raises questions of what premium is charged for the new policy, since at least some portion of the benefits were originally sold at a younger age. Similarly, the question of how commissions should be paid on the new policy, where it is a replacement, must be addressed. In the latter question most companies pay new-business commissions on only the increase in premium and continue the commission schedule runoff on the old-policy basis. This naturally involves administrative difficulties in setting up the new-policy record.

BILLING AND COLLECTIONS

Once the contract has been underwritten, prepared, and placed with the insured, the maintenance procedures take hold. There are very few differences in the billing and collection activities in disability income and in life insurance.

The modes of premium payment choices are almost identical. The persistency experience by mode type also follows the same pattern—annual being the most favorable, quarterly obviously the least persistent. Contractual language normally provides the same type of grace period in disability income that is found in life insurance. Most companies usually offer an extension beyond the normal grace period to allow reinstatement without evidence of insurability.

In many companies life and health billing systems are one in the same, and the insurance client prefers that it be this way. Similar to life insurance more and more disability income policyholders in recent years have chosen the preauthorized monthly check method of premium payment.

POLICYHOLDER SERVICE

Although some insurance companies are structured differently than others, they all must maintain a function that involves servicing and communicating with existing policyholders. In an age of consumerism the importance of this function cannot be underestimated. It is frequently the consumer's only contact with the insurer and consequently may determine the policyholder's image of the insurance company. Accuracy, speed, and concern are more important qualities in this process during an age of greater public expectation than at any time in the past.

In this function many of the questions and activities performed are also similar to those of life insurance. Inquiries as to premium-paying status, questions about changes in premium payments, questions about policy contract language, changes in beneficiary designations, address changes, name changes, and so on are all frequent and routine activities in the policyholder services function.

Since most disability income contracts do not have cash value benefits, this is not an area of consumer inquiry in disability income, but it is a very active one in life insurance.

Conversely, since contractholders in disability income have more concerns about whether or not they will qualify for claim payments under different circumstances, there is much more activity in the area of letters of interpretation for claim purposes. Most of this correspondence and inquiry occurs within the first few months after the original issuance of the contract, but questions arising during its lifetime may also require letters of interpretation. The questions come in many forms. The insured has changed occupation and wants to make certain that he or she is still covered under the contract. The insured wants an explanation of partial disability versus total disability. The policyholder inquires about when and under what circumstances some of the extra benefits in the contract are payable. The number and nature of inquiries for interpretation in the disability contract stem from the following: it involves more variables; the determination of claim is frequently a subjective one; and there is a high frequency of claims.

CLAIMS ADMINISTRATION

Claims administration (which will be dealt with in more detail in the claims chapter in this book) represents a significant administrative activity in the disability income operation and a level of expense that is much more substantial than found in life insurance. The number of claims examiners necessary for a mature block of disability income policies is almost equal in number to the number of underwriters needed to process the new business.

The claims administrative process, therefore, also has many functions in general similar to the new-business function. It involves the receipt of the notice of claim, checking its accuracy and completeness, setting up a claim file, searching the master record for information on the policyholder, and obtaining records of previous claim files if they are of significance. It generally involves an entire set of functions to establish the claim file for the claim examiner, very similar to the process followed in setting up the new-business file for the underwriter.

If there is an area of the disability operation that requires unparalleled service and accuracy, it is in its claim function. Here the true worth of the policy is measured, and it is here the insurer has its most important communication and interface with the policyholder.

It is critical for the reader to remember the importance and magnitude of the claim function in the disability income process. In contrast to most other administrative processes and particularly in contrast to the limited administrative activity required to process life insurance claims, the disability claim process is the cornerstone of the true purpose of the disability contract.

POLICY CHANGES

There is a more frequent policy-change activity for disability income than for life insurance, and again the principal reason is clearly the large number of variables present in the disability contract. Disability income contracts once issued may provide for changes in benefit period, elimination period, indemnity amounts, extra benefits, occupation class, guaranteed insurability options, and so on. Guaranteed-insurability options, particularly in the professional and white-collar occupation groupings, are an increasing policy-change activity.

A second characteristic of disability income that generates more policy changes is the regular and frequent product development enhancements that are made available to in-force contracts. New types of policy benefits, extension of policy language, modification of contract provisions, and a relaxation of underwriting rules may all be available to in-force contract owners. They may wish to change their in-force contracts to take advantage of the new benefits. Policy-change applications are routinely required, normally involving minimal underwriting and selection.

REINSTATEMENTS

The reinstatement function in disability follows the same type of procedure and frequently the same reinstatement form as used in life insurance. As already mentioned, the grace period and an extension for reinstatement follow similar patterns to life insurance, and both the field and home office procedures are similar. In addition to an evaluation of the reinstatement application before approving reinstatement, the disability underwriter will also wish to examine the applicant's claim record. The claim history may provide significant information that will affect the approval of the reinstatement.

The variety and frequency of the various disability administrative functions require a core of experienced and knowledgeable clerical personnel. Companies who have been active in the disability business for more than two decades will still have in force many different policy forms with a great variety of policy provisions as well as numerous extra benefit provisions that have been provided during that time.

To a great extent the true efficiency of an insurer can be measured by the accuracy, promptness, and importance it places on its administrative functions.

Claims

14

Probably no other area of disability insurance has more differences from life insurance than does the claim operation. The level of activity, the expense of the activity, and the training required introduce a specialty that does not have a counterpart in life operations. There may be a dozen or more disability claims during the 30-year lifetime of a disability contract. Each requires some sort of regular processing and the attention of an experienced professional claims examiner. The training and position of the disability income claim examiner is equal in professional status to that of the disability underwriter. It requires a substantial knowledge of medicine, with particular emphasis on the expected duration of different disabilities. Perhaps one way of explaining the magnitude of disability income claim operations is to remember that the number of claim examiners necessary to perform the claim function in a mature disability income operation is roughly equivalent to the size of the underwriting department's staff in the same company.

To the contract owner the service and performance by the claim department is the true measure of the value of the contract. It therefore requires an administrative and an examination process that is efficient, accurate, and responsive to the policyholder's needs. Indeed, claim department time service and quality should be at the optimum level of any service performed in an insurance company.

MOTIVATION AND STABILITY

At claim time the motivation and stability of the disability income policyholder can be observed firsthand. The determination of a legitimate disability is not always crystal clear and identifiable but frequently has many subjective qualities. Does the claimant's back truly hurt enough to cause total disability; or has business activity dropped off to the point where it's time to take several weeks off, and the claim is one element in the decision? Is the 55-year-old with a full-disability program and a history of cardiac insufficiency truly totally disabled, or has the claimant elected this particular time to turn the business over to a young relative and retire early? Is the individual with the recent hernia surgery still totally disabled, or is the person extending the claim a few weeks because the level of benefit payments is adequate to provide a comfortable life-style?

Even when the existence of a disability is fairly straightforward to determine, another whole series of questions emerges at the time the disability would normally be expected to terminate. What special circumstances are extending the disability? Is the claimant receiving disability benefits from other private or governmental sources that may be a deterrent to recovery?

How do you treat the situation of the applicant who can return to work but only on a limited or partial basis? How do you determine exactly how much time the applicant is spending at the place of employment and what percent of the job he or she is able to perform? All of these questions, and of course many others, are normal, everyday considerations for the claim examiner. Although contract language and definition help to resolve many potential problems, since we are insuring individuals and since each individual has a set of complex circumstances and motivations, claim examiners must rely in many instances on their own experience and professional judgment.

ACCIDENT VERSUS SICKNESS DISABILITIES

One other interesting facet of the claim examiner's analysis is the importance of distinguishing whether a disability is an accident or a sickness. Since the elimination period and the benefit period under the same disability contract may be different for accident and sickness, it is important that this distinction be established early in the disability. The individual who has lifetime accident coverage but only a five-year sickness benefit period is motivated to have a claim considered as an accident, rather than as a sickness. Although the difference might appear quite simple on the surface, a claim examiner will tell you this is not the case. The claimant who has chronic low-back problems and who suffers a disability caused by low-back pain, but without a specific incident of an accident, can often legitimately be considered a sickness claim.

The individual with chronic bursitis of the shoulder who suffers a mild blow to the shoulder represents a situation where the claim might not have occurred or have been as serious without the bursitis condition. When does it become an accident or a sickness claim? The individual with arthritic changes in the knee is more susceptible to disability as a result of slight blows to the knee. Would the disability be caused by accident or sickness? Even the most carefully worded contracts with precise definitions cannot entirely clarify how a particular set of circumstances should be treated at claim time. The claim examiner must collect the specific details necessary before making the claim judgment by using experience, remembering the intent of the contract language, and adding a generous dose of common sense.

Sometimes a claim examiner faces the situation of a claimant disabled for more than one impairment during a period of disability. An example is the individual who was initially disabled by an obvious accident and who, while disabled, suffers a sickness that prolongs disability. The claim examiner is then faced with determining whether the accident or the illness is really disabling the individual. Recent court decisions have tended to blur traditional distinctions between accident and sickness claims, and as a result the industry in recent years has tended to move more and more toward requiring benefit periods that terminate at the same time. This tends to remove the circumstance of the policyholder benefiting from the election of accident versus sickness disability.

RECESSIONS AND THE ECONOMY

This book has pointed out on several occasions the impact of economic recessions and unemployment on disability income claims experience. Recessions tend to cause both an increase in the frequency of claims and a general slowdown in the average recovery rate for claimants. The unemployed worker, the worker whose hours have been reduced, the small businessperson whose revenues have decreased sharply—all may be motivated differently during a recessionary period than during healthy economic times. The underwriting department, if it is performing its function properly, should have screened out in the selection process those risks most highly prone to unemployment during recessionary periods. However, not all such risks will be identified, and circumstances present at original underwriting time may have changed by the time the claim occurs. In addition, the magnitude of the frequency of claim and rate of recovery problems move in direct proportion to the severity of the recession.

Claim examiners, therefore, play a most significant role in a recessionary period. They must be alert to identify potential situations of claim abuse caused from malingering. Claim department management may wish to increase investigative procedures because of the increased number of situations in which abuse may be present. Even if it were possible to identify those claim situations of obvious abuse during a recession, there will also tend to be an increase in legitimate claims in recessionary periods. The individual who has a physical impairment that requires surgery may choose this time to elect the surgical procedure. In addition, the pressures of recessionary times tend to increase the number of claims for such subjective impairments as emotional and nervous problems and digestive problems. Although these impairments and disabilities may well be the result of economic pressures from a recession, they are in fact legitimate disabilities. At the same time, their subjectivity increases the claim examiner's problems in determining the degree of disability and the continuing length of the disability.

The most important fact to understand is that, although the claim examiner must always strive to be objective, the role involves a great deal of subjectivity and that the problems in the profession are magnified during recessionary periods.

CLAIM PROCEDURES

The specific procedures to be followed by the policyholder at claim time are spelled out in the disability insurance contract. The notice of claim payment, the time allowed to notify the company of the claim, and other procedures are areas defined in the contract. Companies generally do not adhere strictly to the time period required for notification of claim but frequently accept claim notices beyond the period specified in the policy. There are extreme circumstances in which many months may have passed before notice of claim is received, and this presents substantial difficulty for the claim examiner to adequately investigate the claim. The notice of claim includes identification information, dates of disability, nature of disability, physicians who have given treatment, hospitals where hospitalized, expected length of disability, and so on. Depending upon the nature of the claim, a more detailed physician's certification may be required in order to get specific details and an estimate as to the length of disability. Disabilities that will continue for several months will not normally require a physician's statement each month, but the company will require a progress report completed by the claimant. An individual who has suffered a coronary and is facing six months of recovery may not need a doctor's report each month; however, the individual with a sprained knee who has been disabled for one month will indeed require a physician's statement if that disability continues.

It is important for the claim examiner to make a careful assessment of the claim at the time of its first handling. Similar to the importance of the underwriter determining what investigation is necessary when first evaluating the insurance application, the claim examiner must make a determination as to the legitimacy and severity of the disability early in the claim process. To do otherwise could establish a pattern of claim payments that would be difficult to contest and control later on in the claim. Once the company is committed to the claim payment, it is much more difficult to contest its legitimacy. The percentage of problem claims is an extremely small percentage of the total claims handled by a claim department, but the proper handling of the small percentage of problem claims by the claim examiner will have a significant impact upon the company's claim results. Recalling that the 35-year-old claimant with a $5,000-a-month policy and a to-age-65 benefit period represents a potential total liability of close to $2 million reminds us that each individual claim is of great importance.

TRAINING

The claim department must have established training procedures for its claim examiners and formal guidelines for the evaluation and investigation of claims. The claim examiner must have a thorough background in lay medicine to be able to evaluate and make judgments concerning the severity of a particular claim circumstance and the potential length of disability. Follow-up procedures for open claims, regular review, specific guidelines as to when additional investigation is necessary, and field handling when circumstances indicate are all parts of a claim manual of procedures that must be as detailed as the underwriting medical manual.

CONTESTABLE CLAIMS

Another difference in the claim process from that of life insurance revolves around the contestable period in the disability income contract. Both disability and life insurance have a two-year contestable period. However, the number of claims that occur during the two-year period may be several in number for disability income, whereas for life insurance there will never be more than one—and this one quite a final one! Consequently, the investigation of contestable claims is a frequent activity of disability claim departments and an extensive one. Some companies employ their own field claim representatives to handle problem claim cases, and others use the services of independent adjusters. It should be emphasized that in most claim departments no more than 3 to 5 percent of all claims require field attention.

The higher percentage of contestable claims naturally results in a higher percentage of litigated claims in the disability business. This circumstance tends to be compounded further by the subjectivity of the claim evidence, raising the potential for more misunderstanding and disagreement.

It is important for the underwriter to recognize that the larger potential for claims in the early years of a disability policy's life (perhaps several of them occurring during the contestable period) make it extremely important for the underwriter's investigation to be thorough, logical, and well documented. Sloppy underwriting in chasing down inaccurate or incomplete application information may well restrict the claim examiner from taking the necessary action on a claim during the contestable period. The applicant who stated on the application "mild upset stomach with three days of disability" and who was issued a standard contract may represent a serious problem to the claim examiner if a claim is presented during the contestable period for peptic ulcer. Even though claim investigation may prove that the "mild upset stomach" with the three days of disability was a peptic ulcer attack, the fact that the underwriting department did not investigate thoroughly may present problems to the claim examiner in making the "contestable clause" stick. It is in this area that the claim examiner and the underwriter must work closely together to make certain that the underwriter's intent is in fact consistent with the facts at claim time.

CLAIM INVESTIGATION

Proper investigation and analysis of available information and *planning* this investigation are of paramount importance in the proper handling of the claim. Naturally, the depth and detail of the investigation depends upon the circumstances of the claim—particularly the projected length of disability, the severity of the disability, and the subjectivity of the impairment. All of these variables necessarily must be weighed against other variables, such as the claimant's occupation and age.

Initial claim information comes from the applicant, and in some instances, this may be adequate information on which to pay the claim, particularly if it is an objective, short-term claim. Medical evidence of disability is normally required through the completion of a physician's report certifying to the disability, its nature, and its length. In some instances, particularly for claims occurring during the contestable period, more detailed attending physician's statements may be requested. Hospital records are commonly checked for detailed information concerning prior medical history.

Inspection reports are not routinely used but are used when there is a question of the degree of disability, verification of occupation information, income questions, or possible overinsurance. The nature and extent of the inspection report will naturally vary depending upon the type of information desired and the amount at risk for the insurance company.

Medical examinations are not routinely requested but are reserved for those instances where a disability is of potentially long-term duration and where the degree of recovery is in question. An independent medical examination at the insurer's expense is an important method of obtaining third-party input concerning the severity of the disability.

In recent years direct telephone contact has increasingly been initiated between the insurer and the claimant. For many years it was thought that information collected on the telephone would not be reliable and that inspection report sources provided better detailed information. With increased restrictions and limitations placed upon the inspection report industry from the Fair Credit Reporting Act, more companies began to experiment with use of the telephone. So far insurers have found that they are able to develop important and reliable information by dealing directly with the claimant over the telephone. Such contact speeds up the processing of the claim and cuts down on the handling expense.

The Health Insurance Association of America encouraged development of a Disability Insurance Records System in the late 1970s, and such a system was ultimately introduced under the management of the Medical Information Bureau. The primary purpose of this record system (DIRS) is to alert insurers to problems of overinsurance, particularly during the contestable period. Most large individual disability income insurers now participate in the DIRS system and find that it does provide valuable protective information.

One important facility in claim investigation is the option of direct personal contact where the circumstances warrant it. Although only a small percentage of claims warrant a personal visit and contact from a claim department representative, face-to-face verification of the circumstances surrounding the claim are necessary in some situations. In most companies no more than 3 to 5 percent of all claims are handled in this manner.

CLAIM EXAMINER SKILLS

The educational background of the career claim examiner must be parallel to that of the career underwriter. Many companies find this position to be a good entry-level training ground for future management personnel, since it allows an individual to become familiar with various elements of the insurance business and at the same time to hold down a responsible decision-making position. The training period for the claim examiner continues for many years. Intensive training occurs during the first three to six months, and towards the end of this period, the examiner begins to make significant decisions. It is only after several years, however, that he or she is given the authority to personally approve claims with large liabilities, and the largest and most complex claims will routinely be seen by at least two experienced examiners.

In addition to the depth of medical knowledge required, the experienced claim examiner must also develop a detailed background in contractual language and its interpretation. The examiner is the first line of such interpretation and as such does become somewhat of a lay attorney. This contractual knowledge extends back to all contracts that the company has in force on which there may be disability claims. If one pauses for a minute and considers the evolution and changes in contractual language and benefits during the past 30 years, it is easier to appreciate the complexity of the claim examiner's position. Although the advent of the computer creates an environment in which the examiner will be able to depend upon automatic screening of a particular claim circumstance against the characteristics of the insurance contract, there is still much required of the individual examiner in interpreting contractual language and how it affects the specific claim at hand.

In our current environment of substantial punitive damage risks if claims are mishandled, the examiner must be particularly sensitive in administering the claim. Skills must include accurate documentation, precise interpretation of contract language, and clear communications with the claimant.

The administrative support required in the claim department must include the same degree of attention to timeliness and accuracy that has been mentioned as a requirement of the entire claims process. Various forms, questionnaires, and claim information must be accurately and quickly processed and placed in the hands of the claims examiner. Communications with the contract owner and the claimant must be of high quality and clearly communicate the company's intent. The actual preparation of the check for claim payment must naturally be accurate and clear.

It is important to remember that the claim department through its service is the most accurate measure of the reliability and performance of the disability insurance contract.

INTERPRETATION AND DEFINITION OF BENEFITS

The claim examiner is called upon daily to interpret various clauses within the disability income contract, and almost every clause within the contract may raise some questions of clarity. Policyholders frequently request letters interpreting the definition of disability, the contestable period, the recurrent provision, and the definition of total versus partial disability, all of which may involve the claim department. In the handling of specific claims, interpretation must be consistent, and this requires that the claim examiner work closely with the law department. It is important for the reader to remember that the subjectivity of many claim situations complicate the degree of interpretive problems that must be addressed.

The contract approved with an exclusion endorsement by the underwriting department, excluding coverage for a specific physical impairment, frequently presents additional sets of problems for the claim examiner. It is not always possible to clearly determine whether or not the endorsement covers the claim in question. Is the current claim for gastritis the result of the claimant's history of peptic ulcer? Is the disability of the low back the result of a physical blow received or from the policyholder's past history of back problems, which are excluded under the contract? All such questions require sensible and sensitive handling by the claim examiner.

As in the underwriting process, where we found that back histories represented some 15 percent of all substandard approvals, similarly some 15 percent of all disability claims involve disorders of the back. Disorders and disabilities of the nervous system present a particularly difficult claim situation for the examiner to evaluate. The subjectivity in nervous system disorders is as great as for any other group of impairments. How serious is the anxiety state, nervous disorder, or psychoneurosis? Is the claimant suffering from this nervous problem truly totally disabled? It is almost impossible to project the normal length of disability for various nervous disorders. Again, the skill and training of the claim examiner are of primary importance in the handling of such situations.

REHABILITATION

It has only been in recent years that most companies have given serious consideration to rehabilitation programs. Most professional claim examiners believe that substantial activity and success will be attained in this area during the next decade. When we remember the subjectivity of disability and the importance of stability, motivation, and the will to work, then we can begin to appreciate the variety of factors that must be addressed in a successful and comprehensive rehabilitation effort. It is more than physical rehabilitation! It is more than financial rehabilitation! Indeed, the most important element may be psychological rehabilitation. The preparation for a successful rehabilitation effort frequently requires several months of development. It requires an evaluation of the individual circumstances and characteristics of the particular claimant. Above all, it requires an approach that assumes that successful rehabilitation is in the best interests of both the company and the claimant. It must assume that almost all claimants are candidates for rehabilitation, given the proper circumstances.

If there is one phrase that best describes the necessary characteristics of disability income claim departments, it is *accurate and timely service.*

Actuarial

15

The two most significant factors for the disability income actuary (in comparison with the life insurance actuary) are the lack of substantial and reliable data and the high level of subjectivity in determining claim costs. Life insurance mortality data is voluminous and quite dependable, the volume large enough so that accurate mortality projections can be developed for several different areas of risk. Industry figures, many through Society of Actuary studies, present reliable mortality statistics for medical-examined business, nonmedical business, type of plan, standard issues, and substandard issues. Many of these items can be broken down by the nature of specific impairments. As I have stressed before, no such reliable studies are available to the disability income actuary.

AVAILABLE MORBIDITY DATA

The valuation table in use in the 1980s is the 1964 Commissioner's Disability Table (CDT), which was developed under the auspices of the Health Insurance Association of America. There was a 1971 modification of the 1964 CDT table, but it continues to serve as the primary table for the industry. It is important to note that this table is based primarily upon 1950 data. The business has changed very dramatically since that time, particularly in average length of benefit period, average elimination period, and indemnities, which have steadily increased. It is no wonder that the Society of Actuaries is currently promoting development of a new disability income table based on more current information. Reliable morbidity tables based upon sex, occupation class, benefit period, elimination period, and size of indemnity are important and necessary for the disability actuary.

Although the Social Security Administration in recent years has published some morbidity data, the social characteristics of the Social Security system make this information somewhat less than reliable for industry use. However, the Social Security Administration has the largest volume of data available, and as their volume of experience grows, it is hoped that the information may become more useful.

The Society of Actuaries has conducted a few disability income studies, and because of the scarcity of data, such studies tend to be devoured by the industry and perhaps overutilized. An example is the group long-term disability study conducted in the early 1970s and then published by the Society of Actuaries in 1975. The study indicated a definite correlation between morbidity and the level of the replacement ratio. Table 15–1 indicates that when the replacement ratio (ratio of indemnity paid to predisability income) exceeds 50 percent, then the actual morbidity escalates sharply above the expected level. The greater the replacement ratio, the more adverse the actual to expected ratio. This study has tended to affect both group and individual disability pricing during the past five years. Although there are no individual disability studies that formally confirm this trend, further quantification and evaluation would indeed be helpful in pricing.

In recent years some of the larger disability income writers have noted that their own claim studies show increased morbidity as the indemnity increases, even without regard to the replacement ratio. In other words, there is some evidence that the larger the indemnity, the greater the unit claim cost, without taking into consideration the claimant's income prior to disability. Data in this area is still very scarce, and some

TABLE 15–1
Group Long-Term Disability Experience, 1969–1973

Percent of gross income insured	Ratio of actual/expected claims
50% or less	.88
More than 50%	1.09
More than 60%	1.42
More than 70%	2.19

Source: *Transactions, Society of Actuaries, 1975,* "Reports of Mortality and Morbidity Experience," p. 226.

industry actuaries wonder whether this is truly a trend or rather an indication that expected morbidity levels in the past for large indemnities were unrealistically low.

VARIABLE FACTORS

Motivation, stability, and their related impact upon the work ethic are, of course, particular problems for the disability actuary. In a mathematical science, where scientific and logical principles are a foundation of the profession, it is indeed somewhat uncomfortable for the actuary to be faced with so many subjective characteristics. The subjective motivation and stability factors vary by age, income, occupation class, sex, marital status, physical health, and so on. If we pause for a minute and think about how the same factors are more objective in mortality determination, then we can see that there is a great deal more art involved in the disability actuary's profession.

It should also be pointed out that these variable factors continue to be in a constant state of flux for the actuary. Changes in social mores and norms will necessarily change the underlying assumptions in disability-rate development. Perhaps the best recent example of such changes occurred during the 1970s. As a result of the steep recession of the mid 1970s, the disability industry found that it had to adjust many of the assumptions that had been used for decades. Short elimination period policies could no longer be sold profitably. Premium rates for risks in lower-occupation classes increased sharply. How much of this change in experience was the result of changes in the work ethic as a result of basic changes in our society from the mid 1960s through the mid 1970s? How much was the result of overinsurance problems caused by significant liberalizations in the Social Security system? What will be the future trends of both? How do we measure the short- and long-term impacts upon morbidity?

During this same period of time, actuaries were asked to price disability products that were more liberal and with different types of definitions than in the past. The "own occupation" definition and various presumptive disability definitions are such examples. Without previous morbidity studies on which to base any projections of experience under such definitions, the actuary operates in an environment of subjectivity, best judgment, and common sense. Only successors in future decades will be able to accurately determine whether or not the actuary's assumptions were correct.

As mentioned previously, by the mid 1980s another set of assumptions were being questioned. Professional risks, physicians and especially dentists, who had always generated excellent morbidity results, were going through social changes. These changes in income, group practice, and malpractice risks were changing traditional morbidity patterns.

PRICING CHALLENGES

Fine tuning and quick reaction to social and economic changes are a necessity for disability income actuaries. They must understand the cyclical nature of the business. They must accept the fact that during good economic times claims experience and profits will prove more favorable than what they assumed in their rates. Conversely, during bad economic times the rates may not prove adequate because of higher morbidity. Actuaries must be ready to change basic assumptions when long-term social trends are evident. On the other hand, they must resist the strong temptation to relax assumptions during good economic times or tighten them during bad economic times without evidence of permanent trends.

The industry has, historically, not shown the discipline to avoid overreaction in either good or bad economic times. Rather, it has tended to relax its product language, underwriting, and rates during good times and to tighten them excessively in reaction to the inevitable recession. Part of this phenomenon results from the lack of mature data in the industry, part from inexperienced industry personnel, and part from the general immature nature of disability insurance.

An excellent example of the pricing problems facing the actuary is responding to recent product development trends in partial or residual benefits. Very little partial disability experience and data is available anywhere in the industry, and where available at all, it is for short periods, usually less than six months. New contractual benefits in recent years (frequently called residual benefits) provide for long-term partial benefits that may run for the lifetime of the insured. These partial or residual benefits may be payable based upon the inability of the insured to perform certain important duties of his or her occupation. In other contracts they may be payable based upon the degree of reduction in the insured's earnings, or they may be based on some combination of both factors. The variable combinations that must be addressed in solving the pricing problem for these new coverages pose a challenge to the actuary, and the accuracy of the actuary's assumptions will not be able to be fully evaluated for some 10 to 20 years!

Unfortunately, the subjectivity and variety of disability income pricing problems are complicated by the fact that many companies tend to assign an inexperienced actuary to this product line. Since disability income is a secondary or tertiary product in most companies, representing only a fraction of the company's total premium income, its total impact upon the company results is not primary. Ironically, the lack of objective approaches and reliable and mature data requires an experienced actuary who can call upon years of exposure to a variety of actuarial problems in order to weed through the pricing uncertainties. For this reason, many companies' significant disability losses may be tied directly to the tendency to assign their less-experienced and immature personnel in all areas of disability income administration.

Whether discussing disability income underwriting professionals, claim professionals, or actuaries, the risks and the volatility of the disability product line requires experienced personnel who have the courage to resist overliberal or overconservative reactions. In an industry where little reliable data is available, the financial risks are accelerated when inexperienced personnel are assigned to key positions.

DISABILITY RESERVES

There are two significant reserves in disability income insurance. The active life reserve is similar to its counterpart in life insurance. The typical disability income policy is on a level-premium basis. In the early years somewhat more premium than is necessary for actual morbidity is charged. This excess premium must be set aside to offset the greater morbidity at the older ages when the premium will prove inadequate. The active life reserve is the depository for this excess premium and, of course, the actuary's premium-rate assumptions assume a certain level of interest earnings on these reserves. It should be pointed out that this reserve does not build up either a cash or a surrender value in most disability policies. Some contracts in recent years do offer a return of premium benefit, which does provide for a surrender value of sorts. The size of the active life reserve varies by age and indemnity size but also varies significantly by the length of the benefit period. Problems in projecting levels of interest rates for many years in the future are present in pricing for the active life reserve, as they are in life insurance.

The second disability income reserve is the disabled life reserve, and it does not have its counterpart in life insurance, except for the life reserve set aside for waiver of premium. The disabled life reserve is established reflecting each disability claim and its projected length. The basis for the reserve is the 1964 Commissioner's Disability Table, although companies may establish more conservative or more liberal disabled life reserves if they can demonstrate that their experience substantiates different assumptions. The significance of the disabled life reserve for many disability income writers has only become evident in recent years. With the substantial increase in both monthly indemnity levels and the length of the average benefit period issued, the impact on the claim reserve has taken quantum leaps. For example, in 1960 when the maximum long-term benefit was commonly 10 years and the maximum indemnity $300 per month, the total company liability on a single claim was some $36,000. However, today a disability income policyholder may have an indemnity of $10,000 per month with a to-age-65 benefit period and represent a potential liability to the company in excess of $3–$5 million at age 35. It is more and more frequent for companies to incur claim reserves in excess of $500,000 for one open claim, which can naturally cause tremendous swings in the size of total company claim reserves from month to month and year to year. Reinsurance has become more important as a way of diminishing the impact of large swings in the disabled life or claim reserve of small- and medium-sized companies.

EXPERIENCE STUDIES

A variety of morbidity studies have been employed in the disability business in the past. Until recent years loss ratio experience was probably the most common method of tracking claim experience. Loss ratios tend to be less than satisfactory methods of study because of the many variable factors associated with disability income—length of benefit period, length of elimination period, duration, and so on. Morbidity studies, based upon actual to expected experience for rates of disablement and rates of recovery, are indeed the more reliable methods for evaluating experience and building rates. As has already been emphasized, there is little data currently available on a morbidity basis. The new valuation tables currently under development by the Society of Actuaries (which, it is hoped, will be adopted by the National Association of Insurance Commissioners at some time in the future) will be an important step in this direction.

Even with the development of more reliable actual to expected morbidity tables, the disability actuary will still be faced with substantial areas that require subjective judgment. Differences in extra-benefit riders and basic contract language will continue to call heavily upon the disability actuary's personal experience and judgment.

One area receiving a substantial amount of attention in recent years is the difference in the claim costs by sex. The state of New York conducted an extensive study of industry data in the late 1970s and, on the basis of the results of this study, passed regulations concerning rate differentials by sex. This study as well as other industry studies indicates a different pattern of morbidity in the claim cost for women. The higher claim cost for women in recent studies tends to disappear by the middle-50 ages and falls below male rates in the older ages.

The adage that insurance is a business of delayed rewards and delayed penalties is indeed true in disability income. The non-cancellable contract issued today, particularly because of its subjective qualities and lack of reliable data, cannot be accurately evaluated for several years. I believe a minimum of five years is needed before any intelligent judgment can be made about the profitability of a particular contract or the accuracy of original pricing assumptions. Depending upon the nature of contractual guarantees, the length of time required for reliable experience to emerge may be 10 years or more—another reason for experienced professionals to be pricing, underwriting, and administering the claims for this product line.

PRICING FACTORS

The elements that must be examined in the disability income pricing process have their comparable factors in pricing for life insurance. This book has discussed at length the importance of morbidity assumptions and the fact that they have a high degree of subjectivity. Persistency assumptions are also important in the disability pricing process and also vary in different parameters. Generally speaking, lower-occupation classes, lower incomes, younger ages, smaller premiums, quarterly premium modes, shorter benefit periods, shorter elimination period contracts, all tend to have poorer persistency. Expense rates and costs must, of course, be analyzed as they are in life insurance pricing, and a basic decision that the life company must reach is how it will allocate expenses to the disability income product line. Can a small product line afford to carry its full share of overhead? On the other hand, the actuary must take care not to use consistently liberal assumptions that will eventually result in a loss leader. The estimate of the cost of taxes must be built into the premium. The interest-rate assumptions, again similar to life insurance, make up an integral part of the pricing process that has taken on greater importance with interest-rate fluctuations. Finally, premium volume must be factored into the asset-share analysis and indeed must show the variations by occupation class, age, indemnity, and so on.

Last but not least, the actuary must build a profit margin into the asset share. This subject of itself could generate a separate chapter discussing basic profit margins, contingencies, return on investment, and a variety of modifications and techniques in the pricing process. Suffice it to say that a stock company must build into its premium a specific amount for profit, and a mutual company must build into its margin an amount that represents the expected dividend. Whether the pricing is for a stock or a mutual company, the actuary must build into the profit margin a greater contingency factor than is normally the case in life insurance. The volatility of the disability income product, the lack of reliable morbidity data, and the large number of variable factors that can affect basic assumptions all combine to require a contingency factor for disability income. The greater the unknowns, the more liberal the contract, the greater the need for a contingency margin.

COMPANY PHILOSOPHY

All through this pricing process some key background assumptions of company philosophy must be identified and kept in mind by the actuary. What is the quality and experience of disability underwriting?

How competitive is the marketplace in which the product is to be sold? What is the claims philosophy of the company? Does the company adhere rigidly to contract language, or does it interpret language liberally, or is its philosophy somewhere in between? What is the quality and experience of the salespeople marketing the product? Are they familiar with disability income? Are they familiar with completing a disability income application? Do they do a high quality job of field selection?

Once the product has been placed, approved, and sold in the marketplace, there must be periodic and consistent evaluation of the results to determine whether or not the pricing assumptions are achieving the proper result. In a volatile product line, to ignore such necessary evaluation may cause serious financial problems as the line matures.

One thing is certain in any pricing of a disability product: None of the specific assumptions will prove to be accurate. The hope and expectation is that, in the aggregate, the assumptions will generate the necessary profit margin. The greater the unknowns in a particular product, the greater the risks, the greater the contingency margin that should be built in. It is reasonable to expect that, for any product pricing activity, the company should build in a greater margin for those products with which it is assuming a greater risk. Disability income is one such product.

Law Department Function

16

The role and responsibility of the law department in the disability income product line is directly affected by the nature and risk of this product. The subjective nature of the disability claim demands particular attention from the attorney in designing and writing contract language. Interpretation of contract language, particularly in conjunction with the claim situation, is a frequent role for the disability attorney. This is caused by the wide variety of circumstances that may be involved in a disability claim and by the consequent opportunities for a variety of interpretations. All of these factors tend to lead toward an environment in which significant disagreements are common, and the frequency of suits is more common than is found in life insurance. The disability product line responsibility requires an experienced attorney, since he or she will be frequently called upon to make judgments and offer opinions involving tens and hundreds of thousands of dollars of potential liability.

STATE REGULATION

As with life insurance, disability income is state regulated as provided under the provisions of the McCarran Act of 1945, which strengthened the position of state regulation of the insurance industry. As mentioned in Chapter 1, the primary law regulating the disability income contract is the Uniform Individual Accident and Sickness Policy Provi-

150

sions Law, which was adopted by the National Association of Insurance Commissioners in 1950. Throughout the 1950s the various states adopted the provisions of the Uniform Law, and it stands today as the primary body of law governing the individual disability business.

It contains both General and Optional provisions, and the reader will find many similarities between this and the body of law governing life insurance contracts. Provisions relating to the Entire Contract, Contestability, Grace Period, Reinstatements, Claim Procedures, Change of Beneficiary, Physical Examination, and Autopsy all represent sections of the General Provisions found in life insurance. The claim provisions in the disability Uniform Provisions are obviously more extensive than found in life insurance because of the greater frequency and subjectivity of the disability claim. In addition, the Uniform Provisions provide optional provision language that may be included at the option of the insured. They include language relating to change of occupation, misstatement of age, relation of earnings to insurance, cancellation, and so on. Most of these optional provisions have been driven from the marketplace as a result of competition. The Uniform Provisions have remained essentially intact for 35 years. In recent years many states have promulgated Minimum Standards Regulations, which mandate specific contract language in such areas as preexisting conditions.

CONTRACT LANGUAGE

The disability income attorney's role in the product development process is also a more critical one than in life insurance because of the subjective nature of the product. Although the Uniform Provisions provide and specify language for basic sections of the contract, there still remain large sections in which contractual language must be developed to reflect the decisions of the insurer and define the extent and breadth of coverage.

Defining Disability

For example, one of the key provisions that must be discussed by all interested parties in the product development process is the definition of disability. This definition to a considerable extent represents a decision of company policy. Disability can be total or partial, and each element must be specifically defined. Does total disability occur when an individual can no longer work at *any* occupation because of accident or sickness? Does disability occur when an individual cannot perform the duties of his or her *specific* occupation because of accident or sickness? Does total disability occur when the individual's income is impaired and reduced because of accident or sickness? What degree of income loss must be suffered before a person is considered totally disabled? What specific duties in an individual's occupation represent total disability when they cannot be performed? If a person is only able to work a limited number of hours per week because of accident or sickness, how many hours should still be considered total disability? The company position on total disability must consider all of these elements before attempting to draft language. Once the company's position has been determined, then it is up to the disability attorney to make certain that the language clearly represents what it is intended to represent.

The contract must address a definition of accident disability. In order to be considered an accident claim, must the individual have suffered a specific *physical* injury? Does the back injury that results from bending over represent a true accident, or rather is it a sickness claim resulting from a previous structural weakness of the back? Are self-inflicted injuries covered? Are unintentional self-inflicted injuries covered but intentional injuries not covered? The contract language must be drafted in such a way as to clearly define the company's intent.

Defining Sickness

A similar series of questions must be addressed in determining the company's definition of sickness. At what point does the chronic condition of arthritis, which may have been originally caused from a physical blow, become a sickness rather than an accident? How does the company wish to treat a situation in which a person was originally totally disabled from an accident but subsequently suffers a sickness that prolongs the disability? The individual who suffered a serious accident with a long disability may have recovery impaired because of psychological problems that developed during recovery. Does this claim continue to be an accident, or is it a sickness? Again, the disability attorney must carefully design language that represents the company's intent. It should be emphasized that even under the best of circumstances contractual language will leave unanswered questions and will not address every specific claim situation. The multitude of various accident and sickness claims, the motivation of the claimant, and the nature of the claimant's occupation are only some of the factors that come to play in a live claim situation and that emphasize the subjective nature of disability insurance.

Defining Loss of Income and Benefits

The contract must address and define what is considered to be loss of income if the contract bases claim payments on the degree of income loss. Is a specific percent of income loss established as a measure? What types of income are considered during a period of disability? In the case of a professional person, is income received from accounts receivable counted as income during a period of disability, or does the insurer only consider income actually generated from activities *during* the disability period?

If the contract contains a provision for partial payment of benefits in the event of partial disability, the specific circumstances under which these benefits are payable must be delineated. Is the payment of partial benefits dependent upon the amount of time the claimant spends at his or her place of employment? Is it dependent upon the number or types of duties the claimant is unable to perform? Is it based upon a percent of income loss that occurs as a result of the disability?

CONTRACT DRAFTING

The disability income attorney faces a further complication in the drafting of contract language. Even after receiving clear guidance as to company policy and direction, and even after expressing company direction accurately in contractual language, the attorney must address the competitive environment. It has been an historical fact throughout the history of disability insurance that competition focuses on contract language. This is not to say that premium rates, issue limits, substandard underwriting, and the quality of service are not important in the competitive disability environment. They are important, but the specific language used in defining the provisions mentioned above is more often than not the primary area on which competition will focus. The way in which total disability, accident, sickness, partial disability, income loss, and other contractual provisions are verbalized in the contract will be the focal point around which competition will build its strategy. A semicolon, a comma, or a preposition may loom much larger in the competitive environment than was intended during contract drafting. The highly tuned nature of this contract language competition is frequently the primary stimulus behind new product-development approaches. One company will develop a new clause or benefit to specifically take advantage of or to exaggerate a weakness in a competitor's contract.

The importance of contract language in the competitive environment is more significant in disability income than in life insurance. Competition in life insurance primarily revolves around premium rates, cash values, and the underwriting decision. Rarely does the contractual language play an important role in the competitive sales process.

DRAFTING FORMS

One other area of the attorney's involvement in language drafting is language for various forms, the most important of which is the application itself. Since the application is a legal document and becomes a part of the insurance contract, it must meet the requirements of the various state jurisdictions, as well as elicit information necessary for the underwriter to make a decision. Similarly, the language must be clear and precise enough to minimize claim problems that may result from misunderstandings on the application. Ambiguous questions may lead to significant problems during the contestable period of the contract. A carefully prepared application protects the interests of both the applicant and the insurer.

Similar to life insurance requirements, some state jurisdictions in recent years have introduced specific regulations governing the language to be used on premium deposit receipts attached to the application and on authorizations to obtain information from other sources. The language on these forms must conform to state requirements and, at the same time, meet the objectives of the company within the boundaries of those regulations.

A variety of other forms will involve the disability attorney. They range from forms to be used in the underwriting process (similar to those found in life insurance) to a variety of claim forms. Language in medical examinations, medical questionnaires, income statements, and so on must at least receive approval of the legal department and frequently contain specific language drafted by it. Claim forms range all the way from forms for the applicant to complete alone, to forms for physicians to complete, to perhaps forms to verify employment. More and more, the attorney must be sensitive to legislative and regulatory requirements that limit and restrict the nature of questions that can be asked in order to protect the privacy of the consumer.

FILING OF FORMS AND PROCEDURES

Once the law department has completed its contract drafting, then it must proceed with the necessary filing procedures in the various state jurisdictions. Similar to life insurance, a few states simply require that the form be filed, and others require written approval of the policy form before it can be marketed. Some states employ large staffs of policy examiners and do a thorough job of policy contract review, and other states perform only a superficial review. The company law department, in any event, must keep track of its state approvals and establish a procedure for follow-up and for answering questions that may arise during the policy approval process. The subjectivity of disability income is obviously a factor that enters into the policy approval process since questions of interpretation arise frequently. The skilled legal staff can avoid much delay and irritation through accurate policy drafting before filing, followed by skilled responses to questions that emerge during the policy approval process.

The lack of uniformity of state regulation presents a variety of problems to the legal staff. Although a primary function of the National Association of Insurance Commissioners is intended to encourage uniformity, in recent years there appears to have been a trend toward greater divergence in both legislation and regulation. It is common for a company operating in all 51 jurisdictions (including the District of Columbia) to have at least six varieties of its basic disability policy form in order to comply with various jurisdictional requirements. Most often the differences are minor and of secondary importance, but the insurer faced with either developing a separate form or not marketing the product in the particular state chooses the first alternative. A skilled legal staff may be successful in convincing a state insurance department that there is no need for a separate policy form, but frequently such arguments are unsuccessful. In any event, the individual responsible for a company's contract filing must anticipate these kinds of problems.

As mentioned earlier in this text, New York State serves as the most strict regulatory authority of all jurisdictions. As a result, similar to the pattern in life insurance, many companies operate and market their disability income products in all states except New York. Conversely, a company that designs its product to meet the requirements of New York will find that in doing so it has met the requirements of most other jurisdictions.

Consumerism and privacy trends during the past decade have undoubtedly contributed to the divergence of regulatory requirements from one state to another. In order to respond to the needs of their own state constituents, insurance departments have been particularly sensitive to issues (very often sensitive political ones) within their own states. This trend has tended to place greater burdens on insurance companies and has increased their costs for complying with various regulations.

FILING OF PREMIUM RATES

One very important element in the disability income contract filing process that is different from life insurance is the filing and approval of rates. Not all states require approval of premium rates before marketing the contract, but an increasing number of states do so. This change is further evidence of the influence of consumerism. Premium rate filing follows a fairly standardized procedure, with some states demanding a comprehensive actuarial memorandum discussing actuarial approaches and assumptions used in development of the rates. The contract approval process is frequently a separate one from the rate-approval process, and a company must receive both approvals before releasing the contract for issue.

In recent years some states have developed minimum loss ratio requirements that must be met before a contract's rate filing is approved. The actuarial approach and formula used to develop the rates must therefore conform with the minimum loss ratio requirements of that particular state jurisdiction. Most states vary the minimum loss ratio depending upon whether the disability contract is non-cancellable, guaranteed renewable, or optionally renewable. Since the non-cancellable contract is the most liberal for the consumer, state insurance departments generally allow for a lower loss ratio objective here than is allowed for guaranteed-renewable and optional-renewable contracts. The actuary and the attorney must work closely together during this filing process. Careful planning must be done to make certain that the target date for release of the product is consistent with the desired objective of state approvals at the time of release.

It should also be mentioned that those states that have minimum loss ratio requirements also have subsequent requirements to determine whether or not the contract in the future meets the minimum loss ratio objectives.

EXPERIENCE OF INSURANCE DEPARTMENTS

One final comment on the process and procedure of contract filing in disability income is a common problem that has been mentioned for almost all disciplines involved in disability income. The lack of experience, the subjectivity of the product line, the lack of written material, the immaturity of the line, and the scarcity of reliable statistical data all combine to present problems for both the insurer and the state insurance departments in the filing process. A problem may surface because a state insurance contract examiner lacks experience in approving disability income products. Some problems develop during the filing process because state legislation or regulation was designed with either life insurance or medical care insurance in mind, and consequently the regulation may not clearly fit the unique needs present in a disability contract. One good example of such a problem was Regulation 62 in New York, which defined non-cancellable insurance as a product that could not be cancelled and in which the premium could not be changed until age 65 or such earlier date as the individual became eligible for Medicare. Such language might be appropriate for a non-cancellable hospital or medical care contract, but Medicare bears no relationship to a product that is insuring against disability. The regulation would have had much more meaning if it had defined non-cancellable disability income as a product that cannot be cancelled, having rates that cannot be increased until age 65 or until the individual becomes eligible for and elects to receive Social Security retirement benefits. This New York regulation was changed in 1982 to language similar to that described in the preceding sentence.

These types of problems may well surface during the filing process and require the patience of the disability attorney in dealing with state insurance departments. Indeed, they may necessitate a gentle attempt at educating the regulator on the peculiarities and unique differences in the disability product line.

Disability insurance offers its own level of challenges to the disability attorney. The attorney must be knowledgeable and experienced in insurance law, must be creative and flexible in an environment including regulators who may not be knowledgeable, and must call upon his or her legal training in designing contract language in a difficult and subjective environment.

CLAIM HANDLING

The involvement of the law department in the disability income claim process is much more frequent and complicated than is to be found in life insurance. There are more claims to deal with per thousand policies in force, and the actual determination and verification of a claim is less objective than in life insurance.

The disability attorney is frequently called upon by the claim examiner to help in interpreting contract language. Does the nature of the disability, does the nature of the claimant's occupation, do the circumstances surrounding the disability coincide with the intent of the contract? Perhaps fewer than 1 percent of all claims involve the legal staff; however, these claims frequently offer the potential of substantial financial risk both in claim payments and legal costs. The advent of consumerism and the sensitivity to discrimination of any kind has undoubtedly increased the percentage of cases that are presented to the law department for its opinion during the past decade.

Careful documentation in the development of the claim file is a basic necessity. The information provided at application time and the nature of the underwriting response to that information are frequently important factors in determining company liability.

The public is much more sensitive to challenging the insurer's interpretation of the contract and pursuing a suit in our current environment than would have been true a decade ago. In the vast majority of such situations, the law department, upon examining the circumstances of such a case, will conclude that the company's position is a strong and defensible one. However, the lawyer is often faced with the practical problem of whether or not the legal cost of defending the company position may outweigh the actual cost of paying the benefits. Unfortunately, in many instances the insurer finds it is more prudent to pay the claim or reach a compromise settlement because the costs of defending a suit would outweigh the costs of the settlement. The business necessity of such an approach is clear. However, the continued acquiescence of companies and law departments under such circumstances tends to encourage further suits, even though the grounds for such suits are often weak or even nonexistent when examining the contract language. The company must clearly pick and choose those cases to contest based upon a reasonable interpretation of the circumstances surrounding the particular case. Where important issues are at stake, it must be willing to pursue those cases through to a conclusion, even if the legal expenses exceed the potential liability of the claim itself. To do otherwise will increasingly encourage attorneys representing clients with claim situations that are not truly open to question to pursue them in court, not expecting a court decision but rather hoping for the insurer to settle.

INDUSTRY ASSOCIATION ROLE

There are some external sources of information and help for the disability attorney in fulfilling these responsibilities. The Health Insurance Association of America employs a staff of attorneys who monitor both legislative and regulatory developments in each of the various state jurisdictions. They are sensitive to disability income as well as medical care issues and regularly publish newsletters and specific memoranda dealing with state legislative and regulatory developments. They also employ a similar legal staff that monitors the development of federal legislation that may affect our industry.

In addition, a variety of HIAA subcommittees made up of insurance industry personnel operate in a number of different areas to discuss, recommend, and advise on issues affecting the industry and its regulatory environment. The Disability Committee of the HIAA is specifically assigned the task of monitoring and reacting to issues that affect this product line alone. It functions with a series of subcommittees to address temporary and long-range disability problems and concerns.

A second source of information and help for the disability attorney may lie with the reinsurance facility that the company uses for the disability product. Reinsurers, because of their interest and commitment to this product line, should be in a position to give technical advice on some of the more difficult problems that the disability attorney may face.

BUSINESS INSURANCE

A recent development in the disability income business is the growth of a variety of business-insurance–type sales. Earlier in this text I discussed the characteristics of overhead expense and business buy-out coverages. The development of these contracts requires new skills on the part of the disability attorney and particularly a clear understanding of the nature of the risk to be insured.

In the case of the overhead expense contract, the subject to be insured is not earned income, but rather the business expenses that will continue to be incurred when the owner is disabled. The nature of these expenses must be clearly defined. The way in which the expenses are to be determined at claim time and the fact that the contract only reimburses actual expenses are important considerations. The overhead expense contract requires a special application to develop the necessary business expense information.

Similarly, the buy-and-sell contract is designed to help effect a buy-out of a partner's share in the business if one of the partners becomes disabled. The contract depends upon a formal buy-and-sell agreement being in effect on the lives of the partners. The insurer's attorney must make certain that the language in the buy-and-sell agreement that addresses disability is consistent with the provisions in the insurance contract. This adds a significant level of complexity to the insurance sale since two legal documents are involved—(1) the buy-and-sell agreement between the parties involved and (2) the insurance contract itself. Many companies find the buy-and-sell process to be cumbersome and expensive, and it is consequently sold in relatively small volume throughout the marketplace.

DISCLOSURE AND DISCRIMINATION

Similar to the life insurance environment and as already briefly mentioned in this chapter, during the past decade a variety of state legislative and regulatory enactments have surfaced in the area of disclosure and discrimination. Further enactments in these areas appear likely to continue.

Disclosure

Disclosure documents are required in most state jurisdictions and usually accompany the delivery of the disability contract. Some jurisdictions require disclosure information to be presented at time of application. In each instance, the intent is to more clearly and accurately describe for the potential policyholder the benefits, limitations, and restrictions of the contract. Such requirements have involved the legal staff in first interpreting and then drafting the proper disclosure documents.

There has been substantial activity in recent years in most companies to draft contracts in simplified language; this has included disability income contracts. In such a product line as disability income in which careful contract interpretation is frequently necessary and called for, the task of accurately designing a simplified language contract is perhaps even more complex. The difficult job of contractually defining disability, accident, sickness, recurrent disability, and partial disability must all be addressed again in simplified language.

Discrimination

Finally, the area of discrimination has a natural impact upon disability income. In contrast to the premium circumstance in life insurance, the premium charged women in a disability contract is greater than for men, based upon the fact that actuarial data indicate that the morbidity pattern for women is greater. Nevertheless, there have been frequent discussions, and in fact bills filed in some jurisdictions, during the past 10 years to mandate an environment in which both sexes would be charged the same premium rate. However, no such legislation has yet been enacted. Women in similar occupation categories are offered the same benefits in contracts today as are their male counterparts, and the larger disability companies continue to examine their experience to make certain that their underwriting and rating rules reflect current trends.

Another area of legislative activity is that affecting discrimination against the handicapped. No student of the business would take issue with the social value of evaluating and insuring handicapped risks on the same basis as the nonhandicapped. However, difficult practical questions surface in dealing with this issue. First of all, because the disability contract insures an individual's income, before we can consider a person for coverage, there must be an established pattern of stable employment. Second, if a serious impairment exists, how can the company protect itself against the individual who claims total disability based upon a serious handicap, such as blindness or deafness, that existed at the time of application? The disability underwriter's natural approach is to exclude coverage for any disability resulting from a serious impairment; however, such an approach strikes directly at what many feel is the intent of legislation to prevent discrimination against the handicapped. Many discussions, several hearings, and many positions have been stated surrounding this issue. Several states currently have legislation or regulation affecting discrimination against the handicapped, and at the time of this writing, regulators have not mandated full and complete coverage for any handicapped group. Indeed, to define the handicapped in terms of the disability contract becomes quite difficult. Do they include those with high blood pressure, heart disease, diabetes, and perhaps any risks with serious physical impairments? It would appear as though the current trend that requires insurers to base their underwriting decision upon established actuarial or underwriting principles is a sound starting point to address a difficult issue.

In summary, the task of the disability attorney involves a wide variety of functions and responsibilities that may vary in importance and emphasis from the traditional skills necessary in life insurance. The subjectivity, the volatility, the immaturity, and the frequent claim involvement all play important parts in defining the skills necessary for the attorney who is assigned responsibility for the disability income product line.

Product-Development Process

17

The individual disability income marketplace has been very product sensitive throughout its lifetime. Competition at various times during the 20th century has centered around the cancellability of the contract, the guaranteed level premium, the length of the benefit period, the length of the elimination period, the issue limits, the definition of disability, the recurrent clause, the relation-to-earnings clause, definitions of partial disability, and many other factors. Competition will continue to center around the product and product language in the future. A strong argument can be made that the cycle of products will be shorter and product competition even more keen. Alvin Toffler's futuristic book, *Future Shock,* describes an age in which the life span of most consumer products will be much shorter than in the past. I believe we can expect the same phenomenon to exist in the disability income business.

The disability income product, perhaps more than any other individual insurance product line, must be sensitive and respond to the needs of the consumer. Since it is a product that insures the consumer's earning power and occupation, it must be ready to reflect the dynamic changes that take place in our society. As changes occur in work-ethic patterns, as new occupations emerge, as medical technology changes, as the average life span increases, as new avocations and hobbies emerge, as space travel becomes commonplace, the disability income product and its language must be modified to meet the demands of the marketplace.

FACTORS AFFECTING PRODUCT CHANGES

There are four principal factors that will stimulate product development:

1. Responding to competitors' new products.
2. Consumer demands.
3. Claims experience and trends.
4. Governmental influences.

Responding to the Competition

In a marketplace that is so product sensitive, it is vital for the disability income insurer to be quick to react to product changes of its competitors. This is particularly true in the professional and independent business markets where the competitive environment is especially keen. The demands of this marketplace are more highly developed. The high premium involved in the average sale increases the pressure from the salesperson. The salespeople involved in these markets are skilled professionals demanding the best for their clients. The disability income product in such situations represents only a portion of the total premium the client is paying to the particular salesperson for a variety of insurance products. The risk of losing a client because the disability income product doesn't meet the needs of such a competitive environment is an extremely strong motivation for both the salesperson and the company to react quickly to competitive changes.

Consumer Demands

As already mentioned, changes in our society have a most direct impact upon the characteristics of the disability product. As the consumer has become more aware of the need for long-term disability protection during the past two decades, the disability income product has moved through numerous stages. Indemnities offered have increased more than 30-fold, from $300 per month to $10,000 and more per month. Average benefit periods have increased from two years to age 65 and even lifetime. Definitions of disability have been liberalized from insuring an individual in "any occupation" which he or she is capable of performing to insuring and paying for total disability if the person is unable to perform his or her "own occupation." Guaranteed insurability options, cost-of-living benefits, and inflation indexing have been added to contracts to reflect the inflationary environment changes that have occurred in the past decade. Products to cover specific business needs and risks have been added to most company portfolios. To some extent, all of these product enhancements have had an impact on all occupation classes; however, the most liberal and broadest changes have occurred in the professional and independent-business markets.

What further product changes will be necessary to respond to technological advances in consumer travel, longer working-life span, longer life span, and continued inflation that erodes the purchase value of the indemnity insured in the contract? Whatever changes do emerge in the future, the disability income product development process must be responsive.

Claims Experience

Claim trends and experience must be examined and evaluated on an ongoing basis. Assumptions that were made in originally pricing and designing the product will prove to be inaccurate. Although some slight experience trends may begin to emerge if significant volumes of the product have been sold after three years, a broad data base of mature business will not emerge for at least 10 years. When original assumptions prove to be inaccurate, frequently as a result of changes in society that could not have been anticipated, changes in product language and rate structure may be necessary for future sales. Judgments must frequently be made regarding the necessity for such changes based upon something less than ideal data and experience. Fine tuning in the underwriting process can frequently correct some adverse experience trends. Adjustments in occupation class categories, the method of underwriting investigation, the treatment of impaired risks, and the careful selection of groups that may be contributing to adverse experience are examples of the type of fine tuning opportunities that exist for the underwriter.

Governmental Influence

The final element that affects the need for product change is governmental influence. During the 1970s, the growth and expansion of the federal Social Security disability program created serious problems for disability income insurers. Lower-income markets began to disappear as these federal disability benefits extended into higher and higher income levels that had previously been solely the domain of the private sector. Even in the higher-income markets, insurers found it was necessary to program around Social Security benefits in order to avoid overinsurance problems. New contracts and extra benefits began to emerge that allowed companies to program around both federal Social Security, state cash sickness, and Workers' Compensation benefits. All three areas showed substantial growth in the 1970s. Non-cancellable contracts that provide guaranteed benefits at guaranteed premiums cannot be modified once they are on the books. The importance, therefore, of adjusting contract language and limits for future issues in response to governmental change becomes obvious.

A second area of governmental influence is regulatory. Again, the 1970s saw substantial federal and state regulatory activity, particularly in the areas of minimum standards and discrimination. Substantial contract language changes as well as modifications in underwriting procedures were necessary in response to such regulation. An additional element that affects the disability contract is the added cost of complying with such regulation, and this naturally must be reflected in the premium structure.

The decade of the 1980s was a time of active liberal interpretation of contract language. Definitions of disability received interpretation beyond that originally assumed in the rates. Punitive damage awards, especially in California, affected product design, underwriting, and claim handling. The threat of severe "punishment" financial awards, running into multimillions of dollars, raised the cost of doing business in California.

The final government influence is in the area of taxes. Changes in the tax law may impact both the insurer and the insured, and either one or both may require changes in contract language or limits. Tax rules affecting premium income and investment income to the insurer may require a change in the premium assumptions. Changes in the tax code in the treatment of disability payments to the insurer may necessitate a review of existing issue limits as well as modifications in sales approaches and training.

INNOVATION VERSUS REACTION

Since the individual disability income product is dynamic and must be responsive to changes in our environment, it offers opportunities for creative product-development approaches. The subjective nature of the risk to be insured is such that the "ideal" disability income product has not yet been designed. Each decade sees further development and movement toward the ideal, but the perfect contract will continue to be elusive because of the changing environment and the nature of the risk to be insured.

Developing the Ideal Product

We might define the *ideal* product as one that provides 100 percent income replacement during disability throughout the insured's working lifetime, regardless of changes in income pattern during that lifetime. How can such a product be priced in a non-cancellable, guaranteed-renewable environment? How can such a product be priced and underwriting rules established in the volatile environment of continual changes in the motivation and work ethic of a society? How does the insurer adequately reserve for future liabilities where the maximum claim payout cannot be measured?

The ideal product is indeed elusive; however, the product-development process continues to move in that direction, never quite reaching the goal. Yet, such an environment does offer an opportunity for creative approaches to satisfy the demands of the consumer. Those companies with a long history of success in the disability business have a pattern of continual innovation and creativity in the product-development process.

Risks of Product Development

Like all new ventures, the innovative and creative product approach carries with it inherent risks. It is therefore natural that those companies with the most experience and the largest block of disability premium are the ones in a position to assume such risks. This is not to exclude the fact that many significant developments in the disability business have emerged from smaller and medium-size companies. Perhaps the return-of-premium benefit, which was developed in the late 1960s and early 1970s, is such an example. Careful analysis of the risk involved in new-product approaches is critical in a product line that is so volatile. The industry can point to several examples of companies that misjudged the risk of a new idea and suffered serious financial consequences. As a result, there is a natural tendency for companies in the product-development process, even the larger ones, to proceed slowly into uncharted areas. The normal pattern is to introduce the new idea into the more stable and dependable markets and, depending upon its success, to extend it into broader markets.

Listening to the Consumer

The disability industry, similar to the life insurance industry, can be criticized for failing in the past to truly respond to the consumers' needs and wants in its products. The life insurance industry in the late 1970s and early 1980s began to seriously experience the results of such unresponsiveness as it saw large segments of its market erode and be replaced by other financial service vehicles. The American consumer is both more demanding and more knowledgeable concerning financial needs today, and this has a direct impact upon the disability income product-development process. The industry must begin to consider market research techniques used in other industries to learn and better understand the needs and wants of the disability income consumer. We no longer as an industry can afford to design products that we as insurers are comfortable with and expect to market them successfully with the consumer. We rather must listen and measure the consumer demand and then attempt to design the product that best meets those needs, while at the same time safeguarding the company's interests. Not an easy task! We might also conclude that the risks involved are somewhat more enhanced in the disability income product line, where volatility is so great and the unknowns still numerous.

Not only does creative and innovative product development require listening to the needs and wants of traditional markets, it requires that the aggressive company be alert to new market opportunities. New occupations, new and different businesses, new risks in traditional businesses, changes in avocation patterns, changes in living styles all may offer opportunities for changes in traditional marketing approaches. During the 1970s, most companies withdrew from those markets that were adequately insured with governmental benefits. During the early 1980s, the American public showed increasing concern over the future stability of the Social Security system, and indeed there is clear evidence of a tightening and restricting of the payment of Social Security disability benefits. As this trend emerges further, new marketing opportunities may become available.

Responding to Economic Change

Responding to cyclical changes in the economy is a much more difficult problem. By the time changes in underwriting rules and premium structure have been made, the chances are that we have moved from one phase of the economic cycle to another. It is a fundamental necessity in disability insurance to accept the inevitability of economic cycles and the fact that they will have both adverse and favorable impacts upon experience. Profits will be greater than anticipated during economic growth periods and high employment. Profits will be less than expected—and perhaps even losses will be experienced—during economic recessions. As has already been mentioned in this text, the deeper the recession, the more severe the losses; the stronger the recovery, the greater the profits.

The disability industry unfortunately has a historical pattern of overreacting at both ends of the cycle. The stronger and longer the economic recovery period and the greater the profits, the greater the tendency for product liberalizations. Not infrequently such liberalizations proved to be unsound during the next economic recession. Conversely, the steeper the economic recession and the greater the company losses, the greater the tendency for companies to introduce product and underwriting restrictions, frequently overreacting in the conservative direction.

Therefore, a most important management discipline in the disability industry is for company management to resist the tendency to overreact at either end of the economic cycle.

The industry has not demonstrated the discipline and maturity to manage in such a manner in the past. The overreaction in product, rate, and underwriting liberalizations prior to the steep recession of the mid 1970s and the consequent overreaction in the restriction of product, rate, and underwriting in the late 1970s is only the most recent example of such tendencies. It might be emphasized that even the most experienced management approach will find the pressure and temptation toward overreaction to be very strong and real ones at both extremes of economic cycles.

DETERMINING THE MARKETS

For the new company entering the disability business or for the company that plans to expand its disability product line, the first step is to analyze and determine where its markets are. Such a basic step should be obvious to any experienced insurance manager, but it represents an area in which most companies spend inadequate time for careful evaluation. One major problem in accurately determining where the markets are is that frequently the pressure for product and underwriting change comes from the minority of the sales force. Since the professional and independent business markets are the most highly competitive of all disability markets, it is natural for salespeople operating in these markets to be most demanding for competitive and liberal products. But if only 10 percent of a company's distribution system is operating in these markets, it may be a poor decision to concentrate product-development activity and innovation in this area. A better decision might be to direct the innovative enhancement and effective promotion to capture a larger share of the market represented by 90 percent of the distribution force.

An analysis of a company's life insurance markets is not only the most logical but the most reliable source of information for determining where a company's disability markets will be. The distribution force—whether general agency, personal-producing general agent, or brokerage—will market the disability product to its established clients. What is the average size of the life insurance policy? What is the average income of the purchaser? What types of occupations are represented? What is the average age? What does competition offer in these markets? What unique penetration does your company have in these markets that other companies do not have? What strengths are evident in the way in which the company markets, services, promotes, and underwrites its life products that may be adaptable to disability income?

It is only after such a careful analysis that a company can then address exactly what the nature of its disability product should be. The simple guide of "know your market and know your competition" should be the constant measure throughout the product-development process. Indeed it affects not only product language, rating, and promotion, but also the underwriting and service structure.

WHO PARTICIPATES IN THE PROCESS?

The product-development process for disability income follows a pattern similar to that for life insurance and involves similar home office disciplines. The volatile and subjective nature of the product, however, necessitates more active and early involvement of underwriting and claims personnel than might normally be found in life insurance.

Sales and Marketing Personnel

The process must start with sales and marketing, since it is close to the pulse beat of the consumer and competition. Product ideas and competitive trends represent a continual flow of information from most knowledgeable and active disability sales forces. Most often, however, such product recommendations tend to be reactive rather than innovative. The effective and progressive product-development process almost always takes the input from the sales organization and considers it carefully, but it must also be alert to innovative and creative new approaches. Leadership in the marketplace requires innovation, not simply reaction.

Other Home Office Disciplines

Once the new product idea has been generally defined and accepted as something desirable from a sales and marketing prospective, then several other home office disciplines must become involved before serious development can begin. The actuary must determine how the product is to be priced, whether it can be priced safely, and what safeguards may be necessary to develop competitive rates. The underwriter must be consulted to determine whether or not new underwriting approaches are necessary, how to treat additional risks that the new product represents, and what safeguards should be introduced to satisfy the selection needs. The claim department must be consulted to determine what new risks and factors it will face in administering the claims. In each instance comments, suggestions, and concerns will be expressed regarding certain characteristics of the product, which will then necessitate discussion, modification, compromise, and finally agreement. To bypass or limit the input of any of these disciplines in the product process will increase the financial risk of success of the product. A product designed and developed entirely by sales and marketing personnel may generate tremendous premium volume but may not meet the profit projections assumed for the product. Conversely, a product designed and developed by actuaries, underwriters, and claims personnel may well protect the company's margin but prove to be unsalable. The key to success is the proper involvement and balance of all such disciplines, and inevitably the successful product-development process must involve a good amount of compromise and a good amount of cooperation.

Data Processing and Systems Personnel

In an age of increased computer automation, it is important that data processing and systems personnel be involved early in the product-development process. Innovative and new product approaches may require substantial modifications to existing systems. The cost and time commitment involved in building and modifying existing systems must be determined early in the process, and the expense of system modification may preclude the development of some products. Similarly, a complex systems project may substantially affect the time schedule for developing and releasing the product. Early involvement of data processing personnel and identification of problem areas may offer alternative approaches and options in the product design that pose fewer problems for data processing personnel. To identify such options early may reduce the cost of the project and enhance its early release. Most product-development activities require substantial data processing resource, so that the sooner the magnitude of the project can be quantified, the greater the opportunity for the future resource to be identified and scheduled.

Law Department

As was discussed in the previous chapter, the law department fills an important role in the development of disability income products. The participation of the disability income attorney in product-development discussions is important if he or she is expected to draft contract language reflecting the desires of the product development group. In addition, some product ideas may present special legislative and regulatory problems for the attorney. Similar to the role of other insurance professions, the attorney's input in such situations may identify alternative approaches or solutions early in the process that avoid problems in state filing and approval.

The investment department has not normally been considered a participant in the product process. During times of high yields on investments and reserves, however, the impact on the rate structure from the leverage of investment returns becomes more and more important. In the life insurance industry the development of products whose price is tied more directly to investment yield has certainly increased the importance of the investment function in the product-development process. Similar trends in disability income will require similar involvement.

TRAINING, EDUCATION, AND PROMOTION

The success of the new product does not end with the conclusion of the activities outlined on the foregoing pages. A well-designed product, responsive to the consumer's needs, carefully designed for the markets a company wishes to penetrate, and providing adequate safeguards for the company, will not assure sales success. Perhaps one of the greatest faults of many companies in marketing their disability product is that they fall short of providing adequate training, education, and promotion to assure its success. Some home office management whose disability income line is secondary or tertiary tend to underestimate the complexity of the product in the marketplace.

Training the Field Force

The highly competitive environment requires salespeople not only to be knowledgeable regarding their own product but also to be knowledgeable about competition. A product line where competition frequently centers around product language requires salespeople to have well-developed technical knowledge of the strengths and weaknesses of their product language versus that of the competition. The inexperienced home office manager will tend to narrowly look at the disability product. Too many such managers measure its complexity based upon the calculation of premium, the calculation of the indemnity to be provided, and the benefit period and elimination period variables, but with little regard for such things as the definition of disability, the definition of accident and sickness, and recurrent clauses.

Sales Support

The company that wishes to see its disability product line grow must be prepared to invest in adequately training its field force, providing the necessary sales support material, and generally promoting the product. Sales brochures and sales ideas must be developed and designed consistent with the company's marketing direction in order to create the need for the product and enhance the sale. Support material stressing the strengths of the product, particularly in comparison with competition, must be close at hand for the agent. Proposal capability designed to meet the needs of the various disability markets must be developed. Personal disability income requires different proposal attention than does business disability. Professional proposals must be designed differently than proposals for other markets.

In many companies where the disability sale is a fraction of a producer's life insurance sales, the company cannot expect to develop its salespeoples' expertise to a level that can adequately compete with salespeople who are concentrating in the disability income product line. In such instances, the company must provide specialist support in their field offices or in the home office for their producers to call upon to obtain help and advice in individual sales situations.

MOTIVATION FOR PRODUCT DEVELOPMENT

Perhaps one of the most serious mistakes that company management frequently makes is being primarily motivated to develop or enhance its disability income product line by the desire to "accommodate" the field force. Such a posture is usually a subconscious or unintentional one, but the resulting lack of commitment is the same as if it were deliberate. Companies who develop the disability product line in order to discourage their agents from brokering the product with disability specialty companies, but without the commitment to fully support such a volatile product, simply increase the risk of financial loss. There is no surer way to encourage product failure than to ignore the necessary commitment to training, support, and promotion.

In summary, in order to be successful, the product-development process must be a dynamic one, responsive to changes in the disability income environment. To make major penetrations and increases in market share, it must be innovative and creative and responsive to consumer demand. A company must carefully analyze where its market truly is before designing its product and marketing approach. In order for the product process to be successful, it must encourage a balance of input from various home office disciplines in the design process. Finally, a carefully laid out process in the previous steps will prove unsuccessful if the company short-cuts the training, support, and promotion phase.

Evaluation of Results

18

The evaluation of individual disability income results has been limited by the scarcity of reliable data. This factor has been discussed at several points throughout this book, and its importance is accentuated by the volatility of the product itself. Indeed, the volume of group disability income data is larger and has been the source of more recent disability studies than individual data. For example, the 1976 study by the Society of Actuaries on group long-term disability claims experience indicated the importance of replacement ratios on morbidity. This valuable report, which has been referred to on numerous occasions since it was published, confirmed a fact that had long been suspected in the industry but had been supported by little statistical verification.

The Commissioner's Disability Table of 1964 still serves as the primary morbidity table on which company valuation tables are based. A new disability table developed by the Society of Actuaries is based upon more current and broader data. This new table was accepted by the National Association of Insurance Commissioners (NAIC) in 1986, and was subsequently implemented in the various state jurisdictions. It provides new and different morbidity tables based upon occupation class and also bases its valuation of longer-term claims on actual data.

172

LIFE VERSUS DISABILITY VOLATILITY

Mortality studies in life insurance are extremely comprehensive based on a variety of parameters. Age, sex, medical, nonmedical, standard, substandard, permanent, and term are only some of the factors that are regularly examined and for which significant data exists for reliable statistical results. There is a need for an even greater number of parameters to be studied in disability income—elimination period, benefit period, occupation, income, indemnity, classification, along with all of the variables listed for life insurance. Essentially, no industry-wide data exists in all of these areas, although some of the larger companies have a broad enough data base to have developed some trends and information.

The volatility of the disability income product line not only makes such studies particularly desirable, but also demands that the analyst of such data be alert to the fact that the environment in the future will clearly be different than the environment at the time the data was accumulated. In the very best of circumstances, therefore, morbidity and loss ratio data only reflect experience and trends based on the period of time under study.

Projecting Trends

Subjective judgment and management experience must take hold as trends are projected into the future. Statistical trends for disability income are less reliable for projecting the future than would be true for life insurance, where the volatility is not as extreme. Even in such a limited environment, statistical evidence and trends make up the important and necessary starting place for projecting the future. The person analyzing the data must necessarily have a clear historical familiarity with the period being studied and must be knowledgeable about changes that have taken place in the marketplace since that study, as well as have enough experience in the disability business to make some judgments about the future. I am describing a true professional in the disability business, one experienced in the many peculiarities of the product line.

Period of Study

In order for studies to be valid and for sound conclusions to be drawn, any individual disability income statistical analysis must be done over a period of years, preferably a minimum of five years. Social changes that take place in our society tend to evolve over a period of years, and the progress of trends is important in helping to project the future. Because the direct impact of economic swings, either up or down, is a fact of life in the disability business, the period of study must be broad enough to blunt the peaks and valleys of such economic swings. The analyst must be cognizant of these economic swings in drawing conclusions. Neither good nor bad experience in a particular policy form, occupation class, or geographical area in one or even two calendar years can be taken as evidence to support either elation or dejection. Unfortunately, because of the lack of valid data and the inexperience of analysts, the industry has tended to overreact to temporary trends. Two or three years of good claim results frequently generate liberalizations in product, rates, and underwriting. Conversely, two or three years of poor experience frequently cause sharp retraction with the resulting increase in rates and tightening of contract language and underwriting. Human nature and business pressures cause even an experienced analyst to sometimes succumb to short-term experience trends. Mature and sound judgment would demand that experience always be looked at over a five-year period and then sound judgment applied.

MORBIDITY VERSUS LOSS RATIO STUDIES

Morbidity

Actual to expected morbidity studies are by far the most preferable method of examining disability income experience. There are two basic elements in disability morbidity: the rate of disability and the rate of recovery. The rate of disability is simply the number of disabled lives per thousand lives exposed. Changes in the rate of disability can often be determined early in an economic cycle, since the individual claimant becomes a part of the rate-of-disability study with his or her first day of disability.

The rate of recovery is simply a measurement of the length of disability. It is the number of disabled lives that will recover after one, two, three days of disability; or one, two, six months of disability; or 1, 2, 5, 10 years of disability per thousand disabled lives. The determination of changes in the rate of recovery takes a much longer period of time to emerge, since the statistic is based upon months and years of study of disabled lives. It is important to understand that changes can occur in the rate of disability without changes necessarily occurring in the rate of recovery, and vice versa.

Although changes in the rate of disability can frequently be noticed early in a change of the economic cycle or the unemployment rate, they may be only temporary. Such changes normally occur first in those occupational groupings that are most immediately affected by economic fluctuations, such as the unskilled employee group. The rate of disability may therefore show patterns of increase and decrease over a period of several years, depending upon the economic climate.

However, not only may the rate of recovery show changes in the early months of disability as a result of economic-cycle changes, but it is also a more volatile measure of social change in the public's work-ethic attitude and motivation.

Unfortunately, the data base necessary for valid morbidity studies is a large one, and few companies have the exposure to develop such meaningful data. Even those few industry studies based upon morbidity tend to lose credibility and value as they attempt to break down the data into smaller cells. As more and more companies automate their disability income data bases and claim records, such studies may become more productive.

Loss Ratios

Because of these problems in developing adequate morbidity data, by far the majority of industry and company disability studies are based upon loss ratio studies—the ratio of claims to premium. There are two basic types of claims ratios: cash claims ratio and incurred claims ratio. The cash ratio is simply the cash claim dollars paid out during the period of study divided by the earned premiums during the period of study. The incurred claims ratio, by far the more reliable of the two, is the cash claims plus the active life reserve plus the claims reserve divided by the earned premium during the period of study.

The cash ratio is inadequate because it fails to measure the future liability of open claims that will continue beyond the period of study since it does not consider the claim reserve. It also uses total premium, some portion of which on a level premium policy represents payments for claims to be incurred in the future. It therefore understates the true loss ratio. During the early years of a disability policy, when underwriting selection has not yet worn off, the cash claims ratio will be extremely low. Similarly, a policy with a long benefit period that has a larger portion of its premiums set aside for future claims and under which open claims have a much larger potential claim liability will show a lower cash ratio. Conversely, a policy with a short benefit period, in which a smaller portion of the premium represents reserves for future claims and the potential of a long-term claim is limited by the short benefit period, will show a higher cash loss ratio.

The incurred loss ratio, in counting both the active life and the disabled life claim reserves as part of the claims liability, is a sounder method of determining actual claims experience.

Sensitivity to Trends

The disability income business is clearly one of deferred rewards and deferred penalties. Consequently, the analyst of claim loss ratios or morbidity experience must always be cautious in drawing conclusions from short-term results and must be sensitive to trends in comparison with data from a variety of sources. Trends based upon past experience may be valuable indicators of direction, as long as the analyst is knowledgeable concerning the economic and social variables that may be affect-

FIGURE 18-1

ANNUAL STATEMENT FOR THE YEAR 1982 OF THE _____ (Name)

SCHEDULE H—ACCIDENT AND HEALTH EXHIBIT

	1 Total		2 Group Accident and Health		3 Credit* (Group and Individual)		4 Collectively Renewable		5 Non-Cancellable		6 Guaranteed Renewable		7 Non Renewable for Stated Reasons Only		8 Other Accident Only		9 All Other	
													Other Individual Policies					
	Amount	%†	Amount	%†	Amount	%†	Amount	%†	Amount	%†	Amount	%†	Amount	%†	Amount	%†	Amount	%†

PART 1.—ANALYSIS OF UNDERWRITING OPERATIONS

1 Premiums written
2 Premiums earned (see note b)
3 Incurred claims
4 Increase in policy reserves
5 Commissions*
6 General insurance expenses
7 Taxes, licenses and fees
8 Total expenses incurred
9 Gain from underwriting before dividends to policyholders
10 Dividends to policyholders
11 Gain from underwriting after dividends to policyholders

PART 2.—RESERVES AND LIABILITIES

A Premium Reserves
  1 Unearned premiums
  2 Advance premiums
  3 Reserve for rate credits
  4 Total premium reserves, current year
  5 Total premium reserves, previous year
  6 Increase in total premium reserves

B Policy Reserves
  1 Additional reserves
  2 Reserve for future contingent benefits (deferred maternity and other similar benefits)**
  3 Total policy reserves, current year
  4 Total policy reserves, previous year
  5 Increase in policy reserves

C Claim Reserves and Liabilities
  1 Total current year
  2 Total previous year
  3 Increase

PART 3.—TEST OF PREVIOUS YEAR'S CLAIM RESERVES AND LIABILITIES

1 Claims paid during the year
  a On claims incurred prior to current year
  b On claims incurred during current year
2 Claim reserves and liabilities, December 31, current year
  a On claims incurred prior to current year
  b On claims incurred during current year
3 Test
  a Line 1a and 2a
  b Claim reserves and liabilities, December 31, previous year
  c Line a minus Line b

PART 4.—REINSURANCE

A Reinsurance Assumed
  1 Premiums written
  2 Premiums earned (see note b)
  3 Incurred claims
  4 Commissions

B Reinsurance Ceded
  1 Premiums written
  2 Premiums earned (see note b)
  3 Incurred claims
  4 Commissions

a Business not exceeding 120 months duration

*Includes $ _____ reported as "Policy, membership and other fees retained by agents."

**If not included in claim reserves.

(b) Premiums earned are before adjustment for the increase in policy reserves which has been treated as a separate deduction.

†In each column of Part 1, show the percentages of Line 2 for Lines 3 through 11 inclusive

ing the period under study. Comparison with other companies' experience through annual statements may also give some clue as to a company's performance. However, analysts must be aware of characteristics in the other company's block of business that may be quite different from their own company's. The average age of a competitor's block of business, the mix by occupation class, the benefit period mix, the income range, and so on are all variable elements that analysts must keep in mind when comparing their loss ratio results to those of other companies.

Annual Statement Schedules

Schedule H in the convention blank provides the primary data available for this type of intercompany analysis (see Figure 18–1). Since it only contains loss ratio data, it is naturally less reliable than morbidity statistics would be. Similarly, since it makes no differentiation based upon the duration of a block of business, it presents natural weaknesses in direct loss ratio comparison. Nevertheless, significant trends on a year-to-year basis can be examined and should generate questions concerning differences in a company's trends versus those of the rest of the industry. Schedule O in the convention blank is a good measure of whether or not your own company or the competitor's is setting aside large enough claim reserves to have covered open claims for previous years (see Figure 18–2). If one finds that additional reserves must be established at year end for previous claim-year liabilities, then obviously the formula for reserving must be strengthened. It can be expected that during poor economic times Schedule O will show a shortfall in reserves, whereas the converse may be true during good economic periods.

CLAIM STUDY PARAMETERS

There are a variety of important parameters or areas to study and analyze in one's disability portfolio. In an industry where reliable and sufficient data is less than desirable, the problem becomes naturally more acute when one attempts to break down the data into smaller cells. Nevertheless, to the extent possible the disability analyst must attempt to study more than simply aggregate or total experience. The medium- or small-size company is at a particular disadvantage in this regard. The larger writers of disability tend to keep their experience confidential, particularly the more detailed and specific experience found in small cells. Disability reinsurance companies should have available more reliable data for the small or medium company and should provide such data to their clients, for both their clients' benefit and their own benefit as a reinsurer. The recent work by the Society of Actuaries to develop a new morbidity table to replace the 1964 CDT Table provides information on some cells that was not previously available. Some of

FIGURE 18–2

SCHEDULE O

Development of Incurred Losses

Non-Cancellable, Guaranteed Renewable, and Non-Renewable for Stated Reasons Only, Accident and Health Insurance

1 Years in Which Losses Were Incurred	Sum of Net Amount Paid Policyholders and Claim Liability and Reserve Outstanding at End of Year				
	2 1983	3 1984	4 1985	5 1986	6 1987
1983	X X X				X X X
1984	X X X	X X X			X X X
1985	X X X	X X X	X X X		
1986	X X X	X X X	X X X	X X X	
1987					•

*Equals the sum of Lines 1b and 2b, Columns 5, 6 and 7 of Schedule H, Part 3.

the best data available in recent years has been accumulated and distributed by John Miller, FSA, in his monthly *Disability Newsletter*. Mr. Miller has provided a most valuable service for the disability industry in his attempt to accumulate and analyze a variety of data based upon his many years of disability experience.

Some of the more important parameters or cells to examine are the following:

Occupation Class— Since there are significant differences in morbidity and claims experience, as well as underwriting rules and approaches from one occupation class to another, separate data on each class is necessary for both rating and for the setting of underwriting requirements. Changes in trends in one class may not result in similar changes in other classes, since the socioeconomic impact may be considerably different. Perhaps a perfect example of this sort of trend occurred in the 1970s, when the impact of overinsurance as a result of federal and state disability programs caused a deterioration in claims experience more in the lower classes than in the upper-occupation groupings.

Occupation— Each occupation class is made up of several dozen different occupations, and each one may perform somewhat differently, again based upon socioeconomic trends. Although it is much more difficult to obtain reliable data in such small cells, the larger insurers should be able to obtain some indication of significant trends by observing and combining experience over a period of years. If one compares occupation classifications commonly in use now with those used some 20 years ago, it can be quickly observed that there have been many changes and adjustments. Such factors as changes in the nature of occupations, changes in the work ethic, and changes in the general socioeconomic climate have clearly had their impact and caused the need for occupation-class adjustments.

Policy Form— Most companies will attempt to study their claims results based upon different policy forms. Each policy form has some unique characteristics, and the introduction of a new policy form always carries with it some unknown risks. Consequently, the examination by form is a necessary method of attempting to determine whether or not the assumptions made in designing the policy form have proven sound based upon actual experience. If adverse trends are identified early in the policy form's life, it may be possible to adjust underwriting requirements to improve the experience.

Extra Benefits— Optional or additional benefits, such as residual, cost of living, and future income options, require significant reserve allocations, and therefore, should be tracked and studied separately. In some situations the claim reserve levels required for these extra benefits may even exceed those required for the basic policy indemnity.

Age— Since one of the rate variables is age, experience in this specific cell is particularly important. Changes in medical treatment and technology will have an impact upon age experience as will socioeconomic changes that affect one age group differently than another. As the average age of our population increases, we may find early retirement less desirable, and this may consequently have a favorable impact upon older-age morbidity. Similarly, as the number of younger people in the work force diminishes, we may find more stability in their employment as a result of demand, and this may improve morbidity. Conversely, if older workers tend to remain in the work force longer, thereby keeping younger workers out of their higher-paying and perhaps more stable positions, then this may have an adverse impact upon younger-age morbidity.

Duration— The importance of duration has already been mentioned and cannot be underestimated. To study claims experience without regard to the age of the business under study will run the risk of more inaccurate conclusions than perhaps any other variable element. Loss ratios will naturally be higher on an older block of business and extremely low on a new block, where the effect of underwriting selection has not worn off. In spite of the more reliable results one might expect from incurred ratios, they will also have this tendency of higher ratios for older age blocks. Morbidity studies by their nature are more accurate because the effect of duration can be more easily built into the results.

Elimination Period— Similar to several of the other variable elements, studies by elimination period are important because premiums vary depending upon elimination period length. Changes in experience may occur at one elimination period and not at another, particularly dependent upon the characteristics of the group purchasing a particular elimination period. Short-term elimination periods, less than 30 days, were commonly sold until the mid 1970s for individual disability coverage. Experience on 7-day and 15-day elimination periods deteriorated through the 1970s, perhaps affected by two elements. I believe the first factor was the sharp increase in short-term group and employer salary continuation programs, which tended to cause overinsurance when coupled with individual contracts. Second, a change in the public work ethic through the late 1960s and 1970s may have adversely affected the short elimination period experience.

Benefit Period— Since rates vary by benefit period, experience must be studied for each separate period. Large volumes of long-benefit coverage, to age 65 and lifetime, have been sold only in recent years. Consequently, reliable data over extended periods of time is still scarce but growing rapidly with each passing year. However, no company has accumulated enough to-age-65 sickness experience on large blocks of business in the mid and upper ages to determine what impact the election of early retirement may have on rate assumptions.

Indemnity— Does experience vary based upon the amount of monthly indemnity available under the contract? Prior to the past 10 years there was little statistical evidence that the level of indemnity affected morbidity. However, in recent years some studies have shown that the larger the indemnity, the poorer the experience. This trend must be watched closely.

Income— The income of the insured is closely related to the previous item, indemnity, but it may also be a measure of the stability of the insured in his/her occupation. What is the relationship of indemnity to income; i.e., the replacement ratio? The Society of Actuaries study on long-term disability indicates that higher morbidity may be expected as the replacement ratio increases. Is there a different pattern of such morbidity based upon the income of the insured? The answer to this question would be particularly valuable to the industry, but data does not exist in volumes large enough to be credible.

Geographic— Does morbidity or claims experience vary depending upon geographic area? There is some indication that the densely populated areas may provide somewhat higher morbidity than less-populated areas. Although there have been a few attempts at setting rates based upon geographic area, such attempts have been based upon sparse data and competitively have proven quite difficult.

Agent and Agency— Experience studies by agency and agent represent particularly valuable information indicating the quality of field selection of the producer. The size of the cell under study is usually so small that the reliability of the data must be questioned, but an agent or agency that produces a large volume of business over a period of time will generate enough experience for some conclusions to be drawn. To be able to identify those 10 percent of producers who present significant and serious field selection and quality problems is important, even if the remaining 90 percent may be inconclusive.

Sex— Since premiums differ by sex, separate studies should be conducted. Female morbidity studies have been conducted in recent years, particularly the New York study. Higher morbidity does exist for women and can be demonstrated at least up until the mid-50 age grouping. As women become a more stable part of the work force and move into positions of greater responsibility and income, there may be some improvement in their morbidity that is normally associated with higher-income risks.

Mode— Mode of premium payment is one of those other variable factors that may be of interest in claims analysis. Large-company experience tends to indicate that the annual premium payment mode generates more favorable experience than any other mode. Conversely, the quarterly mode presents the least favorable. The mode chosen probably is a reflection of the stability of the buyer, since the higher-income, more stable risk tends to purchase the longer mode.

There are several other parameters that might be examined if data is large enough and reliable; however, the above represent by far the most important and the most common.

Combination of Parameters

One other factor is particularly important in this discussion, and that is the combination of various parameters in examining morbidity or claims experience. Accurate information by occupation class, elimination period, benefit period, age, and duration is indeed valuable to the disability analyst. However, the value is greatly enhanced if one can study the experience by one cell as it is affected by variations in other cells. For example: How does benefit period experience vary by elimination period? How does occupation class experience vary by age? How does indemnity experience vary by income? The natural problem is that this further breakdown results in even smaller cells to study with less credible data.

The reader should be impressed by the fact that there is a large variety of areas in which useful information is desirable in the analysis of disability experience. The need for great volumes of data in order to make such studies reliable is a serious problem at the present time that will continue into the indefinite future. Such shortfalls in data, however, should not deter the analyst from making an attempt to examine results, always recognizing the limitations of small data and the importance of relying on experience and judgment in the final analysis.

PERSISTENCY STUDIES

The examination and analysis of persistency in disability experience is as important as studying claims experience. It suffers from some of the same weaknesses as does claim experience for lack of large data bases. On the other hand, persistency trends emerge early in a contract's life, and therefore more definitive conclusions can be drawn. The same list of parameters that was mentioned above for claim studies is also important for persistency examination. Persistency does vary by occupation class, occupation, elimination period, benefit period, age, and duration. It is clearly a reflection of the buyer.

There does seem to be some close relationship between persistency and claims experience. Those blocks of business that generate poor persistency generally result in poorer claims experience. This should be no surprise to the analyst, since the critical importance of stability and motivation of the insured are factors that affect both persistency and morbidity. The less stable risk is more apt to lapse, and the less stable risk is more apt to claim.

Some companies have begun to introduce a stability or persistency rater in measuring an applicant prior to issue. It is in many ways an outgrowth of the stability rater used by some companies in life insurance. Because of its close correlation to claims experience, it may have even more value for disability income. To evaluate and rate for persistency based upon length of employment, occupation class, income, marital status, and mode of premium payment may prove to be a reliable under-writing tool. The use of such stability raters is uncommon at the present time and still relatively unscientific. However, the importance of stability and motivation in disability experience makes this route a logical one to examine and pursue.

The disability actuary knows well the importance of persistency in the rate structure. The impact of heavy front-end acquisition expense requires a policy to be in force for several years before the company begins to generate a return on its investment. In such a circumstance the premium is significantly affected by persistency. High lapse rates in excess of 30 percent during the first year may make it almost impossible for the actuary to construct a premium that will meet the minimal loss ratio requirements in some state jurisdictions. Attempts to analyze and then improve upon persistency are well worth the effort. Finding ways to identify the poor-persistency characteristics at underwriting time and if possible to make adjustments that will improve persistency are impor-tant problems for further industry study.

ROLES OF ACTUARIAL, UNDERWRITING, AND CLAIMS

The evaluation of disability results is not solely an actuarial func-tion. In life insurance such studies are almost exclusively perceived to be actuarial responsibilities. Indeed, the more objective characteristics of life insurance cause this to be the most logical approach. The subjectiv-ity of disability income and the scarcity of reliable data require that the underwriter and the claims examiner both assume a role in the evaluation of results.

The purely statistical evaluation of morbidity in claims experience is an actuarial one, but the analysis of these studies requires input from underwriters and claim examiners as well. Both professions, who on a day-to-day basis are in a position to observe and sense trends over an extended period of time, are a valuable resource in quantifying the importance of various studies. Changes in underwriting rules may have affected the experience of a particular cell, and this knowledge is critical in forming conclusions. The claim examiner may be able to observe certain characteristics or problems with particular contract forms or clauses within a contract early in its life, and this information is a necessary part of any conclusions.

In addition to the importance of underwriter and claims examiner analysis of specific morbidity and experience studies is the more subjective ongoing analysis that both disciplines can and must contribute. Since the business of disability income is one of deferred rewards and deferred penalties, the underwriter and claims examiner may be able to observe trends that will not be evident in claims analysis for some time. An environment must exist, therefore, where these two disciplines are encouraged to make such subjective analysis on an ongoing basis and communicate them to each other and to the actuary.

Most results of such analyses will be in the nature of pointing out areas to observe for possible problems, rather than listing definitive conclusions and action to be taken. If the proper environment exists, serious trends may surface early enough so that minor adjustments may be made to correct the problems. The following are examples of problems that might surface: the agent who is doing a poor job of field underwriting, geographic problems that may be a reflection of socioeconomic trends, changes in the behavior and characteristics of occupational groupings. It is important for the underwriter and claim examiner to understand that they have roles to play in this evaluation of results, and the actuary must understand that their input is valuable.

IMPAIRED-RISK EXPERIENCE

One other grouping of variable factors that must be studied in order to draw accurate conclusions on one's disability portfolio is in the area of impaired risks. In life insurance some 3 to 5 percent of all applicants are approved other than standard. In disability income the percentage frequently runs in excess of 20 percent. Where such a large percentage of a company's block of premium is concentrated on impaired risks, it is important that this cell be studied by itself.

The same problems exist for studying impaired risk as for examining the other cells or parameters already discussed. The scarcity of data becomes a particular problem as one attempts to break the impaired-risk group into smaller, specific impairment cells. The problem of reliably determining the loss ratio or morbidity experience for several hundred possible impairments is obvious. Furthermore, within each impairment there is a variety of possible underwriting actions from full-exclusion endorsement, to limited-exclusion endorsements, to extra premiums, to a combination of both, to a combination of exclusion endorsements, extra premiums, and a change in policy benefits.

The more common impairments, such as low-back problems, mental and nervous disorders, obesity, and hypertension, can be studied with some reliability by the larger companies. In addition, companies can group impairments into various "physical system" studies and identify some general areas where attention may be necessary. Making experience studies on all risks who were substandard because of digestive-system problems, or urinary problems, or nervous-system problems is an initial method of analysis. If one particular area stands out as generating poorer experience than the total, then specific action can be directed at the types of impairments found in this one system.

The underwriter must play a major role in such analysis, along with the claim examiner and the actuary. It is important for the company in building its data base not only to record the type of underwriting action taken on substandard risks, but also to record those cases in which an impairment history existed, but the underwriter for whatever reason decided to approve on a standard basis. The experience on this particular cell is as important as that on risks who were approved on a highly impaired basis.

Here again is an area where the reinsurer should be able to provide more reliable information than should any individual company. Since the reinsurer specializes in handling the more complex risk and is more frequently asked to participate in insuring such risks, it should develop such a data base more quickly.

The evaluation of results in disability income insurance is done by using proven technical and analytical disciplines combined with the subjective input of experienced professionals in the business. A product line that carries with it substantial volatility demands regular and ongoing analysis and decisions based upon that analysis. More often than not, the decision is based upon a significant degree of subjectivity, but this should not deter the experienced disability manager and professional from making decisions. Not to make the decision may result in growing adverse experience or an increased competitive problem. The decision maker must be careful not to overreact based upon short-term data in either the liberal or conservative direction, although he or she must recognize that the pressures at times will be great. The fine tuning of underwriting limits and requirements and even of claim handling are critical and important steps for the successful company to consider and implement between major rate revisions. Finally, the close cooperation and interdependence of the actuary, the underwriter, and the claims examiner must be understood and recognized in any successful attempt at evaluating experience results.

Reinsurance

19

The function of reinsurance is to provide a facility to pass on a part of the claim risk to one or more other companies. It is most obviously used in a situation where the amount at risk on a particular policyholder is unusually high in relationship to the average amount at risk. A life insurance company whose average face amount is $100,000 may wish to reinsure a significant portion of all applicants for face amounts of $500,000 or more. Anyone familiar with the life insurance business recognizes that the point at which a company reinsures some portion of a policy depends upon both the size of the company and the face amount at risk. The small company may wish to reinsure for face amounts in excess of $100,000, and the large company may believe it can stand the risk of all claims up to $1 million.

A similar need for reinsurance exists in disability income. It is not infrequent for the company to have a potential liability for one long-term disability claim in excess of $2 million, and in some instances more than $5 million. Even though the claim payment is not made in a lump sum as it is in life insurance, the liability must be recognized by setting up substantial reserves. It is this potential for very large claim reserves that is a primary stimulus for disability income reinsurance.

REINSURANCE HISTORY

Prior to the 1960s, very little disability reinsurance existed in the United States since the indemnity amounts and the length of benefit periods did not involve large potential claim liabilities. For example, the most common maximum long-term indemnity in 1960 was $400 per month of to-age-65 coverage. The maximum liability for any one claim under such a contract rarely exceeded $100,000, and the claim reserve required to support such a potential claim payout was much less than $100,000 for any one claim. Most companies were therefore comfortable in retaining all of the disability income risk. The acceptable system of issue and participation limits by its nature avoided the need for reinsurance. Although the typical issue limit was $400 per month of to-age-65 coverage in any one company, most companies would participate up to $1,000 per month when coverage with other companies was included. This method of spreading the risk through issue and participation limits avoided the need for reinsurance.

As already described in Chapter 1, there was tremendous growth in issue and participation limits during the 1970s and 1980s. The primary factor that caused the indemnity levels to grow to current levels of $10,000 per month was an increased competitive environment, particularly in the professional and white-collar occupation groups. In the early and mid 1960s, companies began to ask this question: If we're willing to participate to $1,000 per month, why not write it all in our company and reinsure the excess? As the demand for reinsurance for disability income grew, reinsurance facilities in the United States grew to meet the challenge. Traditional life reinsurers were the early entrants into the marketplace—The Lincoln National Life Insurance Company, the Connecticut General Life Insurance Company, and the North American Reassurance Company. Early in the 1970s, The Paul Revere Life Insurance Company entered the reinsurance marketplace.

As issue limits grew steadily during the 1960s and 1970s, almost all disability income insurers took steps to establish a reinsurance treaty. Even the largest writers of disability income recognized that there was a clear need to consider spreading the risk when the potential claim liability for any one claim reached amounts well in excess of $1 million.

OTHER REASONS FOR REINSURANCE

In addition to the protection provided by the reinsurer in the case of unusually large claim loss, disability reinsurance served other purposes, as does life reinsurance. The large front-end strain caused by heavy acquisition expense causes substantial statutory strain on surplus. Reinsurance offers a method of spreading this strain to the reinsurer so that a company does not have to be as concerned about rapid growth. A second purpose of disability reinsurance, again similar to life insurance, is the technical support and training that is available. The underwriting of disability income requires different skills than underwriting life insurance, and indeed the subjective nature of the product complicates the underwriting process. Reinsurers therefore provide a necessary facility in helping client companies establish underwriting rules and requirements and providing them a medical underwriting manual. The reinsurer also provides advice to its clients on highly substandard disability income cases, similar to the same type of facility offered in life reinsurance. It is probably true that the disability reinsurer is called upon to provide more information and training in the underwriting area than is true in life insurance because most companies lack experience in the underwriting of disability insurance.

The disability reinsurer is called upon to provide other assistance to its client companies. The major role of the claim function in disability insurance naturally makes the claim function of greater importance in disability reinsurance than is the case in life insurance. The importance of claim investigation, evaluation, and technique are all areas in which the reinsurer can and should provide necessary training to its client companies. In addition, and similar to life reinsurance functions, the disability reinsurer is expected to provide consulting facilities for actuarial questions, product development, and market analysis.

The disability reinsurer, therefore, provides two basic functions: protection and education. The education function tends to be a larger one in disability reinsurance, simply because there is a scarcity of written information, reliable data, and general experience and knowledge. In the life reinsurance environment, there tends to be a hesitancy on the part of the reinsurer to impose its own philosophies and requirements rigidly upon its client companies, and most client companies tend to resist such interference. The typical life company is generally confident regarding its own philosophy of operation and its ability to manage its product line profitably. It looks to the reinsurer primarily for the protection element and for help in the more complex substandard risks. The medium- and small-size disability insurers are much less confident of their philosophy and of their ability to manage the product line profitably. Consequently, they tend to lean more on their reinsurer for basic guidance and direction.

The life insurer bases selection of a reinsurance treaty on an evaluation of the cost, service, and competitiveness of the reinsurer's impaired-risk underwriting. The cost is frequently the primary consideration. In disability reinsurance these three elements are also important in the evaluation, but the ability of the reinsurer to evaluate results, determine market trends, and give advice on future direction plays a much larger role. These elements are naturally more subjective, as is the product line itself; but the typical client company must feel secure about the reinsurer's ability to help manage the product line to achieve the long-term profit objective. Therefore, the cost is frequently of secondary importance.

There is another significant difference between life and disability reinsurance treaties. The typical life treaty establishes a face amount beyond which some portion of the face amount is reinsured. This face amount is usually lower for impaired risks than for standard risks. In disability reinsurance the ceding company tends to retain the same level of coverage regardless of whether the risk is standard or substandard.

AUTOMATIC AND FACULTATIVE

Both life and disability treaties normally provide both automatic and facultative arrangements in the treaty language. The automatic facility is simply the maximum amount that the ceding company can bind the reinsurer for coverage without the reinsurer individually underwriting and evaluating the risk. The facultative capability represents the circumstance in which the reinsurer itself wishes to make some evaluation of the risk before agreeing to assume it. Naturally, the point at which the ceding company elects to reinsure varies according to a company's size. For example, a small company may wish to reinsure fully any long-term indemnities over $500 per month, while retaining the first $500. The reinsurer then may agree to accept the ceding company's underwriting on all cases up to $1,000 (the automatic limit) but become involved in the underwriting process over the $1,000 point (the facultative area). A larger disability income company may retain $2,500 per month of long-term coverage, have an automatic limit of $4,000 per month, and then have facultative coverage beyond this point.

Many life reinsurers will agree to accept the entire risk on highly substandard cases in which the ceding company does not wish to participate. This is not a common arrangement in disability insurance since the disability reinsurer normally wishes to have the ceding company participate to some extent on all risks. Most disability reinsurers expect client companies to insure a minimum of 20 percent of the indemnity at risk.

In life reinsurance the key variables in the reinsurance treaty are face amount and the degree of substandard underwriting. In disability income the variables are the monthly indemnity amount, the length of the benefit period, and frequently the occupation class. In life insurance the face amount alone determines the amount at risk, whereas in disability insurance it is a combination of the monthly indemnity and the length of the benefit period. The greater volatility of the lower-occupation classes to changes in the economic cycle is the primary reason some treaties establish lower retention amounts for the lower-occupation classes.

SPECIFIC TREATIES AND
THEIR CHARACTERISTICS

The specific types of treaty arrangements available in disability reinsurance are similar to those in life insurance. However, there are some variations resulting from the difference in the nature of the risk to be insured.

Coinsurance

In the coinsurance treaty both the ceding company and the reinsurer share not only the morbidity risk, but also the expense and investment risk. The premium is split in proportion to the indemnity risk assumed by each party—50 percent if each party insures half of the indemnity or a one third/two thirds split if one party holds one third of the indemnity and the other holds two thirds. The reinsurer returns to the ceding company some agreed-upon portion of its premium to cover the acquisition expense incurred by the ceding company. Each company establishes active life reserves based upon its proportion of the premium and accumulates interest on these reserves according to its own investment experience and philosophy. Similarly, each company establishes claims reserves based upon its percentage of the indemnity under claim, and the reinsurer reimburses the client company, usually monthly, for its share in the cash claims during that month.

The coinsurance treaty not only provides claim protection, but also, as stated above, assumes a portion of the initial acquisition strain and the strain of establishing the active life reserve. The small company experiencing rapid growth has a clear need for easing the drain on surplus caused by acquisition strain as well as claim protection. One important element of the coinsurance treaty is that the reinsurer assumes the rates of the ceding company, rather than charging a separate rate for its portion of the coverage.

Term Insurance

The term reinsurance treaty has characteristics similar to term life insurance. It is pure insurance in the sense that the reinsurer charges a set premium per $100 of indemnity to cover the claim risk during a particular year, plus an additional amount representing the reinsurer's administrative expenses. The term treaty premium on a particular case increases each year as the insured's age increases and the morbidity risk becomes greater. The term premium is usually calculated to reflect very low anticipated morbidity in the early years of a policy where underwriting selection tends to keep the morbidity at a lower than ultimate level. It does not provide protection for acquisition strain, but it does provide full protection for claim loss according to the indemnity amount reinsured. The reinsurer establishes a claim reserve for each claimant based upon the amount of indemnity and the length of the disability. Since morbidity experience is so volatile in disability insurance, and since the amount of the claim reserve can reach levels in excess of $1 million and $2 million on a single disabled life, many disability insurers prefer this type of treaty to coinsurance. It clearly isolates the claim risk from expense and investment risks and allows the ceding company to manage and control its investment of the entire active life reserve.

For medium- and certainly for larger-size companies, this type of treaty arrangement allows greater control as long as their surplus is such that they can absorb the strain of acquisition expense. It provides more flexibility for the ceding company to recapture some portion of its reinsurance at a later date, since the reinsurer's premium only covers the risk for a given period of time. In coinsurance, on the other hand, any attempt at recapture must also focus on the value of the active life reserve being held for future claims, and recapturing this reserve frequently proves difficult.

Extended Elimination Period

There are several modifications of both the coinsurance and term treaty that are available with most reinsurers. The Extended Elimination Period Treaty is one of these that is most often available on term treaties. Since the claim cost as reflected in the growth of the claim reserve increases sharply as the length of disability increases, some companies prefer to defer the point at which the reinsurer becomes involved for a longer period of time than the elimination period on the contract itself. For example, the company may desire a treaty arrangement where the reinsurer does not participate in any claim until the insured has been disabled for six months or even one year. During the first six months or one year, the ceding company is responsible for all claim payments, but beyond this point the reinsurer is responsible for a specified proportion. Even though the reinsurer is not responsible for cash claim payments until the six-month or one-year point, it must be aware as soon as is the client company of the existence of the claim so that it can begin to establish its own claim reserve based upon the probability of the claim continuing beyond the six-month or one-year period. Since only a small percentage of total claims extend beyond six months or one year, there is a savings to both the ceding company and the reinsurer in avoiding the administrative cost of establishing two sets of records on every claim.

Excess Risk

The claimant with a $2,000-per-month indemnity and a five-year benefit period represents a potential total liability of $120,000 for any one claim. The claimant with a $2,000 indemnity and a to-age-65 benefit period at age 35 represents a potential liability of $720,000. Many disability insurers are willing to accept the total risk with a five-year benefit period and would be willing to accept the first five years of claim liability for all policyholders regardless of the benefit period. The excess-risk treaty, therefore, provides a facility where the ceding company assumes all the risk for two, three, or five years, and at that point the reinsurer steps in and covers the remaining period of the disability. One difference between this treaty and extended-elimination period treaties is that under excess risk arrangements the reinsurer may assume all of the risk beyond the initial period that the ceding company covers.

Quota Share

The term *quota share* defines the nature of the indemnity split within the reinsurance treaty. In this arrangement, regardless of the indemnity amount on a particular case, the treaty language indicates that a specified percent is retained by the ceding company, and the remainder goes to the reinsurer—that is, 50–50 percent split, or 25–75 percent split, or 30–70 percent split. The same percentage distribution occurs regardless of whether the indemnity is $500 or $7,000 per month.

The more common method of sharing the risk is the one previously described, in which the ceding company always retains a specified indemnity level, and the reinsurer assumes the entire indemnity amount above that point.

RECAPTURE

Most reinsurance treaties provide arrangements for the ceding company to recapture some portion of the indemnity it had previously reinsured. As the block of a company's disability insurance grows in premium, it can normally afford to assume a greater percentage of the risk and a greater percentage of the strain. Reinsurance arrangements normally provide for recapture on the anniversary date of the treaty and require notification of such recapture some period of time prior to the anniversary date. At the time of recapture a company normally establishes a new and higher retention level, but a new retention level can, of course, be established without recapturing any portion of policies already reinsured at a lower amount.

The act of recapturing does not involve the ceding company assuming a higher level of liability on any open claims. As has already been mentioned, the process of recapture is somewhat more complex for coinsurance treaties than for term treaties. This is because there is an active life reserve that must be reapportioned according to the new retention level in a coinsurance arrangement.

EXPERIENCE REFUNDS

Some reinsurance treaties contain language providing for a refund of the premium depending upon the morbidity experience on the ceding company's business. Such experience refunds are calculated using a specified formula. Because of the nature of the disability business being one of deferred rewards and deferred penalties, experience refunds are normally not provided until a block of business has been in force for a minimum of two to five years. Its purpose is to reward the ceding company for the quality of its business when its experience is more favorable than the morbidity calculated in the reinsurance rate.

REINSURANCE SERVICES

The quality and timeliness of service is as important in disability reinsurance as in life reinsurance. The ceding company demands and deserves consistency in the various elements of service from the reinsurer, and the competitive nature of the disability business requires that the selection process not be unduly delayed by the reinsurer. In addition to the underwriting and selection service, there are a variety of other services provided by disability reinsurers.

Market Analysis

The nature of the disability product and the nature of the underwriting rules and requirements vary according to the market in which a company operates. A company operating primarily in the blue-collar or skilled-trades markets requires a different product than one specializing in the medical professions. Although it is very fundamental to emphasize that a company must "know its market" before it begins to design its product, market analysis is frequently given too little attention. Often a company listens to a minority of its field force engaged in a competitive market and reacts to such pressure out of proportion to the premium generated. It is only the very large companies that can offer a broad portfolio competitive in all markets. The moderate- and small-size companies must determine where their markets are and where they wish to stress their competitive posture.

Product Development

Although reinsurers do not "develop" the product for their client companies, they must fill an active role of giving advice and counsel in a volatile and competitive activity. No two disability income contracts are identical, and there continue to exist great opportunities for innovation. After determining where its markets are, a company must address what opportunities exist in product development to meet the particular needs of the consumer. Some product ideas will prove too risky in some markets, and all product ideas must receive the careful scrutiny of accurate language drafting. The reinsurer can fill an important role as a consultant in all of these areas.

Pricing

Reinsurers do not normally develop rates for client companies, but they will provide consulting support for the analysis of rates and the assumptions underlying the rates. Those companies who lack experienced disability income actuaries can call upon the services of several independent actuarial firms for rate development.

Underwriting Support

Reinsurers provide extensive underwriting training and support for client companies. In addition to providing a medical underwriting guidebook, the reinsurer offers its services in establishing underwriting rules, limits, and procedures. The experienced reinsurer will have an established underwriting training program for client companies that will be based on a sound depth of experience and provide specific case examples in the training process.

Claims Support

The importance of the claims function in disability income has already been emphasized, and the ceding company must be able to look to its reinsurer to provide guidance and counsel—which includes training of claim examiners, establishing claim rules and procedures, help in the design of forms, and advice on specific claim problems as they occur.

Evaluation

In a volatile product line the reinsurer's responsibility does not end when the claim is paid. It must include an analysis of the experience of the particular client company as well as an analysis of general industry trends. In order to protect the investments of both the client company and itself, the reinsurer must continually inform client companies of trends, rather than reacting only when circumstances dictate.

Disability income morbidity is significantly affected by field selection, and the reinsurer must always keep this fact in mind when evaluating a client company. The skill and quality of field selection will vary from company to company and will require that underwriting rules and procedures, and perhaps even rates, be adjusted as experience dictates.

FUTURE TRENDS AND SUPPORT

The volatile nature of the disability business places a significant responsibility on reinsurers. Their role in guiding client companies, helping to establish underwriting rules and limits, giving advice on product language, and making judgments concerning future industry trends places them in a position where the future success of a block of business depends significantly on them. Reinsurers must understand the sharp cyclical nature of the disability business, and they must resist the strong temptation to overreact at the cyclical valley or the cyclical peak of experience. Client companies, because of the scarcity of data and experience in disability income, depend more upon the reinsurer than is true in life insurance and should expect sound advice and guidance in addition to the basic element of protection provided in all reinsurance treaties.

Governmental
Disability Programs

20

The development of various social programs in the United States is most often traced back to the mid 1930s and the passage of Social Security legislation in 1935. The enactment of that first program provided only old-age and survivor's benefits. Since then, Social Security has been periodically enhanced and expanded into other areas, including medical care and disability insurance. The development of such social programs in the United States parallels similar developments throughout the Western world. Great Britain, Germany, France, and other Western nations all have developed extensive social programs during the past five decades to provide benefits for retirement and medical care and, in some instances, disability income. The nature of the programs differs from one country to another, some being more extensive than others. However, in all instances, retirement and medical care programs tend to take precedence over disability programs. The one exception to this is in the area of government disability programs that provide disability benefits for employees who are disabled because of on-the-job accidents or illnesses.

The emergence of Social Security retirement and old-age benefits in the 1930s significantly affected the life insurance industry. Although some industry observers at the time believed that the future growth of the life insurance industry would be severely impaired, the opposite result occurred. Greater public awareness and acceptance of the need for life insurance generated greater life insurance growth during the four decades following the 1930s than anyone at that time could have imagined.

Broad public awareness and acceptance of the need for full disability income protection lagged significantly behind the public's attitude toward both life insurance and medical care coverages. The substantial growth of disability income in the 1960s and 1970s, however, followed closely the 1956 legislation that initially added disability coverage to the Social Security program. It appears that in both life insurance and disability insurance the introduction of governmental social programs caused increased public awareness and acceptance, which resulted in increased growth in the private insurance industry. It is, therefore, somewhat ironic that in 1935 the life insurance industry and in 1956 the disability insurance industry expressed great apprehension over governmental encroachment of their markets.

WORKERS' COMPENSATION

Workers' Compensation coverage was the first broad-based governmental disability program enacted in the United States. Workers' Compensation programs represent 51 separate programs, 50 of which are controlled by state governments and 1 controlled by the District of Columbia. The programs differ significantly from one state jurisdiction to another, both in the level of benefits payable and the administrative rules governing payment. The growth and influence of the labor union movement in the early 20th century culminated in broad acceptance of Workers' Compensation benefits in the 1930s.

Logically, the more highly developed industrial states were the first to enact such legislation, and those less industrialized jurisdictions were the last to pass legislation. There is a tendency for the more industrialized states to provide more liberal benefits.

Provisions

Paralleling the substantial growth of Social Security disability benefits during the late 1960s and the 1970s, Workers' Compensation benefits were substantially increased during the same period. However, even today there continues to be a substantial difference in the level of Workers' Compensation benefits from one state jurisdiction to another. The more liberal programs provide up to two thirds of a worker's predisability income, but every program has some sort of a maximum benefit payment cap. All programs are designed to primarily cover the needs of the lower-middle- and lower-income working class and are not designed to fully cover the needs of the upper-middle- and high-income earners. The length of benefit payments has gradually been liberalized over the past several decades and is, in most cases, coordinated with Social Security disability benefits, so that the two programs do not pay simultaneously.

The Social Security program is the primary payor, so that Workers' Compensation benefits generally cease when an individual is accepted for Social Security disability benefits.

One of the areas of greatest difference from one state program to another is in the amount of increased benefits based upon the number of dependents. In some jurisdictions the basic benefits are increased by a specific percentage for each dependent. In others each dependent results in an increase of the benefit payment by a flat dollar amount, and this dollar amount varies widely from state to state. In most instances the level of benefits is adjusted substantially, based upon the number of dependents of the disabled individual.

Factors Affecting Workers' Compensation

Similar to private disability insurance experience, Workers' Compensation benefit payments are impacted by subjective factors, even though disability payments are payable on the more objective on-the-job illness or accident. Workers' Compensation statistics indicate an increase in claim activity during recessions and, conversely, much improved experience during periods of low unemployment. Similar to the circumstances in private disability experience, both the frequency and length of Workers' Compensation payments are affected by the economic cycle.

A second subjective factor that has become of increasing importance during the past several years is the increasing public awareness of the availability of Workers' Compensation benefits. In addition, there is increased awareness and knowledge of the circumstances that may qualify a person for benefit payments. These factors, along with the increased "entitlement ethic," have had the same adverse impact upon Workers' Compensation benefit payments as on the private sector.

Coordinating Benefits

With the substantial growth in the percentage of income covered under Workers' Compensation benefits, private insurers during the 1970s began to recognize that they could no longer ignore such potential benefit payments in their own underwriting process. To do so would cause overinsurance when Workers' Compensation benefits were payable along with private disability benefits. Naturally, this duplication of payments carried with it the inevitable increase in morbidity as it became more profitable for the claimant to remain disabled rather than return to work. Since Workers' Compensation only pays benefits for on-the-job accidents or illnesses, it was not possible for the private insurer to simply subtract the potential amount of benefits coming from this government program from what the insurer would normally approve for an applicant. To have done so would have resulted in an underinsurance circumstance when the individual suffered a nonoccupational disability. Many companies, therefore, developed either special contracts or special amendments to contracts that guaranteed to pay the indemnity when Workers' Compensation benefits were not payable. Such contracts or amendments are frequently referred to as nonoccupation coverage since they are designed and priced to pay benefits for accidents and illnesses that occur away from the insured's occupation, leaving the on-the-job accident to be covered by Workers' Compensation. These nonoccupational coverages are frequently the only type of private insurance available in the lower-occupation classes in which earned incomes are less than $15,000 per year.

Although there continue to be substantial differences from one state jurisdiction to another in the level of benefits payable for Workers' Compensation disabilities, the wide differences that existed two and three decades ago have tended to narrow as our entire country has become more industrialized.

SOCIAL SECURITY DISABILITY PROGRAM

With the passage of the 1956 legislation that first added disability income benefits to the Social Security program came marked changes upon the private insurance sector. Similar to the intent of the initial Social Security retirement and old-age legislation, Social Security disability benefits were intended to be only a "floor of coverage." As the years passed, this proved not to be the case as far as Social Security disability benefits were concerned. The initial 1956 legislation provided disability coverage for only those disabilities that occurred over age 50, lasted more than 12 months, and were expected to be total and permanent. The level of benefits was modest, and individual insurers of disability income essentially ignored potential benefits from this source in their underwriting limits. Then in the 1960s, the program was expanded to cover all Social Security covered workers, regardless of age, and the period at which benefits could become payable was reduced from one year to six months. Later on in the 1960s and continuing at a more rapid rate throughout the 1970s, Congress passed a series of bills that increased the level of benefit payments under the Social Security program, including disability income. With such an expansion of government benefits, it was no longer possible for private insurers to ignore the potential benefit payments from Social Security disability because of the dangers of overinsurance.

Definition of Disability

The definition of disability under Social Security has been changed slightly since its inception in 1956. The current definition provides for disability benefits to commence after five months of disability if it can be presumed that the disability either will last more than 12 months or will end in death. At the one-year point the requirement that the disability be permanent is no longer applicable. As long as the disability is total and the claimant is unable to engage in another occupation, benefits are normally payable. It is in this area of whether or not the claimant can engage in another occupation that the greatest differences exist between Social Security disability and private insurance programs. Private insurers, under their definition of total disability, usually require that the claimant be unable to engage in any occupation for which he or she was reasonably fitted by education, training, experience, and prior economic status. This definition tends to be somewhat more liberal in granting disability benefits than is Social Security, which essentially requires that the claimant be unable to engage in "any occupation."

Program Characteristics

It should be remembered that the Social Security program has two important characteristics that are fundamental with most government programs: (1) It is a social program primarily designed for the lower- or lower-middle-income worker, and (2) in its administration, its rules and its guidelines are designed in this direction. The determination of disability is frequently based upon a grid of three factors: age, nature of disability, and the skilled nature of one's occupation. Two individuals with the same physical disability may be treated differently as far as their eligibility for benefits, based upon their age or the nature of their occupations. Two people with the same impairment and the same occupation may be treated differently depending upon their age. The grid approach is an attempt to remove some of the subjectivity from claim determination. In doing so, however, it will in some instances provide disability benefits for an individual who is able to work at some other occupation or even in his or her own occupation.

The second fundamental factor where Social Security disability differs from private programs is in its size. The number of insureds represents the major portion of the entire American working force, and the number of claimants at any one time is in the tens of millions. There are consequently enormous administrative problems associated with managing a program of this size. Such a problem is aggravated in a benefit environment where subjectivity is an essential characteristic of disability and ideally requires individual attention to evaluate accurately each individual case. This latter factor has caused substantial problems, pressures, and public misunderstanding with the disability program in recent years.

Expansion of Benefits

The greatest expansion of Social Security disability benefits occurred as a result of congressional legislation in 1972 that introduced automatic annual increases in benefits based upon inflationary factors. This 1972 indexing was designed with the retirement program in mind and, once implemented, was found to be inaccurate for disability income benefits. The result was that the indexing formula when used for disability income benefits caused an increase in benefits close to two times the rate of inflation. Thus throughout the remainder of the 1970s, disability benefits escalated rapidly, causing substantial overinsurance problems within the system itself, greater overinsurance problems when coupled with private insurance coverage, and a general increase in morbidity trends. This situation was severely aggravated by the fact that it occurred during the deep recession of the mid 1970s, the deepest recession since the 1930s.

Social Security disability benefits increased so rapidly during this period that the private sector found that the market for risks with incomes less than $15,000 had essentially disappeared by 1978. In some instances, not only were younger risks with incomes less than $15,000 eligible for more in Social Security disability benefits than their net take-home pay before disability, but these benefits occasionally exceeded gross income. The Social Security formula was constructed in such a way that the younger claimant received more benefits than the older claimant, since the older risk had all of his or her prior low or average yearly earnings added into the calculation of benefits. This was another inequity that became particularly evident in the disability program.

The serious indexing problem with Social Security was finally corrected by legislation in late 1977 that removed the previous error in the 1972 law and treated the growth in disability benefits similarly to what was originally intended. However, since that time benefits have continued to increase, although at a slower pace. Congressional changes in the Social Security law in 1983 had little effect on the level of disability benefits.

Social Security experience during the mid and late 1970s confirmed claim trends that the private sector had worked with for years. As the replacement ratio increased, morbidity increased. As unemployment increased, morbidity increased. As a recession became deeper, morbidity increased further. As the public became more aware of the availability of benefits, morbidity increased. All of these factors came to play to one degree or another during the recession of the mid 70s and placed tremendous strains upon the Social Security disability income trust fund. Indeed, without the changes in Social Security legislation in 1977, the disability income trust fund would have been exhausted.

Subsequent modifications to the disability program were made in the early 1980s and brought the replacement ratios under the disability program more in line with objectives to prevent overinsurance. This legislation also helped to remove the inequities that existed between benefits payable to younger versus older claimants. Although there are still some desirable corrections that should be made within the disability program, it is clearly much sounder today than prior to 1977. The Social Security Disability Trust Fund must be kept strong in order to meet long-term and deferred obligations. Unfortunately, legislators with little understanding of this need seize upon a growing Fund as a reason to politically liberalize benefits for their constituents. The result in the past has always been the subsequent need to increase taxes to strengthen the Fund.

State Responsibility

Although Social Security is a federal program, it is administered by the various state jurisdictions. The initial review and determination of claim is made at the state level and by state employees. As a result of this diffusion of responsibility, there have tended to be significant differences from one state jurisdiction to another in the administrative process. Because of the subjective nature of disability, even with the attempt to more objectly set Social Security guidelines, there is still substantial room for interpretation and difference from one jurisdiction to another. That the monies expended are federal but the employees administering the program are state employees naturally removes important controls and safeguards.

Administrative Changes

In recent years because of the substantial difference in administration and because of substantial claim problems in the 1970s, the Social Security administration has attempted to implement tighter administrative rules, more audits, and generally greater control. By the early 1980s these administrative steps appeared to be having some impact, since the number of Social Security disability awards and the total dollars expended had reversed their previous steep increase trend.

The enormous size of the Social Security program must be understood and accepted as a major problem in efficiently managing the system in a manner comparable with the private sector. When one accepts this and also recognizes that the program is administered by an entirely separate governmental unit, one can begin to understand the risks, the dangers, and the problems within the Social Security disability income program.

Coordinating Benefits

Similar to Workers' Compensation benefits, the Social Security program provides additional monthly payments to the dependents of disabled workers up to a maximum dollar figure. These dependency benefits are payable only if the child is under age 18 and cease when the child reaches that age.

As the Social Security disability program grew in size, scope, and level of benefits in the late 1960s, private insurers began to include the potential Social Security disability payments in their issue limits. Group disability insurers were able to provide coordination of benefits language within their contracts that directly offset dollar-for-dollar the actual Social Security payments. Several state jurisdictions prevent such coordination in individual disability programs, and as a result, individual insurers have attempted to develop other techniques.

Subtracting potential Social Security benefits from normal issue limits is one such technique, but it has several drawbacks. The person who would normally be eligible for $2,000 per month of individual disability coverage might have this amount reduced by $750 if the insurer concluded that $750 is the amount the individual might expect to receive from Social Security because of a disability. One problem with such an arrangement is that the Social Security benefit amount is not fixed. It varies depending upon the number of dependents. It will increase with inflation. It varies as the insured's income grows. Therefore, there is no specific figure that the underwriter can determine at underwriting time that accurately reflects the future potential benefits for the applicant. In addition, even if such a figure were available, it has already been stated that Social Security may pay benefits that are not payable by private insurers and at other times may not make payments where the private insurer would.

In order to correct the inequities of simply reducing the normal issue limit to reflect Social Security, most individual insurers today attempt to solve the problem by adding an additional benefit to their basic disability contract. This benefit operates similarly to the nonoccupational contract mentioned previously for Workers' Compensation. In the previous example of a $750 amount as the offset amount, an extra benefit for $750 would be added to the basic insurance policy. It would provide that if the claimant was not eligible for benefits under Social Security disability, then the company would pay an additional $750 as long as the individual was disabled or until Social Security commenced payments. This is still not as flexible as a dollar-for-dollar coordination of benefits, but it goes a long way toward solving the problem. No insurer can safely ignore Social Security benefits today because of the gross overinsurance problem.

This overinsurance problem not only exists in incomes below $20,000, but as annual indexing increases the level of Social Security benefits, overinsurance may exist even at income levels of $50,000 and above. Underwriters must therefore consider Social Security in their issue limits as well as provide a Social Security offset rider that will pay when Social Security does not. The pricing of such an offset rider carries with it certain difficulties for the actuary since the eligibility for benefits will tend to vary and change with changes in legislation and administrative procedures. Such a change in Social Security direction, which came in the late 1970s and early 1980s, has already been mentioned. As a result of these changes, the actual insurance company payments under Social Security offset riders has increased since Social Security administration has become more strict.

STATE CASH SICKNESS BENEFITS

Five states have enacted legislation that provides disability benefits for its constituents in instances where Workers' Compensation does not pay. Those states are California, New York, New Jersey, Rhode Island, and Hawaii. Such benefits are normally coordinated with both Workers' Compensation and Social Security and, consequently, are paid for relatively short periods of time up to one year. However, most disability claims are of short duration, and most claims are nonoccupational; therefore those states that do provide such coverage represent significant additional disability benefits.

State-to-State Variations

As with Workers' Compensation, these benefits vary substantially from one state jurisdiction to another—California has the most liberal benefit payments. This liberal program in the state of California is probably one reason industry morbidity in this state tends to run higher than the rest of the country. Some companies pulled out of the state of California entirely during the late 1970s; others restricted their business substantially; and still others increased their rates in this state in contrast with the rest of the country.

There was substantial activity during the 1960s and early 1970s for other states to enact cash sickness legislation. Although many bills were filed in successive years in many states, no additional state has enacted cash sickness legislation since the state of Hawaii in 1969.

Like Workers' Compensation and Social Security, those five state cash sickness jurisdictions vary their benefits according to income and number of dependents. The elimination period is normally of short term, either first day or seventh day.

Private insurers tend to offset state cash sickness benefits in their issue limits. A few companies use contractual language to provide for extra benefits similar to those used to program around Workers' Compensation and Social Security. The contract language indicates that the company will pay an additional specified amount if the individual is not eligible for state cash sickness coverage.

The level of benefits in each of the five states is such that potential overinsurance cannot be ignored, and the existence of this coverage must be recognized in some way in the underwriting process.

NO-FAULT AUTO COVERAGE

The most recent governmental disability program is no-fault automobile insurance. Some of those states that have enacted no-fault automobile insurance provide disability coverage for disability resulting from an automobile accident. The level of these benefits and the length of payment varies considerably from one state jurisdiction to another, and they are not generally coordinated with other governmental coverages. They represent a true overinsurance problem. Fortunately, the frequency of automobile accident disability is a small portion of total disabilities, and most state jurisdictions do not provide such coverage.

Most insurers today ignore the potential of no-fault auto coverages in their underwriting rules. If such benefits become more widely enacted throughout the country and provide for increased amounts and durations, then insurers will logically need to address the overinsurance problem.

OTHER GOVERNMENTAL DISABILITY COVERAGES

The three other federal programs that provide disability benefits must be included in any discussion of this kind. They are the various pieces of special federal legislation providing disability benefits for members of the military and civil service employees and the Railroad Retirement Act. Each one represents a special and distinct occupational grouping, and until 1983 neither group was covered under the Social Security program for either retirement or disability.

The benefits available under all three programs generally involve unusually high replacement ratios and do not leave room for any significant amount of additional private disability coverage. In some instances, the programs have maximum income caps, which may allow private insurers to cover disability above this income cap or maximum. However, this amount represents a very small percentage of the total income covered under these programs. Consequently most companies will not insure any of these groups for individual disability income.

SUMMARY

The various governmental disability programs are broad based and to some extent cover every American worker. Private insurers today must consider the availability of such coverage during the underwriting process and in the drafting of contract language. The industry must be alert to further expansion of such programs and their further encroaching on the private sector's marketplace. At the same time, insurers must be quick to adjust underwriting rules and contract language as the various governmental programs are modified and changed.

Page 206 — Chapter 20

The Health Insurance Association of America has played a major role both in informing its membership of legislative and regulatory activity affecting disability income and in taking an active lobbying role in presenting the industry position before various regulatory and legislative groups. The HIAA has in the past and continues to have an important impact at both the state and federal levels, and the industry must support its continual monitoring of all of the governmental programs discussed in this chapter.

Group Disability
Benefits

21

HISTORY

Group disability benefits began to emerge in a limited way in the 1920s, after individual disability income contracts were quite well established. These group benefits had limited growth until the 1950s and experienced particularly rapid growth in the 1960s, 1970s, and 1980s. Similar to the stimulus in the growth of group medical care coverages, the labor union movement had a substantial impact upon both group weekly income and group LTD coverages. During the 1950s and 1960s disability coverage became a popular fringe benefit to add to employee benefit programs, and it quickly grew to insure more people than did individual contracts.

Another external development affected the growth of group disability benefits during the same period. This was the continued expansion of Workers' Compensation coverages and the emergence of disability benefits under the federal Social Security program and state cash sickness benefits in some states. The growth of such programs made the public and employers more aware of the gaps in their governmental programs, and they, consequently, sought to close these gaps with group coverage. In those states mandating cash sickness on nonoccupational coverages (New York, New Jersey, California, Rhode Island, and Hawaii), the laws and regulations usually allow an employer to meet the requirements of the law by purchasing private group insurance coverage. In Rhode

Island, however, all covered employees are within the state sponsored plan. Group insurers were naturally quick to offer such insurance consistent with the various state requirements as the legislation was passed.

Similar to the pattern of development in individual disability income, group disability coverages initially emerged as quite limited protection and then gradually expanded as insurers gained more confidence and expertise. Early coverages had very short benefit periods, usually 13 or 26 weeks, with quite modest weekly or monthly indemnities. Group short-term disability contracts are normally defined as those with benefit periods of 13, 26, or 52 weeks. Group long-term disability contracts have longer benefit periods, typically to retirement age, although some two- and five-year benefit periods are still written. The premium growth of both group short-term and group long-term disability programs over the past two decades has been very substantial, outpacing that of individual disability income. Table 21–1 will give the reader some appreciation of this growth. Without the efficiencies and economies that group disability programs offer to employers and employees, much of the population would be grossly underinsured for disability income. Group insurance coverages can be marketed profitably at relatively low cost in comparison with individual contracts; therefore, needed coverage can be provided to higher income risks as well as middle- and low-income risks. The expense of providing small indemnity contracts on an individual basis to such risks is increasingly prohibitive.

TABLE 21–1
Growth of Group Disability Coverages (number of persons with disability coverage, in thousands)

Year	Group policies	Individual policies
1946	7,135	8,684
1950	15,104	13,067
1955	19,171	13,642
1960	20,970	14,298
1965	24,273	14,587
1970	34,830	18,913
1975	40,133	21,894
1980	45,369	21,609
1984	42,045	13,954

Source: *1986–1987 Source Book of Health Insurance Data,* Health Insurance Association of America.

COMPARISON WITH INDIVIDUAL DISABILITY

There are areas of great difference but also areas of similarity between group and individual coverages and approaches. The group contract is generally somewhat more restrictive than the individual contract, and the premium can be adjusted annually on the entire group or the contract cancelled if the insurer so desires. This is in contrast to the individual non-cancellable disability contract, where the premium is guaranteed for the life of the contract, and the contract cannot be cancelled. The ability to adjust rates in the group contract has a very significant impact upon the premium cost since the insurer has the ability to change the rating to reflect experience as it emerges. Commission costs are significantly less generous in group insurance, approximately one quarter to one half the commission typically paid on an individual disability income policy.

The fundamental group insurance principle of the protection of large numbers of risks applying for similar coverage has the effect of limiting or eliminating antiselection, which is a primary concern in individual coverages. Naturally, the greater the number of lives insured under a group case—as a percentage of those eligible to be insured—the greater the protection against antiselection. A minimum of 75 percent participation is usually required. There is minimal or no medical or financial underwriting on the participants under group contracts, except where the number of lives insured in the group is very small—typically fewer than 10 lives. Additionally, with the maximum benefits available under group LTD plans steadily growing, medical and financial underwriting is being required on participants insured for these high maximums.

PREMIUM CONSIDERATIONS

Group premiums are structured with several variable elements. Short-term weekly income premiums are based upon benefit amount, benefit duration, elimination period, age and sex distribution, and, sometimes, adjustments for specific industries. LTD premiums typically reflect additional factors such as more extensive adjustment based on the type of industry, occupation, and the replacement ratio desired.

The premium rate may also be adjusted based upon both the number of lives insured and the percentage participation of all eligible employees in a particular group. As mentioned previously, the greater the number of lives, the smaller the risk of antiselection. Similarly, the greater the percentage of employees participating in a particular program, the less antiselection exists. The most favorable case from a participation perspective is the one in which the employer is paying the entire premium, and therefore all eligible employees are covered under the plan. Yet even in such a situation, the particularly small group (less than 10 lives) presents the potential for the decision maker in the group plan to select against the insurer. In such a situation the danger exists for the president or senior company officer to make the purchase decision in order to provide coverage for a seriously impaired risk, either himself/ herself or another key individual.

UNDERWRITING CONSIDERATIONS

Early group disability programs were primarily 100 percent em- ployee pay-all; the employee paid the premium personally and had the option of participating or not participating in the group. However, in later years more and more group disability programs became at least to some extent contributory; the employer paid all or part of the pre- mium. With the taxability of LTD benefits, employee-pay-all LTD plans are coming back into prominence. The stability of the firm and the industry in which the firm is engaged are important elements in the underwriting evaluation. Is the industry overly sensitive to seasonal or economic changes? Is it the type of firm that is sound financially and a well-managed, growing organization? Is it the type of firm that will experience significant layoffs during recessions? Such occurrences tend to increase morbidity. It is customary in employer-sponsored plans to require a minimum period of service before an individual becomes eligi- ble to be included in the disability income program. Such a time period has traditionally been one year; however, in recent years six months, three months, and even no length-of-service requirement whatsoever are becoming more common.

The group underwriter and the group actuary work very closely, both in the initial underwriting and in the renewal-underwriting process. The evaluation of the numerous variables in each case, particularly those that are unique to the particular case, require consultation between the two disciplines. This is particularly true during the renewal-rating process, when the assessment of experience under the group case and an evaluation of any change in premium necessary involves both under- writing and acturial techniques.

THE GROUP CONTRACT

The provisions of the group insurance contract have many general similarities to those in the individual contact; however, there are also some distinct differences. Perhaps the most significant difference is that the body of state law and regulation governing group insurance is an entirely separate set of statutes and regulations than those governing individual disability income. The magnitude of difference between the two contracts is distinctive enough that separate regulation is necessary.

The contract in group insurance is not between the employee and the insurer but rather between the employer (who is the owner of the contract) and the insurance company. The employee receives a certifi- cate outlining benefits, the identical process that is followed in group medical care coverage. The group insurance contract has an insuring clause, a definition of disability, a description of the benefit period and the elimination period, and the necessary language governing the handling of claims. The preexisting-condition language is customarily somewhat more restrictive than in individual contracts, since in all but the smaller-size group, there is no medical underwriting to exclude or limit those individuals who are in particularly poor health. Therefore, typical group disability contracts exclude or limit the payment of benefits for disabilities that occur during the first year of the contract if the insured had a definite history of the impairment prior to the date of the policy. This preexisting-condition language is sometimes eliminated, however, when the group insurance is replacing an existing group disability income program.

COORDINATION OF BENEFITS

A frequent characteristic of the group disability contract is that it is nonoccupational. The language is worded in such a way that benefits for occupational disabilities are either excluded from coverage, or if payable under Workers' Compensation, are deducted from the normal benefits payable under the contract; thus coverage is primarily for accidents or illnesses that occur away from and are unrelated to the job environment. In addition, some short term and most all LTD group contracts coordinate their payments with other governmental or employer-sponsored programs. Social Security disability payments and state cash sickness disability payments are deducted from the amount otherwise payable, and the group contract is also coordinated with any other employer-sponsored disability program that may exist. In recent years there has been an increasing tendency for employers to provide salary-continuation programs on a self-insured basis for the early days or weeks of a disability, and it is naturally important for the group disability program to avoid duplication of such payments. Typical employer salary-continuation programs may be for as short as four weeks or for as long as one year and are frequently tied to the employee's length of service. The stability of the risk, in this case the nature of the business and its stability, is as important an ingredient in group evaluation as is individual stability underwriting for individual disability income.

SHORT-TERM DISABILITY (WEEKLY INCOME)

Short-term disability income benefits have the longer and more established history of group disability coverages. As mentioned previously, the benefit period for such coverage is typically 13, 26, or 52 weeks. The elimination period may be as short as 0 days for accident and 7 days for sickness, but is rarely more than 15 or 30 days. The definition of disability is an "own occupation" definition, and insured individuals are covered for any disability that prevents them from performing the duties of their normal occupations. Short-term weekly income is often the only coverage available to the lower-income and more hazardous occupations within a group. Since it is during this short-term period that the greatest likelihood of Workers' Compensation, state cash sickness, and salary-continuation programs may be payable, coordination of benefits in plan design plays an active role.

LTD

Providing long-term disability benefits is a more recent development for group insurers. Although some amount of coverage has been issued for the past three decades, the significant growth of LTD began during the 1970s and continues today. Benefit periods are typically 2 years, 5 years, 10 years, or to retirement age, usually to age 65. The most common duration of benefits in recent years has been to age 65; however, as a result of federal age discrimination legislation beginning in 1978, coverage for covered workers may extend to age 70. The elimination periods are normally longer, at least 30 days and frequently three months or even one year. Benefits are coordinated with other governmental coverages and with any other employer-sponsored plan, including, of course, any group short-term weekly income benefit package that may be in effect.

Typical LTD programs offer own-occupation coverage for the first two years of disability, thereafter an any-occupation definition continues to provide benefits if the disabled employee is unable to perform the duties of any occupation for which he or she is reasonably fitted by education, training, and experience. In recent years the length of the own-occupation definition for long-term disability benefits has been extended further, and extension to the end of the benefit period is quite common. The nature of long-term disability and the associated risks result in it being primarily written in the less hazardous and more stable classifications, particularly for the officer and managerial ranks. A typical group insurance disability program might provide weekly income coverage for all employees but provide long-term disability benefits for only the managerial-class employees and higher classes. Other breakdowns of employees may be between salaried and nonsalaried workers.

Because of the additional risk assumed by the insurer, the underwriting restrictions for long-term disability are somewhat more rigid than for weekly income, and therefore the average age, size of the group, participation, and contributory factors tend to play a more important role than in weekly income.

INDEMNITY AMOUNTS

Historically, the maximum level of indemnity available under group disability programs, both weekly income and LTD, has been less than that available under individual contracts. Again, the fact that the group insurer cannot medically evaluate the risk requires a somewhat more cautious approach. On the other hand, group replacement ratios have generally tended to be somewhat higher than those in individual disability contracts, although not by great margins. Weekly income benefits are generally written in lower amounts than long-term disability, and although some long-term disability contracts today may be written for maximum amounts of $10,000, $15,000, or even $20,000 per month, most contracts provide benefits of $5,000 per month or less. Replacement ratios for group weekly income and LTD are tied to *gross* earned income and typically run from 50 to 70 percent. The higher percentage is naturally for the lower-income individuals, since their net take-home pay is a larger percent of their gross income; the lower percent replacement ratio is reserved for those higher-income individuals whose net income is substantially reduced by federal taxes. The replacement ratio for group long-term disability contracts is normally more conservative than for group weekly income. The most common replacement ratio for long-term disability is 60 percent, while it is commonly 66⅔ percent for weekly income.

CLAIM HANDLING

Claim handling of group disability claims follows a similar pattern to that found in any individual claim handling. Except for any differences that may be present in contract language, the same sort of claim investigation is pursued, and the same skills are required. The one additional element that must be recognized is that there is a third party who has an interest in the handling of the group disability claim, and that is the employer. This can be either an asset or a liability, depending upon the particular nature of the claim and the motivation of either the employer or the employee. In any event, the group claim examiner does have an additional interested party to be aware of. The interest and growth of rehabilitation efforts are taking on as much importance in group disability claim handling as in individual claim handling, and here again the employer may play an active and important role.

MULTIPLE-EMPLOYER TRUSTS

In recent years there has been an increased tendency to write weekly income and long-term disability benefits for very small groups, even down to one and two lives. Such small cases are frequently grouped together under an industry or multiple-employer trust agreement, to take advantage of the regulatory and administrative benefits of group insurance. In such small- or baby-group cases (typically less then 10 lives), there is a much greater risk of antiselection. Consequently, the underwriting tends to be more restrictive, the benefits somewhat more restrictive, and the rates higher. This is simply the latest of several excursions of group insurers into new markets; as more experience and confidence is gained in this area, further extensions will occur.

ASSOCIATION/FRANCHISE

Association or franchise coverages are not typical group insurance contracts. However, since they do insure large numbers of people under general group principles, this is an appropriate section in which to discuss them. Group insurance by definition generally requires an employer/employee relationship, but some state group insurance statutes make specific provision for association or franchise groups. Such coverages are regularly offered to local, regional, or national associations of professional people, business people, fraternal orders, civic organizations, or any other group of individuals who are gathered together with a common interest, as long as that interest is other than purely insurance.

Association or franchise contracts are normally issued to the association or to a trust with certificates issued to the individuals. Association coverage, however, does use some group selection and actuarial principles in underwriting and pricing the coverage to be insured. The law of large numbers, if employed properly, can work in such association/franchise situations.

Given the size of the group, the average age, the sex, and the benefits applied for, the underwriter and actuary can determine a rate and a product offering based on a certain level of participation. It is in the area of participation that particular difficulties are encountered in association/franchise coverage. Since there is no employer involved, the motivation to participate is less, the solicitation is normally done through the mail, and consequently the percent of participation is frequently low. A fundamental rule of insurance is that a low level of participation means a high element of antiselection. The most favorable association/franchise opportunity from the insurer's point of view is therefore one in which the association is a strong one that can motivate a high percentage of its members to participate. Such association programs are normally contingent upon a minimum percent of eligible members participating.

Similar to group insurance, association/franchise contracts are subject to premium adjustments on an annual basis, and the entire case may be cancelled if experience proves particularly poor.

The future of both group and association/franchise coverages in the United States appears to be a growing one. As the public becomes more and more aware of the need for long-term disability income, it will demand such coverage at the lowest possible cost. A substantial floor of disability income coverage can be adequately provided through either group or franchise/association benefits at a much less expensive rate than an individual contract. On the other hand, by its nature, the group or association/franchise contract is not designed to meet the specific needs of an individual. It does not have the capability of being tailored to meet individual needs in terms of benefit levels, nor does it provide the greater personal guarantees offered by the individual contract. And it can be cancelled and the premium increased. Both group and individual contracts, therefore, have their place in the marketplace, and group insurance will continue to experience significant growth as it has in the recent past.

Disability Income Future

22

Those who attempt to look ahead and project the environment of the future accept the risk of being proven wrong as time goes by. But because the disability income business is one of deferred rewards and deferred penalties, management must always look into the future and make decisions that affect markets, products, pricing, underwriting, and claims handling. Although no projections or conclusions will ever prove to be entirely accurate, the important objective is to identify significant trends and thereby narrow the margin for serious error. As the disability industry moves through the 1980s, several factors should be addressed in any discussion of the environment of the next 10 years.

ENVIRONMENT

Economic Climate

The economic climate in which we operate and the level of unemployment will continue to have a direct impact upon disability income results. Will double-digit inflation return to impact our economy? If this proves to be the case, it will have a direct effect on expense rates, product design, and the general stability of in-force business. Inflationary periods tend to increase lapses and policy makeovers, since the contract fails to cover the insurer's income needs after a short period of time.

We will continue to experience periodic recessions, some steeper than others, with generally the same effect on our business as in the past. Morbidity will increase during recessionary periods, and the steeper the recession, the higher the morbidity. A true economic depression will have financial consequences similar to those of the 1930s depression. The volatility of disability experience is so directly tied to the economy and unemployment that adverse financial consequences cannot be avoided. The successful disability manager is the one who can significantly blunt such adverse effects.

Stability, Motivation, and Work Ethic

Closely related to the economic factor is the question of what changes will occur in our society that will affect stability, motivation, and work-ethic assumptions. Sharp changes in these factors had a profound effect upon traditional guidelines and characteristics of the disability business from the mid 1960s through the early 1980s. Markets disappeared, underwriting rules changed, pricing patterns changed—all in response to an enhanced entitlement ethic. The steep swing of the pendulum slowed down in the late 1970s as a more conservative attitude took hold in American society. It would appear that the next several years will not see a return to such steep swings in the pendulum and will consequently not demand such sharp changes in our products, our pricing, and our underwriting rules.

However, the industry must be alert to changes in traditional patterns and motivations that affect occupational groupings, geographical areas, or certain age groups. Even though the general trend may be more favorable than in the recent past, changes in technology and changes in demographic trends may adversely impact some segments of the economy.

As mentioned in previous chapters, there are early indications of significant changes in the traditional morbidity levels of professional risks. How extensive will this adverse trend be? At what point will new morbidity levels begin to stabilize? What product, pricing, and underwriting changes must be made to establish acceptable margins?

Governmental Encroachment

The significant growth of governmental disability programs slowed down sharply in the late 1970s and early 1980s. There is no indication yet of a recurrence of sharp acceleration. Indeed there has been some retrenchment and restricting in the Social Security disability income program. This area must be watched closely in a product environment in which private industry indemnity levels are guaranteed for many years into the future at level premiums. If the current government fiscal problems substantially improve with a growing economy, there will be a growing pressure to liberalize and expand government programs, including disability benefits under Social Security.

Perhaps a greater threat of government encroachment exists in the area of regulation. Recent federal and state legislation and regulation in the areas of privacy and discrimination have significantly increased the costs of administering all insurance products. These costs have been passed on to the consumer. When regulation becomes excessive, the result is not in the consumer's best interests. Continual participation and observation of government trends in these areas must be encouraged, and all insurers must accept the responsibility of educating regulators and legislators to avoid excesses.

Competition

The competitive environment for disability income products will continue to increase over the next decade. Several factors will help create such a climate. Sharp changes in the traditional level of profits and stability in life insurance will cause many insurers to look to other product lines for growth, disability income being one of them. There continue to be significant opportunities for disability income sales growth, since many potential markets and marketing opportunities have been only slightly penetrated. Although the professional marketplace is a heavily penetrated market, there remain larger groups of self-employed individuals who lack sufficient disability income protection. Various business uses for disability income have only been lightly penetrated during the past decade.

Increased competition will also be heightened by the entry into the marketplace of other financial institutions offering a full range of financial services, including disability income. It remains to be seen how effective their penetration of the marketplace will be; however, we can at least conclude that their entry will increase public awareness of the disability income product. A final element that will increase competition will be the need for both insurance companies and their salespeople to increase productivity in order for each element to hold its costs of operation at manageable levels. One logical solution to increased productivity is to broaden the product portfolio of the traditional life insurance salesperson to include other product lines, disability income being one of them.

MARKETS

There is a variety of ways to discuss the markets for individual disability income in the next 10 years. Occupation, income, geographic distribution, self-employed versus employee, age, and sex are marketing factors for which some trends are already evident.

Occupation

The blue-collar occupations will offer limited growth for individual disability income, except for the employer and highly paid skilled worker whose income protection needs are not met by governmental programs or group insurance. The independent business market, particularly those businesses with less than 25 employees, offers the greatest growth opportunities. A study conducted by the Life Insurance Management Research Association and published in *U.S. News & World Report* in 1981 indicated that only 10 percent of the 3½ million small businesses in the United States had individual disability income coverage. Aggressive penetration of this market carries with it certain challenges and risks for the insurer, since it does not represent as homogeneous a group or as stable a group as does the professional occupation class. The income ranges of small-business people run from very modest levels to very high levels. The stability of this income is more directly and immediately affected by economic swings. The financial failure rate of small businesses tends to be high. The physical risks vary considerably depending upon the nature of the particular business or industry. Even with all of these variable factors, this market offers considerable opportunity for growth.

The professional marketplace will continue to be the most competitive of all individual disability markets. This market is already substantially penetrated and has heavy replacement activity from one company to another. The large average premium per case, however, will continue to attract keen competition in product, rates, and underwriting.

Income

When we examine markets by income categories, we will find that current trends will continue, strongly affected by government programs. The lower-middle and lower-income markets will represent limited opportunities for growth and premium. Social Security disability benefits, Workers' Compensation, and state cash sickness benefits provide almost full coverage for risks with incomes of less than $25,000. This income floor will gradually increase as automatic cost-of-living increases are affected in the various government programs. Short-term individual disability income for up to one year of benefits can and will be written to cover that period during which Social Security benefits are normally not paid. In addition, some supplementary coverage beyond one year will be sold, providing limited coverage only when governmental benefits are not payable.

The middle-income range of $25,000 to $100,000 is the market in which most of the self-employed independent-business prospects are found. This will represent a growth area for both individual disability income and various types of disability business insurance. The high-income market, in excess of $100,000, is represented by professional risks and some of the more select independent-business markets. This market will be characterized by keen competition, as was mentioned previously.

Geography

Geographically, the markets will naturally follow the movement of the population toward the sunbelt of the South and Southwest. The aggressive competition for disability income premium is primarily in the 40 or 50 largest population centers across the country. The same level of competition will gradually be extended to the top 100 areas of population. Competition and penetration of professional and independent-business markets in the less populated areas is not as keen, and these areas will continue to be somewhat less competitive than the larger metropolitan markets. However, as more companies enter the marketplace and as the public becomes more aware of the need for individual disability income, all geographic areas will tend to increase in the level of competition.

The Self-Employed

The self-employed will continue to be the primary source of individual disability income prospects. They are less likely to be covered under group insurance, less likely to have their income needs fully protected by government programs, and during the past 10 years have come to recognize the need to protect their personal incomes through an individual disability program. It is this same market that offers the opportunity for growth and innovation with various types of disability business insurance. The employee marketplace offers minimal opportunities for growth, since normally it is fully protected by employer salary-continuation programs, group insurance, and the various governmental programs. The exception to this protection in the employee market is the higher-paid, higher-skilled, and more stable risk whose income is at such a level that it is not fully covered by other programs. In addition, the employees of the self-employed small-business person represent potential markets for individual disability income for the same reasons.

Age

Demographic changes in age distribution will offer one of the largest areas for market change and shifts during the next decade. As the age of our population increases, the premium distribution by age will follow the same pattern as the changes in age distribution. More premium will be generated in the over-age-35 and up-to-age-55 group, and less premium in the under-age-35 category. Very little individual disability income is currently written in the age-55-to-70 category, but it may prove to be a growing market as the average American remains in the workplace longer. This trend will be accentuated by the extension of the Social Security retirement age beyond age 65. This market offers special risks and hazards for the insurer since it represents the age group with a much higher percentage of sickness disabilities. Although very little non-cancellable disability income is currently written over age 60, this will tend to change as marketing opportunities become evident to more insurers.

Sex

The female marketplace has been only lightly penetrated and perhaps represents the greatest opportunity for significant market changes between now and the year 2000. As a greater number of women assume permanent roles in the marketplace, more and more disability income will be sold to them. With each passing year, increasing numbers of women will assume positions of more responsibility in various business situations and with increasing incomes. As this occurs and as their average income increasingly approaches that of male workers, their need for greater disability income protection will be evident and their demand will increase.

In all of the market areas discussed above, the public awareness and demand for individual disability protection will increase. Along with increased consumer demand will naturally come a more competitive marketplace and new and more innovative products, all fostering a more mature and healthy business environment.

Finally, new markets may emerge in areas that we are unable to see clearly at this time. The rapid growth of high-technology businesses, the exploration and colonization of outer space, and other changes in our living environment will bring with them new occupations, new industries, and new challenges for the disability income product.

DISTRIBUTION SYSTEMS

In the late 1970s and early 1980s, there began to emerge several factors affecting the traditional distribution of individual life insurance, and, indeed, the emergence of new distribution systems. The same trends affecting life insurance will affect individual disability income. Many questions have been raised concerning the viability of the traditional agency distribution system, its cost effectiveness, and its productivity. At the same time various mass marketing approaches, specifically direct-mail selling, have been extensively broadened to contact large segments of the marketplace. Other financial institutions, banks, and investment houses have entered the life insurance business, and some to a limited extent have entered the disability business. At the very least, one can conclude that there will be a much wider variety of distribution systems and mechanisms available to the consumer than in the past to purchase insurance products.

Individual Agent

The individual agent will continue to perform a necessary role in distributing insurance products into the foreseeable future. Neither life nor disability income insurance is "bought" in great volume, but rather the need must be sold. This process requires the personal attention and service of a skilled, professional, and well-trained career insurance professional. Personally designing an insurance program to meet an individual's estate, tax, and business needs is frequently of such complexity that the consumer will demand the personal services of the insurance salesperson. The market that demands such service is consistent with the professional and independent-business markets, where the greatest growth opportunities for individual disability income lie.

Other Distributors

On the other hand, there will be a substantial increase in the amount of insurance premium, including disability income, that is sold through other distribution mechanisms. Group weekly income and long-term disability programs will continue to generate large amounts of premium and show substantial growth. Franchise disability income, a close sister to group insurance, will also continue to grow and will particularly expand into nonprofessional franchise/association programs. Neither group nor franchise coverages currently offer the same quality of coverage as do individual contracts. Contract language is less liberal, it carries more restrictions, and it is not portable if the insured changes business or profession. These differences will tend to narrow as group and franchise writers liberalize their contracts in both language and portability.

Mass-marketing and direct-mail distribution mechanisms will be broadened but will tend to provide restricted coverage that will be purchased primarily by the middle- and lower-income marketplace. It will, in most cases, represent a basic floor of coverage, rather than a full and complete disability program to meet the personal needs of the consumer. In a few short years more direct selling will be done over the television screen in conjunction with a two-way telecommunication capability. The consumer will be able to observe a sales presentation on a cathode-ray tube, have questions answered over a telecommunications line, and observe a program more personally designed for him or her. The salesperson will use this capability in reaching and selling the client with the aid of the computer.

Banks, stock brokerage firms, and other financial-service firms are entering the life and disability marketplace. They enter with an existing base of clients and will capture some portion of the disability marketplace. They will tend to capture a wider, larger floor of the market than will direct mail. However, the highly personalized and technical sale will still require the personal involvement of highly trained life and disability income specialists. The key to the success of such financial firms in significantly penetrating the insurance marketplace will depend entirely on the degree and level of competent technical support that they can deliver to the consumer in the advanced sales situation.

Some companies are marketing various insurance products through one-stop retail-marketing outlets. Frequently, they are set up at counters in department stores, and their market penetration will primarily be the less-sophisticated and lower-income buyer who is looking for a floor of coverage.

The distribution of life and disability products is proceeding through a period of rapid innovation and change. Some new systems will succeed; others will fail; new ones not yet imagined will emerge and the best segments of existing distribution systems will still remain. Specialty companies, whether life or disability income, will be in demand to deliver their products through both traditional and new distribution systems that meet the personal needs of the consumer.

PRODUCTS

The key element in the products of the future will be those that are responsive to the needs of the consumer. In the past both life and disability insurers have to a great extent designed and manufactured products for the consumer without carefully listening to the consumer's needs and demands. The product revolution in the life industry in the late 1970s and 1980s is indicative of the problems that will emerge when one fails to be responsive to those consumer needs.

The individual disability income marketplace has traditionally been more product-sensitive than has been true of life insurance. Detailed and sometimes minute comparisons of contract language and provisions have played a major role in the competitive selling process. Individual disability income products have matured and progressed to such a point that in many instances, particularly in the professional marketplace, little room for further liberalization of current contracts exists. The definition of disability has reached the point that there is truly no meaningful further step to take. Product and product language may therefore play a somewhat lesser role in the future than in the past. Competition may stress the elements of service, rates, and underwriting more than in the past.

This is not to say that new-product development opportunities do not exist for individual disability income. Just the opposite is true! Since the disability income product directly insures the individual's income, it must continue to be responsive in design to changes in the consumer's needs. Changes in occupation, changes in real-income growth, changes in the length of the workweek, changes in retirement patterns, and changes in avocations must all be considered and affect product design. A period of extended and high inflation will accelerate the need for cost-of-living benefits, guaranteed insurability coverage, and a general indexing of coverage to income.

There is a need for regulators to address the overinsurance problem when governmental coverages and individual contracts are combined. Several states currently have language that prohibits or limits the effective coordination of benefits in individual disability contracts. If these language barriers were removed or eased, it would offer significant opportunities for companies to integrate and innovate product language to more directly meet the consumer's needs, while at the same time lowering the rate.

Perhaps the best way to emphasize the product opportunities that continue to exist in disability income is to point out that the ideal disability product has not yet been designed or marketed. There is no product in the marketplace that will fully protect earned income from the time the consumer enters the working marketplace to retirement, adjusting automatically to the consumer's income changes and needs over a working lifetime.

ADMINISTRATION

The administrative environment for disability income in the future will closely follow the pattern of other individual insurance products. There will clearly be greater automation not only in home office administrative functions, but also in field sales offices. Field entry of application data, and even the image of the application, will be transmitted and automatically stored for automatic retrieval on a terminal screen. Greater computer screening of application data, automatic ordering of underwriting requirements, screening of that information when it is received, and actual approval of the policy will increasingly be automated procedures. Generation of the policy schedule page and policy issue will be accomplished in the field office in most individual insurance applications, where it is not today.

Direct field inquiry and direct policy change will be most commonly accomplished at field terminals. One significant and positive effect of greater automation in the administrative process will be the emergence of more reliable and accurate management information. This is of particular importance in the disability income product line, where management information is so scarce today because of a lack of adequate data.

Consumer demand for quality and efficient service will be the prime catalyst in moving companies toward an environment that can provide such service.

UNDERWRITING

As the underwriting process in the future becomes increasingly more automated, not only will many applications be automatically screened and issued without individual underwriting attention, but the underwriter will personally perform this function in front of the terminal screen and will become increasingly dependent upon the information the screen displays. Technology that enables the image of a document to be actually stored on a disk along with other data and called forward on the same screen at the underwriter's request provides an environment where the tedious shuffling of paper in the underwriting process will disappear. That technology has arrived and when implemented will make paper unnecessary in most insurance processing.

The primary underwriting tools of medical examinations, physician's reports, and personal-history information will continue to be necessary. The major changes will occur in the transmission method for this information, storage, and screening.

Underwriting rules and limits will of necessity change as the consumer environment changes. Issue limits that were $8,000 per month in 1982 will be in the neighborhood of $15,000 per month (assuming a moderate annual rate of inflation) by the year 1990. Stability and motivation will continue to be the main subjective characteristics involved in the underwriting process and will continue to require the judgment of the trained professional disability underwriter.

The increase in the number of wage earners in one family presents a new factor for the underwriter that has not yet been adequately addressed. Is the motivation of the disabled wage earner affected by the fact that the spouse continues to work and earn an income? Is this motivation affected by the level of earnings of each of the spouses? Is this motivation affected by the ages of the wage earners? In some circumstances under today's underwriting rules and limits, the real spendable income of the two-wage–earner family may actually be increased upon the disability of one of the wage earners when we consider the fact that disability income benefits are not taxable (see Table 22–1).

TABLE 22–1
Replacement Ratios for Two-Wage–Earner Family

	Monthly earned income	Monthly take-home pay*	Replacement ratio
Both working:			
Spouse A	$2,500	$1,700	
Spouse B	$2,500	$1,700	
Total	$5,000	$3,400	
One disabled:			
Spouse A	$2,500	$1,800	
Spouse B	Disabled	$1,700 from disability policy	
Total	$2,500	$3,500	103%†

* Monthly earned income less federal, state, and FICA taxes.
† Replacement ratio is regular total income ($3,400) divided into total income when one spouse is disabled.

More reliable data and greater ease in technically retrieving and evaluating the data will help the underwriter in the evaluation of impaired risks. The continued high percentage of impaired-risk cases and rejected applicants in disability income will continue to diminish as more reliable experience becomes available and new underwriting techniques and approaches are developed. Competition will itself require greater innovation in addressing and handling the highly impaired risk.

CLAIMS

The claims environment of the future will follow closely the pattern already discussed in underwriting. It will be highly automated. The claim examiner will work directly at a computer terminal, and the claim payments will be automatically deposited to the claimant's account in a checkless society. There will probably not be an area in which service is more critical than in the ability of the company to promptly and accurately deliver the claim payment to the consumer. The consumer's expectations will increase in this area.

Older Ages

There are many unanswered questions in the disability income claim area that will be answered before the turn of the century. Because of the rapid growth of disability income sales during the early 1980s, the present block of disability premium is still quite immature. Significant product changes that emerged during the late 1970s and 1980s have not had an opportunity to be tested by the passage of time. For most companies a low percentage of in-force premium comes from policyholders older than 50. What effect will the own-occupation definition of disability have on traditional claim patterns between ages 55 and 65? What effect will liberal residual and partial disability income language have on this same age group? Large indemnity amounts providing up to $10,000 per month of benefits have been written only recently. What special problems in the area of motivation and stability will these benefits cause as the business matures or as large groups of policyholders move into the upper ages?

Rehabilitation

One exciting area that will take on greater importance during the next decade is rehabilitation. Activity in this area has already begun with the emergence of many private rehabilitation firms, and most insurers are giving some attention to the importance of this process. It is in many respects a true virgin area. It appears to offer an ideal opportunity since a successful and effective rehabilitation is in the best interests of both the consumer and the insurer. A successful rehabilitation activity improves our responsiveness to the public's needs, and by returning the claimant to the work force it strengthens our economy.

Similar to any new enterprise, initial investments of money and resources are necessary before meaningful and successful returns can be measured. Rehabilitation is an area in which all disability insurers should prudently make an investment for the immediate future.

The need for the skills of the professional disability claim examiner will continue to be important for the financially successful disability insurer.

ACTUARIAL

Many of the elements of the future that will affect the disability actuary have already been discussed. The most important of these is clearly the gradual but constant development of more reliable data on which to price our products and make decisions of policy and direction. Not only will the data be more reliable and greater in volume, but increased data processing facilities will provide for a more responsive environment.

This will come at a time when the need for quicker analysis and more rapid pricing changes will become increasingly important in order to respond to an enhanced competitive atmosphere. Some of the actuarial art of pricing disability products will be replaced by the more reliable science of improved data. However, the analysis and pricing of the disability income product line will still require a generous dose of judgment. The importance of the stability and motivation characteristics are such that the actuary cannot do otherwise!

REGULATORY

The regulatory environment affecting disability income will again tend to follow that of life insurance. It would, of course, be desirable if the various state jurisdictions could, in fact, work more effectively together through the National Association of Insurance Commissioners in order to foster more consistency from one jurisdiction to another. This is as true in disability insurance as it is in life insurance.

Simplified language requirements have progressed through most state jurisdictions and will be enacted nationwide in a few years. Privacy regulations may be expanded, depending upon the national political environment. Various legislative and regulatory actions in the area of the handicapped will be expanded, and insurers must find product, pricing, and selection methods that will meet compliance requirements. Sex discrimination has been eliminated from product design and selection, and there continues to be pressure and consideration to require equal pricing for insurance products. In spite of logical actuarial statistics that clearly prove a difference in morbidity between sexes, the industry may have to face how to respond to mandatory legislation and regulation in this area.

Finally, any discussion of the future of disability income must consider the role of the manager responsible for that product line. The next chapter will discuss the key elements in the management process. In closing this chapter, however, it is important to emphasize the most critical factor in the disability manager's role. It is that managers must, at all costs, avoid overreaction, even when those around them are pressing in that direction. The volatility of the disability income product creates an environment in which overreaction in the direction of liberalizing is a strong temptation during good economic times, and overreaction in the direction of restricting is just as strong a temptation during poor economic times. The sound manager must resist both extremes!

Managing the Disability Product Line

23

This book has dealt with the various characteristics of individual disability income and the important considerations in each of its several disciplines. This text has attempted to compare, whenever possible, the differences between life insurance and disability income insurance, since almost all companies selling this product consider life insurance to be their primary product line. There remains one very basic but overriding function that must be addressed, and that is the management of all the elements to achieve the desired sales, service, and profit results.

The functions and procedures that must be managed are obviously very similar to those in individual life insurance, and the same management techniques and skills must be employed. As with previous chapters, this chapter will not be an attempt to discuss basic or general management principles, but will rather focus on those areas and factors that demand particular attention from the disability income manager. The purpose is to identify those elements where unique risks and problems exist for the disability income manager, particularly those where my own personal experience as well as my observations of other companies has identified items of risk that will significantly affect a sound and profitable operation.

The most basic requirement is that one individual be responsible for the financial results of the disability product line! The volatility of disability income is such that a successful operation requires the overall attention and direction and responsibility of one individual. This is of particular importance where the disability income product is secondary

or tertiary in importance since the diffusion of responsibility and authority will obviously result in the manager giving this product line secondary
or tertiary attention. The president or senior officer in such instances
will tend to give proper management attention to the product line only
when a serious problem has surfaced. At that time the solution to the
problem will be more complex and have more serious financial consequences. It is only in the very small handful of companies for which
disability income is the primary product line that overall responsibility
for management can be logically assumed by a senior officer or the
president. Too many companies make the initial and fundamental error
of ignoring this important requirement, and thus their sales, service,
and financial results are adversely impaired.

ESTABLISHING OBJECTIVES

Profit

The first objective must be to manage the line in order to generate
a profit! Although this would seem to be an accepted requirement of
any product line, too often it is not given proper primary attention,
and company actions are such that a successful financial result cannot
be achieved. A very common error occurs when company management
perceives the disability income product line to be an accommodation
to its field force. In response to pressures from the field force and in
reaction to the fact that the field force may be brokering disability income
through other companies, an insurer may make the decision to either
enter the marketplace or strengthen its disability income product position. If, in such a circumstance, its primary objective is accommodation
and not profit, then the possibility of financial success is indeed question-
able, particularly in a product line that carries with it so much volatility.

There must be a definitive profit goal! The premium structure
must provide for a specific profit element, in the same way the construction of a premium provides for claims, expenses, commissions, and taxes.
The product line must then be managed to achieve this profit over the
lifetime of the particular product. Economic volatility is such that the
success of the profit objective must be measured over a period of time,
an absolute minimum of five years, since year-to-year fluctuations will
be frequent.

Market

The manager must determine where the markets are for the disability product and which markets the company intends to penetrate.
The important consideration here is the careful and objective analysis
of the capabilities of the field force. Except for the largest writers of
disability income, the disability income manager cannot expect to make

a major and significant penetration of all potential markets. The analysis of where the markets are normally requires an analysis of where the company's individual life insurance markets are, since disability income sales will logically and primarily come from these sources. Although this would appear to be a basic and somewhat easy determination, for many companies it is not. The field pressure for new products, new rates, and more liberal underwriting normally comes from those salespeople operating in the more competitive professional marketplace. Even though the percentage of a company's individual life insurance that comes from the professional market may be only a small percentage of its total life sales, it will find its primary pressure for disability income product liberalization to come from this source. The independent-business, skilled-trade, and blue-collar markets are simply less competitive at this point of industry development. Therefore, to concentrate marketing activity in answer to the needs of only a small percentage of the field force would be the wrong decision. The marketing thrust should rather be directed toward the natural and broader market from which the life insurance sales are coming. Indeed, there may be greater opportunity for sales and profits from those markets in which the competition is not so highly developed. This is particularly true when the manager directs his or her activities toward the natural life insurance markets.

ROLE OF THE DISABILITY INCOME MANAGER

Since the disability product is normally marketed through the same distribution system that markets individual life insurance, some obvious problems are present for the disability income manager. The life insurance distribution system, the company's field force, will not usually be under the disability manager's direct control, and yet he/she is given responsibility for the disability product and its sales results. Although perhaps having responsibility for product development, training, promotion, underwriting, claims, and actuarial functions, the manager will not have responsibility for the distribution system, except in those companies where disability is the primary product. He or she must therefore obtain a commitment from company management and from the officer in charge of sales to cooperate in achieving sales objectives. Although this is not the ideal circumstance, the product-line manager can frequently limit potential problems and misunderstandings by establishing clear objectives and guidelines. The success of the sales effort will be dependent upon the training and support the manager can provide to the company's sales force. The disability marketing staff must include disability income specialists who can not only train, but also provide assistance and advice to the salespeople in specific sales situations. The disability sales specialist must serve a role similar to a group sales representative's role and act as the technical specialist upon whom the agent calls for assistance. In most companies the salesperson in the field will not become a disability income specialist, but will look to the disability income marketing department for sales support in the same way he or she seeks the support of advanced life, pension, and group sales-support personnel. The disability income manager, therefore, controls a distribution system made up of a very small handful of disability income specialists who service the company's field force. The manager's ability to meet sales goals is dependent upon two elements: (1) the skill and expertise of these disability specialists in serving the field force and (2) the cooperation of the company sales department in allowing the manager to provide this service and training.

CRITICAL MANAGEMENT CONSIDERATIONS

The disability income manager must recognize the unique characteristics of this product line and then manage to minimize the risks and problems that those characteristics represent.

The Economy

The cyclical nature of claims experience is one important factor. Recessions will come and go, some more severe than others. Each one will have its impact upon claims experience; and the steeper the recession, the more severe the financial impact. The most important discipline for the manager is to avoid that tendency toward overreaction, which has been discussed previously. Following a period of economic growth and good financial results in the product line will come increasing pressure to liberalize products, rates, and underwriting. Following a period of losses caused by a recession will come the opposite pressures to restrict the product, premiums, and underwriting. The manager must avoid both extremes! This is easier said than done since the pressures from either company management or the field force will be strong. Company management, as well as the field force, must be educated to the extent reasonably possible in the normal cyclical patterns and pressures that affect the disability income line in order to better consider and make sound management decisions and provide direction.

As the economy enters a recession, the disability manager should take steps to make certain that underwriting and claim procedures are sound and being administered properly. The manager must make certain the underwriting department is more carefully evaluating those applicants who are particularly susceptible to unemployment and reduced income during a recession and must make certain that the claim department is more sensitive in evaluating those claim situations that are affected by the economic climate. Fine tuning of procedures and administrative rules in both underwriting and claims during recessionary periods may well prevent tens and hundreds of thousands of dollars in losses.

Stability and Motivation

A second critical management consideration is understanding and accepting the importance of stability and motivation in the financial results of the product line. An important part of the training of the sales force must be to emphasize the key role it plays in the selection of the disability income risk. The agent must understand why the risk with characteristics of unstable personal, family, or business factors is a poorer risk for disability income than for life insurance.

The disability manager must be sensitive to socioeconomic changes that affect the traditional work-ethic pattern, whether the change affects a specific group of the population or society as a whole. In some situations the manager will find it necessary to place restrictions upon business submitted by individual salespeople because underwriting and claims experience indicate unusual claim problems. The fine tuning of underwriting rules and the placement of restrictions where necessary is another instance in which proper selection techniques can make a substantial difference in the financial results. It requires judgment, frequently including a significant amount of subjectivity, and then the ability to execute a decision. The manager must use care not to overreact in either direction in the area of stability and motivation.

Strategic Planning

The final critical management consideration has already been alluded to, but requires more detailed comment. The manager must have both a strategic and an operating plan to assure the achievement of objectives. The strategic plan should include those longer-term, perhaps five-year, strategies that will assure the sales and profit goals company management desires. The operating plan will detail those annual objectives to help assure the fulfillment of the longer-range strategic objectives.

The disability product line must include specific sales goals, and I believe that a healthy operation must establish aggressive sales goals, always somewhat greater than the rate of inflation. The plan must also include specific profit goals, and the line must be managed to achieve these profits. To emphasize sales goals without the necessary balance of profit objectives may generate impressive premium revenue, but the success will be short-lived if poor actuarial and underwriting guidelines result in greater-than-anticipated losses with the passage of time. Similarly, too great an emphasis on profits will result in impaired sales growth because of an uncompetitive market position. The key point for the manager to remember is that balance must be maintained between sales and profit, neither one dominating the other.

PRODUCT DEVELOPMENT AND PRODUCT CONTROL

Once having determined where the markets are, the disability manager is ready to design and develop the specific detail of the product. The product design must fit the specific market; it must meet the needs of that market. As has already been stressed throughout this book, the competitive nature of the market varies from the unskilled to the professional market and from the lower-income to the higher-income market. The stability and motivation characteristics vary from one market to another, and consequently liberal features in the product will vary dependent upon that level of stability. The competitive environment differs from one market to another and must be carefully considered in product design. The ideal disability income product has not yet been designed and marketed, and therefore opportunities exist in product design for innovation for almost all products. Different products and product language approaches may offer a marketing advantage, even though they may not carry additional underwriting or claims risk.

Determining Consumer and Field Force Needs

The first step requires listening to and determining the needs of the consumer and the field force, but care must be taken that the loudest voice is indeed coming from the largest market. The product development process must be sensitive to both what the consumer wants and what the agent will sell. Although one might think these would usually be compatible, they may not be. It falls upon those people involved in product development to balance these needs in product design and then support the product through training and education of both the field force and the public.

The product development process also requires the important element of balance. The specific product idea and initial design must be the responsibility of those people charged with the marketing responsibility of the product. They will have analyzed the consumer and the agent needs, looked at various alternatives, and recommended a product approach. In such a discussion, product development includes not only the contract language, rates, and product support, but also underwriting rules and guidelines. Product recommendations will occasionally address only changes in underwriting rules and requirements, at other times changes in the rating structure, and at still other times an entirely new or revised policy form. Occasionally, changes in underwriting rules and requirements or rates or contract language may initially come from actuarial, underwriting, or claim personnel in response to trends they observe in the marketplace or from experience analysis.

Product Design

Once the marketing department has recommended a specific product approach, the approach must then be examined and the detailed design completed. This function requires the cooperation and coordination of marketing, actuarial, underwriting, claims, law, and administrative personnel. These various functions were discussed in detail in the chapter dealing with product development, but it bears repeating that the careful and considered input of all of these disciplines is important for a successful product development activity. A product designed and developed solely by marketing personnel may generate enormous sales revenue but generate financial losses. Similarly, a product developed solely by actuarial personnel may, on paper, generate the desired profit but be priced in such a way that it cannot be sold. Similar statements may be made regarding all of the various disciplines.

The input and influence of the individual representing each discipline must be kept in balance so that no one discipline dominates the others. This is where the role of the disability income manager with overall responsibility for the product line becomes important. The manager has the final responsibility for the design and the financial results that will emerge and thus must be observant and make certain that the advice he or she is receiving about the design of the product is not dangerously out of balance when considering the input of the various disciplines. The stability and motivation sensitivity of the disability product make the underwriting and claims input of greater importance in product development than in life insurance. Some decisions affecting product design will often be based upon the experience and input of underwriting and claims personnel. Although this input cannot be objectively quantified, it must be listened to in the same way the opinion and judgment of marketing personnel must be heard.

Evaluating the Design

The actuary's role is a more objective one, although less so than in life insurance because of the scarcity of data as well as the natural subjective nature of disability income. The disability income manager must be aware of and have discussed the specific pricing assumptions the actuary has made in constructing the premium.

The lawyer plays an important role in drafting contractual language, which is complicated by the subjective nature of many disability claims. The lawyer must be sensitive to the choice of language and how this may be interpreted by both the policyholder and the courts.

The function of the administrator in the product development process is becoming of greater importance because of the increased commitment to automation. Since disability income offers great opportunity for innovation, it presents the potential problem of a product design that cannot be easily administered. The individual representing the administrative function must be familiar with both the capability and limitations of manual and automated systems. If administrative and systems personnel are involved in the product design in the early stages and understand the objectives, they will be able to point out potential administrative difficulties so that alternative solutions can be addressed. Along the same lines, the substantial lead time required to redesign or develop new automated systems will often prove to be a problem when implementing a new product. Detailed specifications must be prepared carefully but promptly and submitted to data processing personnel before a commitment to release of the product can be made.

Therefore, the important element in product development and design is balance! The disability income manager having the final responsibility must create an environment in which this balance is encouraged.

TRAINING AND EDUCATION

The words *training* and *education* in this context affect more than the normal training and support that is required to assure sales success. In a product line that is normally no more than secondary in a company's operation, there is a need for training and education of all individuals involved in the product line to assure its success. Many of the people involved in the disability income product line, whether sales, actuarial, claims, underwriting, or administrative personnel, will have had previous experience in another product line. They must be trained and educated in the unique characteristics of disability income and must understand the company objectives and plans. They must understand the unique characteristics of the product line and its significant risks.

In addition, the disability income manager must in a general way educate other company management. Since disability income is a secondary line, it represents a subject with which many key individuals in the corporate structure will be unfamiliar. Care must be taken to inform them of the general characteristics, the risks, and the goals and objectives of the disability operation. The manager must perceive this to be an important function.

SERVICE

It goes without saying that service to both the policyholder and the salesperson must be at an acceptable level. Since disability income will in most cases be a secondary product line for the agent, it is perhaps even more important that service be at a high level. For a product line with which the agent is somewhat unfamiliar and perhaps uncomfortable, poor or marginal service may quickly turn him or her away from making future sales. Service to the policyholder takes on added importance in the disability claims process. In life insurance there is only one death claim, and in that instance the claim examiner is not dealing with the insured. In disability income there will frequently be many claims during the lifetime of the policy, and the insured is actively involved in the claim process. The timely and accurate servicing of the claim will help assure the confidence and good will of both the policyholder and the salesperson.

The disability manager must be sensitive to these service needs, impress their importance upon personnel, and establish standards to regularly monitor performance.

EVALUATION OF RESULTS

A product line that carries with it significant volatility and subjectivity requires the ongoing evaluation of experience and trends. Although the major responsibility for this evaluation lies within the actuarial function, the underwriting and claims disciplines must be included. Indeed, underwriting and claim personnel must be encouraged and expected to analyze trends in the business and to make recommendations where appropriate. If they perceive their role to be one of reacting to actuarial recommendations, then an important segment of valuable information and input is missing. In a business of delayed rewards and delayed penalties, quantifiable actuarial data may not emerge until well after important trends are evident to the astute claims or underwriting manager.

Morbidity and persistency trends tend to run parallel in disability income. Persistency trends are evident much sooner than morbidity trends and should be regularly evaluated, particularly when new marketing thrusts are being made.

Balance is once again necessary when the disability manager makes decisions based upon recommendations received in the evaluation process. The manager must take action—and take it quickly—when information is serious enough to warrant it and must delay action in other instances. The key question is how to determine when the situation is clearly a serious one, and, of course, this is difficult. The answer comes from experience, knowing the individuals who are making the recommendations, being aware of past trends, being aware of where you are in the economic cycle, and many other variable elements. The manager should remember that fine tuning by making minor adjustments can have great impact and may pay enormous dividends in a product line where one claim may amount to several hundred thousand dollars in claim payments or reserves.

The manager must build an environment of consistency in decision making, rather than one of jumping from one extreme to another based upon little or limited data. Changes and modification in direction will be necessary at times, but they should always be consistent with a properly constructed strategic plan. The successful manager will set the tone and philosophy for the entire disability income operation.

In summary, the product line must be managed by an individual who has responsibility for the entire operation. This person must know where the markets are and must manage to achieve specific sales and profit objectives. The manager must understand the cyclical characteristics of disability income and the subjective impact that stability and motivation have on the financial results. He or she must be sensitive to the need for balance in responding to cyclical changes both in the product development process, and in the evaluation of results. Finally, in most companies where the disability product line is not the primary one, the manager must be conscious of educating senior management to both the risks and goals of disability income.

Index

*Page numbers in bold-face indicate definitions.

239

242   *Index*

Net Worth, 28, 70, **91**
  chart, 92, 103
No-fault auto, **35, 205**
Non-cancellable, 2, 8
Nonoccupational clause, **53,** 198
North American Reassurance Company,
  187
Not takens, 79, 114

O

Occupation, 26, 77, 179
Occupation class, 77, **116,** 179, 190
Occupation schedule, **116**
Occupation stability, 118
Optional extra benefits, 54
Orphan policyholders, 126
Other coverages, 30
Overhead expense; *see* Business overhead
  expense
Overinsurance, 8, 13, 24, 28, 46, **64,** 101,
  144, 224
Over liberalization, 42–43, 45–46, 145
Overreaction, 144, 166, 228, 232
Override commissions, 80
Overweight, 109
Own occupation, 50, 144, 226

P

Paramedical exams, **100**
Partial disability, **55,** 145, 152
Paul Revere Life Insurance Company, 9,
  187
Payment of premium, **52**
Peptic ulcer, 111, 108
Persistency, 41, 104, 148, **182,** 237
Persistency incentives, 80
Persistency rater, 26, 182
  chart, 94
Philosophy, 148
Physical examination, 101
Physical hazard, 116
Physical history, 101, 184
Physical impairments, 121
Physician, 47, 114, 120, 144
Physician reports, 136
Placing the policy, 78
Planning, 232
Policy approval, 154
Policy changes, 94, **131**
Policy form, 180
Policyholder services, **130**
Policy issue, **127**
Preauthorized checks, 130
Preexisting conditions, **52**
Preliminary application, 94
Premium collections, 125
Premium deposit receipts, 154
Premium discount, 36
Premium rate filing, **155**
Premium volume, 148
Premiums (group), 209

Presumptive disability, 53, 144
Pricing, **144,** 193
Pricing factors, 148
Privacy, 155, 227
Procedures for filing, 154
Product development, **161,** 193, 234
Product liberalizations, 43
Products, **18**
Professional market, 162, 219
Profit, 148, 166, 230
Programming the need, 79, 202
Progress reports, 137–138
Promotion, 169
Proposals, 170
Protection, 188
Provident Life and Accident Insurance
  Company, 9
Punitive Damage, 164

Q–R

Qualification period, **53**
Quota share reinsurance, 192
Railroad retirement, 205
Rate
  of disability, 174
  of recovery, 174
Rate-up, 108, **109**
Recapture, 192
Recession–1970s, 14, 41, 44, 135
Recessions, 41, 144, 205, 232
Reconsiderations, 110, 112
Recurrent disability, **51**
Reduced elimination period if hospital con-
  fined, **54**
Registered Health Underwriter, 98
Registration, 126
Regulation, 49, **150,** 163, 217, **227**
Rehabilitation, 19, 141, 226
Reinstatement application, 94, **132**
Reinsurance, 10, 147, 157, 179, 184, **186**
Reinsurance services, 193
Reissues, **129**
Rejections, 18, 113, 226
Relation to earnings, **8, 53**
Renal calculus, 111
Renewal rating, 210
Replacement ratios, 44, 66, 89
  Chart, 67, 69, 143
Replacements, **129**
Reserves, **145**
Residual, definition, 50, **52,** 145, 226
Return of premium, **54,** 146, 165
Rhode Island, 68, 204
RHU, 98

S

Salary allotment, 36
Salary continuation, 218
Salary deduction, 36
Salary savings, 36
Sales, 19, **73**